LYRICS

I found your rain on the sidewalk
found you saw
driving through the night ■ the
border ■ where the waterfall
jury is out ■ flow ■ the moon
glass crowded street below ■ the full
way that's shadow
it is ■ she moved like a
reflected
I found rain in the
is like a field heart where
café ■ hostage ■ a season night trees
driving through
the night ■ the only road across
night street flow like a waterfa
crowded below ■ the full moon in
■ that's just the way it is ■ she moved like a shadow
and then I found you reflected in the glass ■ the pa
is like a that's sown heart's taken hostage
hostage field ■ a season without fear
shadow
shadow

LYRICS
writing better words for your songs

writing **better** words for your songs

by Rikky Rooksby

A BACKBEAT BOOK
First edition 2006
Published by Backbeat Books
7777 West Bluemound Road,
Milwaukee, WI 53213
www.backbeatbooks.com

Published for Backbeat Books by Outline Press (Book Publishers) Ltd,
2A Union Court, 20-22 Union Road, London SW4 6JP, England
www.jawbonepress.com

ISBN: 978-0-87930-885-8

A catalogue record for this book is available from the British Library.

EDITOR John Morrish
EDITORIAL DIRECTOR Tony Bacon
ART DIRECTOR Nigel Osborne
DESIGN Paul Cooper Design

Printed by Regent Publishing Services Limited, China

12 13 14 15 16 6 5 4 3 2

To Paul Ashton-Bridges, for remembering the words, and much else.

contents

preface

"I can't think of anything to write ..."

How often has this thought crossed your mind, just when you need a lyric for a song you're composing? It hits all songwriters at some time or another.

No aspect of songwriting causes more frustration than writing lyrics. You have your chords together, a melody to sing over them, and an arrangement, but no words. So often, lyrics are the last aspect of songwriting to be considered. Frequently a lyric is scribbled at the last minute and you end up singing words you didn't want to say, don't like, or didn't mean. Do you find yourself repeating phrases from other songs, using clichés, and getting stuck for rhymes? Do you feel you're always writing about the same things, perhaps the same themes as everyone else? Or do your lyrics seem a closed book to others? Are members of the audience after a gig saying, "Great music, but what were they were going on about?"

How To Write Lyrics will help songwriters write better lyrics, expand their awareness of the craft of lyric-writing, and develop their own style, images and themes. There are suggestions about how to draft a lyric, how to salvage old lyrics, how to expand your sense of what a lyric can do, how to write new types of lyric, and how to avoid obscurity. The book takes you deeper into lyric-writing to grasp common techniques and subjects. Seeing what others have done with lyrics during the past 50 years will suggest opportunities that could recharge your creativity. Here are many tips and ideas that can find new life in your own lyrics, and pages of encouragement, whatever style of music you play.

You don't have to read *How To Write Lyrics* sequentially; dip straight into any section that interests you. If you have a half-complete lyric that's missing a section, look through these pages and find an idea to complete it. If you seem to get stuck writing about the same subjects, browse the many titles. If short of inspiration, dip into *How To Write Lyrics* at random.

How to use this book

The book has nine sections. **Section One** tells you how to make a start. **Section Two** provides 30 strategies for finding inspiration and helping you avoid writer's block. **Section Three** takes you from writing a simple sketch through to a polished final draft. **Section Four** looks at the magic of titles, and **Section Five** considers specific techniques that affect lyric writing on a line by line basis. **Section Six** deals with how lyrics generate pictures through metaphors, similes, and surveys some of the commonest imagery that songwriters use. **Section Seven** examines story-telling, point-of-view, and character. **Section Eight** discusses some broader issues to do with lyric writing which affect where you direct your songwriting. Throughout the book there are interviews with leading songwriters who discuss how they write lyrics.

Section Nine is a sourcebook of themes, listing hundreds of songs according to their subject-matter, as a source of inspiration: find them on the web and see how leading lyricists have handled those subjects in the past. They are a mixture of singles and album tracks from bands and singers from the 1950s to the present day. The titles also give you a sense of which themes have been most popular, and which are perhaps over-done or have become clichéd. This will help you invent titles sharper and more intelligent than the average.

Titles alone can inspire songs; they can remind you of a song you once knew which might be a starting point for a song of your own. These are not definitive listings. It is inevitable, given the millions of songs in circulation on vinyl, CD, DVD and for download, that every reader will be able to think of alternative examples. You can have fun compiling your own lists for certain subjects.

This book is part of a multi-volume series on songwriting. To find out more on chord sequences, melody, guitar chords and guitar tunings, and writing songs on keyboards (especially if you're a guitarist), seek out *How To Write Songs On Guitar* (2000), *The Songwriting Sourcebook* (2003), *Chord Master* (2004), *Melody* (2005), and *How To Write Songs On Keyboards* (2005). If you write riff-based songs, *Riffs* (2002) is the most encyclopaedic study ever published about them. To learn more about the elements that make a magic recording, 100 songs from 1960 to the present day receive for careful scrutiny in *Inside Classic Rock Tracks* (2001). Information about these titles can be found on www.Backbeatbooks.com and www.rikkyrooksby.com.

Section 1

making a start

Writing lyrics requires completely different skills to those used in other aspects of songwriting. No wonder so many people find it a struggle.

Sometimes I finish the lyrics the month before we go into the studio. But for the most part, 90 per cent of them are done at the last minute." (Kurt Cobain)[2]

"When I look at our first 10 years, I just hear unfinished work, lyrics we never finished because we ran out of studio time." (Bono on U2)[3]

"I did the tune first and wrote words ... later. I called that 'Scrambled Egg' for a long time. I didn't have any words to it." (Paul McCartney on 'Yesterday')[4]

"Some songs come quickly and some songs take forever. 'Sherry' [Four Seasons, US Number One in 1962] was a quickie. It took 15 minutes. I was ready to leave for a rehearsal we were having, and I sat at the piano and it just came out. Not having a tape-recorder in those days, the only way I could remember it was to put a quick lyric to it and remember the melody and the words together. I drove down to rehearsal humming it, trying to keep it in my mind. I had no intention of keeping the lyrics. To my surprise, everybody liked the lyrics so we didn't change anything." (writer Bob Gaudio)[5]

Lyric seems to be the hardest word

Many people find writing lyrics the hardest part of songwriting. If you do too, relax ... you're in good company. Noel Gallagher of Oasis told *Guitar* in May 1996, "The music side of it is easy – it's the lyrics I can't stand writing." A few songwriters deal with this issue by forming a partnership with someone who can supply words. The common division of labour in songwriting partnerships is along the music/lyric divide: one person composes the music, the other writes the words. Think of Burt Bacharach (music) and Hal David (words), or Elton John (music) and Bernie Taupin (words), or John Barry (music) and Leslie Bricusse or Don Black (words). Occasionally, a songwriter who usually does both words *and* music might give the writing of the lyrics to someone for a special project. Brian Wilson asked Tony Asher to write lyrics for the classic *Pet Sounds*. But the majority of songwriters write music *and* lyrics single-handed.

It was in the 1960s that what had often been separate roles of performer and songwriter became fused, primarily owing to the success of The Beatles. Previously there was often a whole team of creative people with individual roles behind a hit song. Each one only needed to excel at one thing. Joni Mitchell is sceptical about the assumption that one or two performers should (or can) fulfil all the creative demands to the highest level:

"Everybody's a singer-songwriter now, but not everybody should be, not everybody can do all of these things, and yet everybody does. And that's why I think music has gone downhill. It used to take three – a great lyricist and a great musician and then a great singer. Like with Frank [Sinatra], and that's why that stuff is so enduring – because you had three gifted people doing it. Now you've got people, they're not really a great singer or a great writer or a great musician doing it, so the standards have dropped severely."[6]

Don't think there's anything wrong in seeking out a partner to share some of the burdens.

Writing lyrics means shaping the meaning of something which, if left as instrumental music, would remain undefined; there is a change of the level of expression. That's one reason why (to play with an Elton John title) for many songwriters 'lyric' seems to be the hardest word. Picture this scene: a songwriter at the piano, or with a guitar, plays with chords and creates an emotion and atmosphere that is creatively inspiring. Our songwriter invents a melody to go with this mood. Then comes the moment where words are required, and that means getting specific. This sad- or happy-sounding chord progression must now direct its general sadness or happiness to a *particular* human situation. A lyric is the place where the emotional suggestions of pure music are defined as concrete human concerns and events. It's like a piece of translation, from one medium into another. The general musical mood is focused by a lyric into a context, a voice, a human drama.

But what if you don't have anything in mind? It happens to everyone, including the professionals. Around the time of *The Soul Cages* album Sting admitted that he had found the album difficult because, while the music came easily, the ideas in his head at the time would not have led easily to lyrics that he could use on an album. He eventually got round this block by drawing on memories of his childhood and youth in Newcastle, in the industrial north of England.

A second reason why writing lyrics is often problematic is because it requires different skills to those for composing. A good lyricist has a multi-faceted sensitivity to language. He or she can write memorable phrases, spot a potential hook or good first line, rhyme competently, handle metaphors and images, and re-shape a phrase while retaining its sense. A lyricist has an ear for words that are awkward to sing, or too abstract, or too obscure, and knows how to organise a lyric around a character, an emotion, a story or an idea so that it makes sense and can speak to a large number of people, even if its origin was personal. Such language-oriented skills are not automatically granted just because you are a good singer, guitarist, keyboard player, or composer. For most songwriters it's necessary to work at acquiring these skills. This book will help you to do that.

Which comes first, music or words?

"The way I write is to sit down with the guitar and keep on writing until it's finished. I've never written a set of lyrics independently of the song. I have to have an idea for the melody and then I'll choose words that sing well. I'm not proud of seeing the lyrics written out, usually, because they need the music to back them up." (Chrissie Hynde of The Pretenders)[7]

"It's a great luxury – at least for a lyricist – to write to [recorded] tracks because you have a much better sense of what the musical mood of the song is. If you're writing with a person who plays piano and they're sitting at the keyboard playing, they may have a whole different sound in their head from what you have in your head when you hear what they play ... Although in some ways, it's a little more demanding because you're now having to fit into something that's complete whereas when you're writing lyrics to a song that has no real arrangement done to it yet, theoretically, what you write can influence what that turns out to be." (Tony Asher on writing with Brian Wilson)[8]

"The rhythm of the words is more important to me than the sense at that [initial] stage ... 'In The Air' was improvised like that, and so were songs like 'I Don't Care Anymore', 'Take Me Home', 'Sussudio' ..." (Phil Collins on improvising nonsense)[9]

You can write a lyric at any stage in the songwriting process. Each has advantages and disadvantages. You can write a lyric first. It doesn't have to be complete; a few lines and images might be enough to sing when you're working on the chord progression and melody. Some people find a title comes as soon as they get an inspiring musical idea, and this title maintains the song's identity until it is finished. Some writers like to develop a lyric with the music, sitting guitar in hand, writing down lyric ideas and chord ideas, or at a keyboard. It's a matter of whatever works for you.

The advantage of starting with a complete lyric is that it can be easier to sing a melody with meaningful words. Lyrics written first can be worked on until they make sense, have memorable lines and images, and are easily set to music because they are singable and don't have awkward phrases or line-lengths. Whatever way you decide to do it, it is certainly a good discipline to keep a notebook and work up ideas so that you have a stock of finished lyrics you can fall back on if need be.

The other method is to either to think of words as you invent the melody, or write the lyrics when the song's music is finished. This could even mean leaving it as late as having the backing track recorded. On the positive side the music may inspire you to come up with a set of good lines; on the other hand, you won't be able to change the music so easily to fit the lyric.

What kinds of lyric are there?

Lyrics can be classified in many ways, especially according to subject matter, as is done in **Section Nine**. But at this point we need a more general answer to the question. Here are four fundamental types of lyric:

- Feeling lyric – expresses emotions, moods, atmosphere.
- Thinking lyric – expresses an idea, insight, realisation, truth, falsity.
- Experiencing lyric – expresses a story, a sequence of events, time-dependent.
- Contemplating lyric – observes, describes, an object or objects, a scene.

These categories are not exclusive of each other. A single lyric could cover all four. But a lyric will tend to gravitate towards one of these, and a songwriter may have a temperamental bias to write more songs of one type than the others. Most songwriters start with a bias toward the feeling lyric, if only for the reason that emotion is the greatest spur to creativity. If we bring in other types of lyric, such as the confessional, comic, satiric, protest, or romantic lyric, you can see that these are subsidiary; they can be experienced through any of the four main types. This is just one aspect to lyric-writing that it may help to keep in mind.

Let's examine the development of a lyric from the first ideas to a final polished draft.

Just write

There are times when writing a lyric is easy. Sometimes songwriters have an urgent sense of what they want to sing about. The likeliest time for this to happen is when they're in love. As Rufus Wainwright put it, using the metaphor of a volcano, "When you have a crush on someone, when you're moved by someone's physical presence, lyrics come like Mount St. Helens, songs come out of your ears!"[10] This can lead to attempts to be spontaneous in the studio, so that a lyric is improvised during recording. Here's Tim Burgess on the recording of The Charlatans' 'Subtitle':

"It was just ... Rob [Collins, keyboards], and a microphone in the middle of the room, and I just sang the first thing that came into my head, based on the sort of mumbo jumbo feeling you get from like a huge crush on someone. Basically, that simple. I just had like 'not the same as everybody else' and 'why talk to her?' written down ... and that was the way it was left. It was supposed to ... get a feel of the song but it just ended up being the song. It was completely spontaneous ..." [11]

Another example of this 'wing-it' procedure would be U2's 'Elvis Presley and America', where Bono's first-take improvised melody and mostly garbled lyric were left unchanged when the song was released on the album *A Sort Of Homecoming*. The public is largely unaware of the hit-and-miss nature of so many lyrics. Cream's 'Badge', for instance, got its title merely because of a misreading of the word 'bridge' on a piece of paper.

The hope in such situations is that inspiration will strike. Willie Nelson once said, "Writing is – I don't know – an instinct, an intuitive thing, you have to be in a receptive mood. Sometimes an idea comes along and you have no control over it. It just overwhelms you, so you just sit down and get on with it ..."[12] Such inspiration will quickly fill a blank page with jottings – complete phrases, incomplete phrases, lines that rhyme, lines that don't rhyme, isolated similes or images, maybe a title. This is what I term a 'sketch', and it can be as haphazard as you like. Here's the important point: once the sketch is done you are no longer looking at a blank sheet of paper.

This makes a huge psychological difference. The hardest part of lyric writing is to get past the intimidating inertia of that blank paper. Once there is a sketch you have surmounted that horrible, numb feeling of "what am I going to write? I can't think of anything ..." The sketch can be expanded, re-written, and generally fiddled with. Gradually, through a series of drafts, decisions are made about the most effective beginning of the lyric, what will be its conclusion, how many lines make a verse, which bits make a chorus, whether there's anything suitable for a bridge, what is the title, etc.

But songwriters don't always feel inspired. So what do you do when you have no theme in mind and can't think of what to write? The answer is: do anything that will result in a sketch, that gets you writing, to side-step the paralysing feeling of staring at blank paper. Nothing more inhibits creativity than the struggle to make a start. You need to find a way round this, as an artist stuck for ideas might simply throw paint at a canvas to begin painting.

One exercise is to write from the present by asking: where are you? What can you see, hear, smell? How are you feeling? What's been on your mind? What time of day, week, season is it? What happened yesterday? What's supposed to happen today? What would you like to happen tomorrow? What do you think likely to happen tomorrow? What's been on the news? What's going on in the lives of your partner, friends, family? What music have you been listening to recently? What do you like about it?
Write anything about any of these things. Don't evaluate what you put down, just write.

Keith Reid

Interviewed by Thomas Jerome

Unusually for a non-performing, behind the scenes lyricist, Keith Reid is actually an integral member of a band. Along with pianist/vocalist Gary Brooker, Reid formed Procol Harum in 1967 as a vehicle for the duo's songs. The band's first recording was of a slice of abstract lyricism Reid titled 'A Whiter Shade Of Pale', which Brooker set to a tune loosely based on Bach's 'Air on a G String' from the *Suite No. 3 in D Major*. It went on to become one of the most successful singles of all time. Other Reid/Brooker penned Procol Harum hits include 'Homburg', 'Conquistador' and 'Pandora's Box'.

Do you want to write, or do you have to write?

Definitely something I want to do, and chose to do. I don't have to do it. Although I don't think it's a bad thing when people have to write to earn a living. That's a very valid impetus for doing things.

I write now because I really want to, and I need to. It's an outlet. If I didn't have this, I'd probably have a lot of frustration.

Do you have a set pattern for writing lyrics?

I go through phases. I get inspired, or something happens – you hear something, read something, see something – and that triggers a response. And the response in my case is to put words down on paper. Whenever I get an idea I'll make some notes, but won't necessarily turn that straight into a song. But I'll accumulate ideas, and then if I feel like writing a song, I'll turn it into a song.

Do you ever force yourself to write, or do you wait for the inspiration to come?

I don't sweat it too much. I've come to realise that you go through periods: sometimes you go through a period of months where it seems like every day you get ideas, and it all feels very creative. And then you go through periods where nothing seems to spark your imagination. So now, I can go through a couple of months where nothing really happens, and it doesn't bother me. Because I know that something will happen, and it does. But having said that sometimes I will just go and put something down on paper, but generally I let it happen, because I know it will at some point.

There used to be a time when I'd rely on keeping an idea in my head for a while, but nowadays I can't remember them. Now I write them down. But it's a funny thing: I only write [ideas] down in pencil. Because it's only an idea. Then I let it germinate. I don't ink it in … I only ever type a song out when it's finished. I suppose it's a bit like with a painting; when you start it's just a sketch, and then as you think about it more, you colour it in.

You discover the song as you write it. You get an idea, but there's no way of knowing what the whole song's going to be about. An idea develops, and then you discover in the writing of it what it is. You get surprised by the stuff that comes out. I see where it is, where it takes me. I don't have much of an idea.

Is there anything that you feel you shouldn't write about?

No. I firmly believe that you have to try to be honest and truthful, and that's the only . . . You have to follow the internal logic to the end, so that there's a sense of truth. You have to be very truthful, whatever line you're pursuing. You might chose at the end of the day not to let something see the light of day, but while I'm working, there isn't anything I wouldn't write about.

Nothing that you wouldn't want put out into the public domain?

Well … a few months before 9/11 I wrote a song called

'American Ugly,' and I really thought it was a good piece of writing. But then 9/11 happened, and I thought 'bang goes that one'. It was just close to the bone. I was going to use it for a record, but you can't.

Not as close to the bone as 'Bomb The Pentagon' by Primal Scream.

I don't know that song, and I don't know why they wrote that line. It depends whether they meant it. I wouldn't do anything if I didn't mean it, and I wouldn't write anything for effect. So I don't know if their song was written for effect. If it is, the way I look at it that makes it a bullshit song. I would never write anything to be controversial.

But if you thought something 'controversial,' would you write about it?

If I honestly felt it, and honestly meant it, I wouldn't back away from it. But at the end of the day, I might decide 'this is insensitive' and put it in the drawer. With 'American Ugly,' events overtook me. But I wouldn't write anything specifically to cause outrage.

Do you write with the singer that you're working with at the time in mind? When the rest of Procol Harum say 'We're going to do a new record', for instance, do you go back over what you're written in the meantime and see what's suitable, or do you start work on a new 'Procol Harum project'?

That's a good question. For the last record that we did, when we started saying we were going to do it, I really sat down and wrote songs for that record. I suppose I was writing for that record, but it isn't a particular style of writing. Procol Harum was formed as a band to do the songs Gary and I had written. So I think of them as my records – as me expressing myself.

So do you write differently if you write for other people?

Yes, actually I probably do. When I'm working with another artist, I try to get into their head. Experience has told me that if I don't get into their head, then what I come up with isn't going to work for them. You try to find out what they're thinking, and try to relate to them. So in a way when I'm writing songs for Procol Harum I'm purely expressing myself. But when I write with and for other artists, I'm trying to see what they're feeling, and trying to add my take on that.

You published a book of your lyrics, which is fairly unusual I think in that a lot of songwriters like the words to be attached to the music as a single entity. A lot of people don't even like having their lyrics printed on their record sleeves. But you must be fairly comfortable with the words on their own?

I am actually. They always have to work on a piece of paper for me to pass them on and have them set to music. If they don't look good on paper, I throw them away.

How much importance do you attach to the title of a song?

Here's the thing … for years and years, I never used to have a title. It always came last, which is why, with a lot of Procol Harum songs, the title is some kind of summation of what the song is about. It used to be the last thing. More recently, the title can be the first thing that comes along. It's been there at the beginning, it's been there at the end. I don't have any rules.

How about the first line? Is it important to start with a bang?

I never used to give it any thought. The first time I ever gave that any thought was a few years ago when I read an interview with George Michael, where he said that his first couple of lines have to have a lot of impact. That never occurred to me, because I try to make every line important. But I know that people do.

Do you think a lot about rhyme and rhythmic patterns as you write?

You have to have a rhythmic pattern; that's why you're writing songs and not something else. Rhyme is very important. There's always some sort of rhyming scheme. It can be odd – there's a Procol Harum song called 'A Salty Dog' [from *A Salty Dog*, 1969] where I had the idea of writing something circular. But there's always a pattern, and that's very important to me.

Which of your lyrics are you most proud of?
That's difficult. But I remember thinking that some of the lyrics to 'Grand Hotel' [from *Grand Hotel*, 1973] were pretty damn clever. I did some rhyming there that I wasn't trying to do, so which wasn't contrived. There's a couplet – "Dover sole, and oeufs mornay / Profiteroles and peach flambé" – that I thought was pretty good! I didn't work on it – it just came out. And I thought, to blow my own trumpet, 'that's as clever as Noel Coward!" There's also a song, 'A Salty Dog,' which I think is the most direct piece of writing I've written. I don't believe I could be more self-revealing. That's as direct and as honest as I think it's possible to be.

Which goes back to what we saying about writing with other people in mind ...
I've never censored myself. Gary was very good. If I gave him something, and he could set it to music, he'd sing it. He didn't seem to mind, and I suppose in a way we were a band, so it was valid for him to sing my lyrics. But I've certainly found, writing with other people, that they may not want to sing what I'm thinking – they may feel uncomfortable because it doesn't reflect where they're coming from.

What other songwriters do you admire? Who did you look to when you first started?
When I started to write I emulated Bob Dylan. He was my inspiration. I wanted to write like him, definitely. After a while I started to find my own voice. There are other writers that I've admired – Randy Newman, Joni Mitchell – but I didn't emulate them, because they were my contemporaries. Any great work is inspiring – music, painting – but Bob Dylan was the only songwriter who inspired me to the point of emulation.

Any more recent writers?
Nowadays you hear songs, but there's no one great writer. I like John Hiatt. I hear tons of stuff, it can be anything.

I read an interview with Brian Eno, where he said that the hardest thing in modern music is to write a great lyric. Do you agree?
Yeah, I think so. As a lyricist, I find that when I write with other musicians they have tracks coming out of theirs ears. It's much easier to write music, particularly nowadays with computers, than to write words. You can get away with crap lyrics if you have a good beat! But, saying that, a great piece of music is also very hard to write.

Are there any terrible lyrical clichés that you try to steer clear of?
There actually aren't, because you can always subvert them. That's something that I've done. There is no cliché that you cannot subvert. You can even have fun with 'moon' and 'June,' the greatest cliché of all time. You can take the greatest cliché, and then the next two lines can be something brilliant. Clichés are there to be exploited, that's my advice to a songwriter!

Any traps and pitfalls that you try to avoid, then?
No, because there's nothing that you can't use to your advantage.

Are lyrics these days less important than they used to be?
Yes and no. If you're a student of music, and you look at the golden age of classic songwriting, it seems that now people can get away with a lot more. There is nothing that can't be a hit song now. You can repeat the same phrase over a loop – you can write three words, and that'll be it, which I guess you couldn't do, in the 1930s, before computers. Even going back to the golden age of song, people got away with some rubbish, but now, at the touch of a button, you can make a sound than sounds impressive. You can get away with more.

Section 2

30 ways to find inspiration

Do not despair. From eavesdropping to watching TV, there are many well-tried techniques that can help you conquer your fear of the blank page.

"Ideas, titles for songs, I would definitely do at home because I would watch the news, the goings-on in the world, movies and listening to conversations between people on the street or in a restaurant. I was always looking for material ... When you're a songwriter you're always very observant of the world around you." (Lamont Dozier of Motown songwriting team Holland-Dozier-Holland)[13]

The inspiration for a lyric can come from many sources. It is said that Roy Orbison wrote one of his biggest hits 'Oh Pretty Woman' when his wife Claudette went out one afternoon shopping. Orbison asked Claudette if she needed any money, but fellow songwriter Bill Dees interjected, "A pretty woman never needs any money.' Dees was struck by the phrase, thinking it would make a good title.

Inspiration could be an idea, a feeling, a phrase, a title, a person (real or imagined) or a story (true or fictional). You can start with a clear theme or none. You can start with words, images or different types of statement, and let the theme rise from them. Here are 30 strategies for inspiring a lyric if there's nothing compelling you to write.

1. Listen to people talking.

"I get ideas from almost everywhere but especially from supermarket queues – I have a talent for eavesdropping and it's amazing what you learn waiting to pay for your fruit juice." (Morrissey 1987)[14]

2. Write a single, evocative phrase. Neil Tennant of The Pet Shop Boys is one of those who claims that most of his lyrics begin with a phrase he's jotted down or an idea for a title.

3. Keep a small notebook and pen in your pocket to write down ideas immediately they occur to you.

"I write passing thoughts, overheard conversations, discovered quotations, advertising signs, mumbled threats, and words of kindness and endearment, on scraps of paper. Sometimes I mutter them into Dictaphones or record them on my answer-machine when there is not even an eyebrow pencil in hand to order to commit them to the page." (Elvis Costello)[15]

"It all usually starts with a riff on a guitar and then I decide I want to write about something and I look through my notebooks and find all the phrases and rhymes. I constantly write down things I like, like 'bereft and adrift'. If I'm missing one line I just flick through my notebook and there's one there ..." (Evan Dando of The Lemonheads)[16]

4. Try writing a lyric sketch in a public place. Bob Dylan is just one of those who would sit in a coffee-house for days at a time, looking at the other customers, making up things about them and writing down whatever came into his head.

5. Listen to music to alter your frame of mind and encourage a receptive mood. Write down the thoughts, feelings and pictures the music evokes. Listen to songs in a language you don't know and write down phrases that the unfamiliar sounds suggest. Brian Wilson famously wrote the whole of the 'Mount Vernon And Fairway' song sequence from The Beach Boys' *Holland* while listening to Randy Newman's *Sail Away* album over and over again.

6. Glance through a newspaper or a magazine. Paul McCartney once said that the first line of a Beatles lyric often came from reading a book or looking at the newspapers.

7. Put your pen down and go to your guitar or keyboard.

"You get ideas for songs from all sorts of situations. I just start playing the piano and the chords start telling me something. Lyrics for me just seem to go with the tune, very much hand in hand." (Kate Bush)[17]

8. Write with the TV on, but with your back to it so you can't see the picture. Keep an ear open for odd phrases you could use or that collide with what you're writing in fruitful ways. John Lennon got the idea for 'Good Morning, Good Morning' from a TV commercial that was on in the background as he sat at the piano.

9. Watch the TV with notebook and pen.

"I write mostly when it's raining or dark, usually after 10 at night. I get a lot of inspiration from watching TV." (Nicky Wire, Manic St Preachers)[18]

"At night … he [John Lennon] loved to channel-surf, and he would pick up phrases from all the shows. One time, he was watching Reverend Ike, a famous black TV evangelist, who was saying, 'Let me tell you guys, it doesn't matter, it's whatever gets you through the night.' John loved it and said, 'I've got to write it down or I'll forget it.' He always kept a pad and pen by the bed. That was the beginning of 'Whatever Gets You Through The Night', an American Number One and UK Top 40 hit for John." (May Pang)[19]

10. Write randomly, the first things that come into your head. This could be prose. Keep going until you have filled every line of the page. Then look for the nugget.

"Lately, I get in a room by myself. No telephone, no TV, not much to look at. I usually by writing down random phrases. Maybe I'll start writing about a certain subject and there's a phrase that strikes me, so I'll spin off from that." (David Byrne of Talking Heads)[20]

Van Morrison described 'Madame George' as "just a stream-of-consciousness thing, as is 'Cyprus Avenue'. Both those songs came right out. I didn't even think about what I was writing. There are some things that you write that just come out all at once, and there's other things that you think about and consider where you'll put each bit."[21]

"I often sit at a typewriter and knock out stream-of-consciousness stuff; it helps clear the head, but often brings forth ideas for songs and so on." (Pete Townshend of The Who)[22]

11. Travel by the transportation of your choice and watch the world shift to reveal new things.

"I've written most of my best songs driving on a long journey scribbling lyrics on cigarette packets whilst steering'. (Neil Young)[23]

12. Imagine an ending or a punchline and work backwards from it. What needs to happen or be said to get there? Stephen Sondheim says that he finds it useful to write backwards, starting with "a climax, a twist, a punch, a joke".

13. Punch the clock: try writing on a regular, timetabled basis. Pretend you're a Brill Building songwriter who is expected to knock out songs every day. Randy Newman worked for years in an office, nine to five. Chris Difford of Squeeze consciously imitated him by establishing an office near his home. Nicky Chinn and Mike Chapman disciplined themselves to start work at 10am every day, beginning with a title and working from there.

14. Cross-fertilise: try writing more than one lyric at a time.

"Lyrics are manna from heaven and you have to interpret them. I always have three or four songs going at once. It's more competitive than confusing; they fight for my attention." (Rufus Wainwright)[24]

15. Think of a childhood memory and either write about it, or take the core feeling of that memory and project it into an imaginary situation.

"I remember looking at the river and thinking how happy I was to be alive. Waterloo Bridge has featured so prominently in my life that I have taken potential girlfriends there just to see how it felt." (Ray Davies of The Kinks, describing a childhood stay in a hospital overlooking the Thames.)[25]

"I had an uncle who used to tell me stories. It seems to me now his sole purpose in life was to scare me witless. A recurring character in his stories was this spider-man. When I was about six or seven, he used to try and scare me and my sister, arriving late at night and whispering. He was my bogeyman." (Robert Smith of The Cure on 'Lullaby')[26]

"A lot of early Move lyrics came from a book of fairy stories for adults that I wrote at school. It ended up in a folder in my bedroom and I drew on it for songs like 'I Can Hear The Grass Grow' and 'Flowers In The Rain'." (Roy Wood of The Move)[27]

16. Go shopping and watch what goes on in shops.

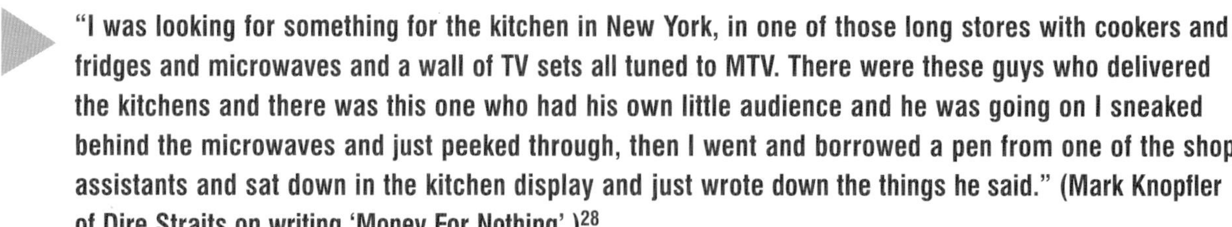

"I was looking for something for the kitchen in New York, in one of those long stores with cookers and fridges and microwaves and a wall of TV sets all tuned to MTV. There were these guys who delivered the kitchens and there was this one who had his own little audience and he was going on I sneaked behind the microwaves and just peeked through, then I went and borrowed a pen from one of the shop assistants and sat down in the kitchen display and just wrote down the things he said." (Mark Knopfler of Dire Straits on writing 'Money For Nothing'.)[28]

"Hudson's was hip, the biggest and best department store in downtown Detroit. The [Christmas] holiday hustle and bustle ... got me to feeling a little better. I avoided the toys and baby department, heading straight for the jewellery counter. Picked out some pearls for Claudette. 'They're beautiful,' I told the saleslady. 'Just hope my wife likes them.' 'I second that emotion,' said Al [Cleveland, fellow Motown songwriter]. What a funny phrase, I kept thinking on the way home, dodging in and out of the holiday traffic. That afternoon we wrote the song. 'I Second That Emotion' was soon a smash for the Miracles." (Smokey Robinson)[29]

17. When you've finished eavesdropping on shop assistants, go and buy a book.

"Years ago, I just went into a shop and picked it [Peter Reich's *A Book Of Dreams*] off the shelf, and really liked the title and the picture on the front. I'd never bought a book before which I hadn't known anything about; I just felt I'd found something special. And nine, ten years later, I re-read it and it turned into a song." (Kate Bush on writing 'Cloudbusting'.)[30]

18. Keep a notebook by your bed in case inspiration strikes in the middle of the night. Freddie Mercury of Queen used to scribble ideas at night without even putting the light on.

"It was 3am when Bobbie Gentry woke up, inspired to write a song for her first Capitol album. A sentence scribbled on a pad of paper supplied the seed: 'Billie Joe McAllister jumped off the Tallahatchee Bridge." (Fred Bronson describing the origin of 1967 US Number One 'Ode To Billie Joe'.)

19. Play some favourite songs by other people to get yourself into a different frame of mind. Many famous songs were inspired by their writers hearing other peoples' songs and hoping to emulate them. Barry Mann and Cynthia Weil got the inspiration for 'You've Lost That Lovin' Feelin'' from The Four Tops' 'Baby I Need Your Loving'. Brian Wilson got the inspiration for 'Don't Worry Baby' from The Ronettes' 'Be My Baby'.

"By attacking [Love's] 'A House Is Not A Motel' or 'Seven And Seven Is' in a rehearsal room I've actually found the means to start writing my own songs again. I always carry a notepad, pencil, rubber, and a French pen-knife, in a little Shure microphone bag, and these old songs have given me back [inspiration], and now I'm scribbling all the time." (Robert Plant)[31]

20. Go for a walk round an art gallery.

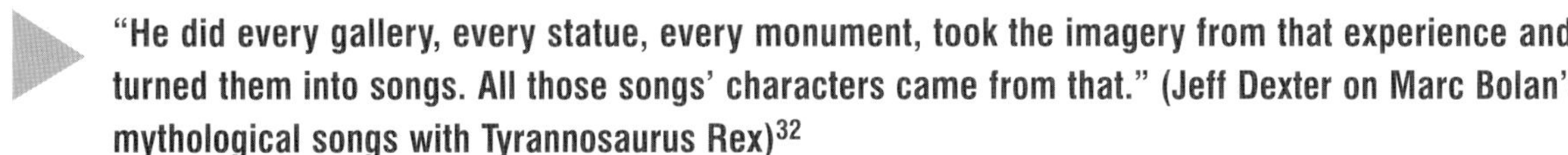

"He did every gallery, every statue, every monument, took the imagery from that experience and turned them into songs. All those songs' characters came from that." (Jeff Dexter on Marc Bolan's mythological songs with Tyrannosaurus Rex)[32]

21. Browse in a copy of *Halliwell's Film Guide* (or similar) and find an exciting title. It's optional whether you watch the film or just work with the title.

"It's about a relationship being a very finely balanced thing that can be easily thrown off by a third party. The whole thing really came from a line in *The Godfather*, during some family argument, where Marlon Brando says 'Don't interfere, it's between a man and a woman'." (Kate Bush on 'Between A Man And A Woman')[33]

22. Free associate to some music and record what you say. Mike Stoller recalls that he would hammer away at the piano while Jerry Leiber paced around the room shouting out lines and phrases that came into his head. Anything promising would be worked on. They wrote 'Hound Dog' in that way. It took only ten minutes.

23. Turn on the radio, at home or in the car. Hear accurately *and* inaccurately. John Gourrier, writer of the 1968 John Fred & The Playboys' hit 'Judy In Disguise (With Glasses)', came up with the title after mishearing The Beatles' 'Lucy In The Sky With Diamonds' as 'Lucy In *Disguise* With Diamonds'.

"When you sit down and wait for inspiration or just fiddle around on the piano, nothing happens. But it's always coincidence [that gets creativity moving). You hear a song on the radio and hear just the word that you've been looking for for three months, or you go to a movie and get something going on in your mind ... all these fluke things that happen that turn into good songs.' Per Gessle (writer of 1991 US Number One 'Joyride'.)[34]

24. Have an emotional crisis. This one carries a health warning.

"I was arguing with my girlfriend. I said, 'Stop in the name of love' and we both started laughing and stopped arguing. I said, 'What did I say?' and she said, 'Something about stop in the name of love.' " (Lamont Dozier)[35]

25. Become a new person ... or a little bit of a new person. Springsteen once said that a new song requires a new idea, and a new idea comes from being a new person. Not a *wholly* new person, just a little bit of a new person, from having areas of new psychological growth.

26. Write with members of your band using a random strategy.

" 'Hallucinating Pluto' came out of this game we sometimes play when we're writing. It's called Exquisite Corpse – the Surrealists invented it, I think. They'd do it with a drawing; one person would

draw a head, then they'd fold the paper and the next person would then draw in a torso. We do that with our lyrics. Everyone writes three or four lines … it leads you to a place you wouldn't normally go." (Keith Strickland of The B52s.)[36]

27. Read the lyrics, and listen to the music, of pre-rock'n'roll songwriters. That was another era when the craft and purpose of lyrics was perceived differently.

"I was listening to Noel Coward last night – incredible, incredible craft, incredible wit, incredible social commentary with humour. Stylistically, the language is a bit more formal than certainly this generation would understand. But beautiful and correct, and internal rhyme, and so much skill and so much to say without being *heavy*." (Joni Mitchell)[37]

"In the past … there was more talent and there was more intelligence when it came to writing a lyric. There was more depth of feeling … It's [the present] a generation that was brought up on TV. They didn't read as much as our generation did." (Barry Mann of Mann and Weil)[38]

28. Find someone to write with.

"Lyrically, it doesn't come as naturally as the music. When you do an album it's 12 sets of lyrics and it's quite intense, so I enjoy writing things with other people to see what they bring out in me." (Ian Brodie of The Lightning Seeds)[39]

"As far as my songwriting is concerned I believed in working with anyone who had something to offer and although I had some regular writing partners like Mike Valvano and Morris Broadnax, I'd work with virtually anyone. (Motown producer Clarence Paul)[40]

29. Try writing a group of lyrics around a theme, story or concept.

"The older I get, the more sense it makes to write several songs about the same subject, and the LP [Stevie Wonder's *The Secret Life Of Plants*] taught me that a good title is an important launch pad for any project … I just don't think there's the space sometimes to deal with the whole of a subject in a single song." (Paddy McAloon of Prefab Sprout)[41]

30. Write more than you need, perhaps in prose, and then edit it down.

"If there are four verses in a song, I'll write 24 verses, then almost line by line I'll go them and cross them out – that's too clever, that's too stupid, that's too arch, that's too cute … and then with the detritus I'm left with I put a song together – which might lead to things that are disjointed, unclear, or whatever, but which would be, if not illuminative of a condition, expressive of it." (Green Gartside of Scritti Politti)[42]

Aimee Mann

Interviewed by David Simons

As the bass-playing singer-songwriter for Boston's 'Til Tuesday, Aimee Mann had a hit with her very first try, *Voices Carry*, in 1985. Her solo albums include *Whatever, I'm With Stupid*, and *The Forgotten Arm* (2005). Nine of her songs were used in the soundtrack to the film Magnolia.

A while back I was reading this Fiona Apple interview and she was talking about making poetry by cutting out headlines from newspapers. So I thought, "That sounds like fun." So I tried that, and I wound up with a couple of the lines for 'Calling It Quits' [*Bachelor No. 2*] that way. I kept working at it like that, and writing stuff down at the same time, until it took a shape that meant something to me. Then I just went back and threw out all the other stuff that was just wordplay.

What's an example of a lyric you've altered to fit the meaning of the song, but maybe kept the initial premise?
For the opening line to 'Red Vines,' [*Bachelor No. 2*] instead of, "They're all still on their honeymoon/just read the dialogue balloon," I'd originally written, "They're all still on their honeymoon/it's Underdog Day Afternoon." [*laughs*] Which I thought was a bit much, although for a while there I was going to call the record *Underdog Day*.

You've had quite an assortment of co-writers over the years.* 'That's Just What You Are,' (I'm With Stupid *1996) for instance, was a song Jon Brion had started, then you came in and wrote the bridge and finished it off. Is that your "favourite" way to collaborate?
A lot of times Jon would do that, just hand me a little chord progression and some words and melody, or some kernel of an idea. And I just always found his music very inspiring, so it was very easy for me to make a whole song out of that. 'Amateur' (*I'm With Stupid*) was like that as well – a lot of it was already there, I just had bring it to the end. The other thing about Jon is that he would always tell me right away what the concept of the lyric was – and I'd always know immediately what he was talking about. Like with 'That's Just What You Are', he's referring to someone who's always acting like a jackass and won't do anything about it; you know, "that's just how I am, and I can't change," that sort of thing. I could relate to that!

So coming into it like that, where you've already got the road map, seems like the most preferable way to go.
Yeah, and it's definitely a lot more fun. Because there's already something there for you to follow.

What about writing with Elvis Costello? Same thing?
It's actually just the opposite with me and Elvis—that's a case where I'll have to come up with the initial framework. Like on 'The Fall of the World's Own Optimist' [*from Bachelor No. 2 2000*], I had like a verse and a chorus, but I couldn't come up with any words for the verses. So then he came along and wrote this whole B-section to the chorus, which was really great, it takes the song in this whole other direction. And then he added in the verse lyrics, which I then had to tailor to get back to the original topic.

It sounds very similar to the way he worked with McCartney.

Yeah, I'll bet it was. Because that seems to be a very effective method for him.

Your husband has helped out instrumentally on your various efforts, and yet there are no Mann-Penn songwriting credits.

We don't really collaborate, mostly because we both like to work in the same style. Also, Michael has a harmonic sensibility that's totally different from mine. He just goes to chord changes that are kind of foreign to me, even though it doesn't sound foreign when you're listening. Still, it's hard when you're writing with someone, and he's going to this chord change and you're thinking, "Wow, I would never go *there*." But of course he can get away with it on his own, because he's got the melodic ideas and the arrangements already in his head—he knows exactly where it's going once it's time to record.

Do you two at least sit down and exchange ideas?

Every now and then there'll be a song that he's working on that'll be close enough to my style of writing, that I'll come in and say, "Look, why don't you try this chord progression," or, "Why don't you do this thing in the middle." And he'll give me advice as well – particularly if I'm stuck, I might ask him what he thinks, and he'll come up with some chord that I hadn't thought of. But in general, I don't think we really click as writers.

One thing you and Michael have in common is the ability to come up with really inventive lyric ideas. "I swore you off, but you climbed back on," for instance,* [from "Long Shot"]*—some people would labour over a line like that for weeks. Did you?

It depends on how bad my writer's block is [*laughs*]. I find that by jotting down ideas in a notebook – which I'll occasionally do when I want to get into the writing process – really helps, it's the kind of thing I should probably utilize more than I actually do. For me, it's usually just a matter of writing down topics, rather than individual phrases. But something like that can really jump-start the creative process – especially when you don't feel like writing at all.

In 'It's Not Safe,'* [I'm With Stupid*] you wrote about an "idiot who keeps believing in luck." Was that you?

In this business, people often say one thing and do another. And for a long time I guess I did believe – until I finally reached the point where I stopped believing and just got out. I'm now satisfied that I can't do anything to make it better, I just equate it with anybody who's ever had to get out of a bad relationship. Believe in luck? Sure, you can be like Annie, you know, the sun will come out tomorrow, but that's crazy. I'd rather be perky and optimistic on my own behalf – and whatever happens, happens.

Section 3

from sketch to final draft

Now you've made a start, it's time to shape, clarify, strengthen, and finally polish your words until you have something you can be proud of.

Silence the perfectionist within

"Don't let the critic become bigger than the creator. Don't let it strangle you. Go ahead and say, 'I saw this girl / She was the best girl in the world.' Let it go. Put a string of stuff together. Go ahead." (Randy Newman)[43]

If you try to write and don't feel inspired, there is an outer and an inner aspect to the initial difficulty of writing. The outer dimension is the inertia that blank paper embodies. The inner dimension is the perfectionist most of us have in our heads. This is the inner critic who, in Randy Newman's words quoted above, must not be allowed to become greater than the creator. In my experience, the worst scenario is if you know you have to write a lyric on a particular theme (for instance, if you are writing on commission, or for a story). A series of unhelpful comments may come into your mind. For instance: "that's stupid", "that's not very profound", "that's been done before" or "you've done that before", "that's not a very interesting theme", "you'll never find a rhyme for that", "it's not as good as the one you wrote last week/month/year", "this will never turn into anything good", "that's not as good as the lyrics to [insert title of current favourite song]", "wouldn't you rather do something else?" (and, last but not least,) "that's not perfect".

But there is a simple phrase that will stop that inner voice interfering with your creativity: shut up, I'm not done yet. You write a cliché – so what? Shut up, I'm not done yet. Here are some tricks to keep self-censorship at bay:

- Never sit chewing your pencil consciously trying to write and rejecting anything that falls short of what you think is sheer brilliance.
- Don't reject the first line that comes to you – write it down and keep going.
- Don't reject ideas and phrases as not good enough or done before until you have written a page or more.
- If necessary, write what you think is rubbish to get you going. You may need to write a couple of pages before anything good comes. Eventually it will.
- Don't necessarily try to set a rhyme pattern at this stage, but if rhymes occur to you naturally, leave them in.
- Don't let the search for a rhyme hold up the flow of thoughts and images.

To summarise: when you sit down to sketch a lyric, just write. Clichés can be cut later. The sketch process is like panning for gold. Few prospectors ever waded into shallow water and immediately picked up gold with their fingers. You have to sift a certain amount of mud to get the couple of gold nuggets that will be the basis of a good lyric. So don't worry about the mud.

Sometimes a bad session, where it seems you've come up with nothing at all, is the prelude to a later breakthrough. Maxi Jazz of Faithless: "I'll start at about midnight and go through until about seven in the morning, writing sheet after sheet, and when I look at it it's garbage ... My ego is constantly getting crushed, y'know? 'Eight hours, no sleep and that's the best I can come up with?' ... But a day or two later, at some point it'll happen. I could be chopping carrots and, bang, there's a line – and I stop what I'm doing and start writing and it all just flows out."[44]

Creativity is about trying things, thinking laterally, allowing for the spontaneous. In his autobiography *To Be Loved*, Berry Gordy spoke of the mood at his Motown label in its 1960s heyday: "Hitsville had an atmosphere that allowed people to experiment creatively and gave them the courage not to be afraid to make mistakes. In fact, I sometimes encouraged mistakes. Everything starts as an idea and as far as I was concerned there were no stupid ones. 'Stupid' ideas are what created the lightbulb, airplanes and the like."[45] Much can spring from a momentary, spontaneous action. Of the writing of their international hit 'I'm Too Sexy', Richard Fairbrass of Right Said Fred remembered:

"We took a tea break and the computer was playing this loop round and round, and right out of the blue – I can't tell you where it came from – I started singing, 'I'm too sexy for my shirt' and we all fell about laughing. Fred ... didn't think we should be frivolous. He thought we should crank on and do our serious music. So Rob [Manzoli] and I convinced Fred [Fairbrass] after three or four days that we should pursue it. And I couldn't get that top line out of my head."[46]

Before it was called 'I'm Too Sexy' the song was called 'Heaven' and its theme was the serious one of looking forward to the afterlife as a leaving behind of the problems of the here and now.

Cut-ups

A cut-up is an artificial way of generating a sketch if you can't write one yourself because the inspiration isn't there. It won't create a lyric for you, but it can act as a stimulus. As an *avant garde* literary technique it was pioneered by William Burroughs, and is related to the art technique of montage. There was a vogue for 'indeterminacy' technique in the arts in the 1960s, because it was (questionably) felt to have an authenticity about it which conscious intention lacked. The most famous cut-up lyric in rock is probably David Bowie's 'Moonage Daydream', with its cut-up-derived squawking pink monkey bird.

This is how it works: choose two or three pieces of writing. These could be your own discarded old lyrics, poems, bits of dialogue, prose from a novel or short story, non-fictional prose, advertising copy, newspaper articles, anything that catches your eye. Copy the words onto paper so that you can cut them into individual bits. Put them in a box, shake them around, and start pulling them out, trying to arrange them in phrases. The result will be peculiar, funny, startling, silly, nonsensical and evocative juxtapositions of words, which constitute a sketch. You will need to turn them into grammatical phrases in the first draft. If a cut-up is productive you will get some imaginative phrases and possibly a theme. A more refined approach would be to choose texts that were thematically related, like three famous poems on political freedom or growing roses. You can experiment with texts written in different time periods, as long as you even out any discrepancies of language in the final drafts (removing archaic or obscure words).

Tools of the trade

"A computer is only of use to me to type a final legible draft ... I find that, despite the variety of fonts available, the ordered appearance of the computer screen kills the rhythm of the written word. Sometimes the page needs to be tiny and crumpled. Sometimes it must be vast and pristine." (Elvis Costello)[47]

"I like to write on notebooks. I generally use the computer a little later on, to move verses around." (Leonard Cohen)[48]

"I love reference books that help me with words, dictionaries of slang, superstition, phrase and fable, the *Book Of Knowledge*, things that help me find words that have a musicality to them." (Tom Waits)[49]

Writing lyrics hardly requires the technology of the recording process, but there are a few tools of the trade, and finding which work best for you is important. First to consider are the materials used to put down your sketch. Songwriters will say that, for them individually, there is a world of difference between lined or unlined paper, narrow or wide feint, margin or unmargined, loose-leaf, spiral-bound, A4 or A5, blue ink, black ink, hard pencil, soft pencil, and so on. Everyone has a preference.

Personally, I find there's something easeful and 'organic' about writing sketches and drafts on paper with a soft, sharp pencil rather than ink. As for paper size and rule, narrow feint paper keeps more lines in front of you at a time, especially if it's A4, though A4 won't fit in a coat-pocket (an A5 notebook might). I never write on a computer screen until the lyric is nearly finished, when type confers a dispassionate perspective that can assist in polishing the lyric. Perhaps a word-processor encourages the wrong part of the brain at the start of writing. If you're reaching for inspiration you need to look inward, into your imagination, not outward at a screen.

If you know how to write melody in conventional notation, a book with lines on one side and music staves on the other, such as Janis Ian used, is handy. Blank guitar chord boxes on one side of the notebook are handy, so you can write the chords down for the song (crucial with altered tunings where none of the shapes are conventional). I also find in drafting that I write out the lyric from start to finish *each time* I re-draft, including lines I'm not changing, because it keeps the conscious mind occupied with the mechanical business of copying what's already there, so that new ideas can pop up from the unconscious to fill in blanks or improve phrases.

If during a later draft you need to reconsider a single word or phrase, because it isn't what you want to say, the tool for the trade is a thesaurus. This is a reference book that gives equivalent or close-related words (known as 'synonyms') from which to select one that is a better fit. When sorting out rhymes you will find a rhyming dictionary extremely helpful. You can even use it to provide a group of effective rhymes before you start writing. A decent dictionary is handy for checking meanings. Books of quotations and proverbs are good sources for finding common phrases.

Writing a sketch

"I usually start with a conversational line and don't stop till I get to the end. I don't worry about whether it's any good or makes sense. Then I review it all." (Chris Difford of Squeeze)[50]

When you are writing a sketch, keep going until you get tired, your attention breaks, or you run out of lines. This phase of the process often feels like a spell cast over you. Stay in it as long as you can. This feeling indicates that unconscious and intuitive parts of the mind are in play. In the 'spell-state' you lose your awareness of time and what is going on around you; concentration develops and deepens. One of the great rewards of any creativity, this state can give a sense of calm, a curious power, a potent balance, such as exhibited by a tightrope walker. Poets and writers often describe it as being like possession by a greater energy. If you find your ideas go off in an unexpected direction, let them. It could be your sketch will result in two or three lyrics, rather than one. Make that decision later.

If you already have a tune, or a chord progression, playing this over, or in your mind, or listening to an instrumental recording, can help bring ideas forward and keep you in the spell-state.

A first look

When the spell-state finally fades, like a glider drifting in to land, you can stop, take a break, make a drink, then come back and glance over your scribbles. What have you got?

- Notice the lines that stand alone, and the others that connect up for four or five or six at a stretch, long enough to make a verse. Do you have a sense of how long the verses will be?
- Look for the lines that could fit together.
- Look for patterns of phrasing, or potential patterns. These could determine the whole structure of the lyric. An obvious example is a list.
- Some single lines will suggest ways in which they could be developed.
- What is the theme or story or mood emerging from the sketch? If you see more than one, either discard the less interesting, or the one for which you have fewer lines. You might be able to use it for the bridge of the song where a contrast might be needed.
- Scan the sketch for a memorable phrase or image that could be the song title, and therefore possibly shape the chorus. This phrase may well sum up what the song is about.
- Think about where the song will start and where it will end. This includes looking for what might be a memorable first line (though this can be developed later – the first thing is to decide where the lyric is going to begin in terms of content. If it is a story, where does the story begin? Take the first line you have and then re-work it to make it striking in a later draft.)
- See if you can decide whether this lyric will have rhyme and, if so, what kind. It is a good idea to bring rhyme in as early as you can if you're going to have it. Trying to turn a later unrhymed draft into a rhymed lyric can be difficult and produce a stilted effect.

After the sketch comes what I call the first draft.

The first draft

Drafting is the process of re-writing a lyric sketch to shape, clarify, improve, and finally polish it. The first draft is when you begin to shape the rough material, laying out a structure that will carry the lyric through the remaining drafts.

I don't call the sketch the first draft, because the sketch is itself a different process, driven by inspiration, not by selective editing of something now in front of you. With the first draft you continue the inspiration of the sketch but go on to shape, select, re-phrase, supplement and eliminate. This is also creative, and should be conducted in as inspired a frame of mind as you can, so that new ideas can feed in. It is desirable to do the first draft of your 'sketch' as soon as possible after the sketch. That way you stay in touch with the inspiration. Try to do as many drafts in one sitting as are necessary to get the basic shape and content of the lyric. Precise corrections and polishing can wait, because the fundamental structure of the lyric is in place.

So as to not encourage destructive self-censorship, reserve judgement about your sketch. Don't be too critical at this stage, and don't agonise over single words. Go for overall sequence, imagery and basic theme. The demands of your critical faculties should increase only with later drafts. The time to agonise over a single word, verb, or adjective, is when the lyric has been through a number of drafts, not on the first. Much more important is finding the central energy of the lyric, as this is the point that people must be able to identify with. The central energy of a lyric is most often located in:

- a chorus
- a repeated refrain (if it doesn't have a chorus)
- a first line and/or a title.

As an example of 'central energy' in a lyric, think about The Beatles' 'All You Need Is Love' (no doubting what *that* song is about) or the climax phrase/title in 'Born To Run'. Think about your favourite songs and identify where this central energy is expressed lyrically.

If you find the sketch won't yield anything coherent, no matter how you look at it, don't worry. Put it aside and if you have the energy, write another one, and start from a different inspiration. If you feel there's no more creative juice, leave it and do something else that benefits your music. Keep your unused sketch. It may be that at a later date, halfway through another lyric, you find lines in this unused sketch that can be salvaged in another lyric. Or it may be that with the passage of time you'll be able to revisit this sketch and find a way to rescue it.

Further drafts

Continue drafting for as long as it takes to get a coherent lyric. If your initial sketch and draft provide a lot of material there may need to be some drastic cutting. The original sketch of Hendrix's 'Purple Haze' ran for pages and pages and had to be boiled down to three verses and a bridge. For Ray Davies of The Kinks, "it's a discipline, like exercising. It's very difficult to get to the nub of what you want to say in three minutes when you want to say hundreds of things. You have to use an editorial system and say in two lines three pages' worth of ideas."[51]

After two or three drafts, it may be that you need only to reconsider the odd word here and there. If you already have music for this lyric you could be checking each draft against the music to see if the words fit or are singable. When a draft is nearly a finished lyric, type it on a word-processor. At this late stage strive for objectivity. Seeing your words in cold type on a screen (or printed out), no longer in your handwriting, depersonalises them.

This is an aid to seeing the effectiveness of the lyric is and whether bits need to be changed.

Finally, a cooling-off period is advised. Come back to the lyric after a few days and see how it looks. You may find that you can fix a problem then that you can't solve now. It may also be that if you go on to compose the music for this lyric the music will dictate changes (such as having too many verses, or too many lines in the chorus). Not all songs can be composed and written in a short space of time.

A final polish

The historian Thomas Carlyle once described genius as "the infinite capacity for taking pains". What seems pure inspiration can often be the result of hard work. Even at a late stage you can, if you wish, take greater trouble to improve your lyric. Since some people think lyrics don't matter, or that audiences don't listen to them, this might be considered artistic ambition going beyond what is pragmatically necessary. The controversy over Bruce Springsteen's 'Born In The USA' (was it anti-American or gung-ho patriotic?) is a salutary warning about how a lyric can be misinterpreted. He always said that the song was not ambiguous: it just needed people to listen to the verses as well as the chorus.

The last touch could be a significant change such as altering the hook-line and title. Thin Lizzy's 'The Boys Are Back In Town' was originally called 'GI Joe Is Back In Town' but bassist and singer Phil Lynott changed it because it didn't sound right. It could be changing a "but" to a "yet". Here are some songwriters describing the final stages in the quest for the finished lyric.

"I worked for two or three nights just to find one line that was right. There were so many alternatives but only a few were right for the song." (Kate Bush on 'Houdini')[52]

"There's a song I really wanted to put on this record [*I'm Alive*] called 'Alive In The World'. It's really good. But there's this one moment, this one line, and it's the kind of line that can be shouted out over the battlements, that can be inscribed on something permanently, that's got to actually stand, like an emblem – and I don't know what the line is. It's the kind of line that you can't just throw off. So I just couldn't finish the song." (Jackson Browne)[53]

Conversely, there is also artistic judgement in knowing when to stop with a lyric. It is possible to over-refine, and lose the freshness of a lyric's earlier drafts. Sometimes the fault in a lyric lies too deep to be able to change it without essentially starting again, like a human hair trapped in the glaze on a pot. Making superficial changes can't always alter such a blemish. Leonard Cohen used a parallel with poetry to remind us that a lyric sometimes needs to be left alone: "[poet W.H.] Auden used to say: the poem is never finished, it's abandoned. At a certain point you've done all you can to bring it into existence and if you go a little further you start ruining it so you pull back."[54]

A related skill is the ability to see when an idea is not worth pursuing. This takes experience. Songwriters have different views on the question of spontaneity versus craftsmanship. Pete Waterman believed, "The best art is always naïve. If I find myself working for a long time on an idea, I abandon it."[55] Sometimes it is a matter of self-awareness, knowing that you are too tired, distracted, or disinclined, to sketch or re-draft. As Madonna says, '... when that happens, you just have to stop and go out or something. Go to a movie ... there are times when you just have to let it alone. And go get some inspiration. Ultimately, you can't force it. But there is a certain amount of discipline required."[56]

Rewriting an old lyric

The skills you develop getting from a sketch to a draft, and then from a first or second draft to a final version, are skills which can be applied to rescuing old lyrics. It is a common experience among songwriters that the lyrics date faster than the music. If you have been writing songs for any length of time it is normal to find that earlier lyrics look feeble, silly, immature and/or incoherent. You may change your mind how you feel about the topic. That young woman (or man) you met at that party who intoxicated you for a month, and half a dozen songs of rapture, turns out to have feet of clay and a real capacity for giving you grief. You can't stand those lyrics; but you still like the music.

Of course, since your audience don't know how things turned out, they may be happy to hear you sing those rapturous love songs with the original words. How things turned out doesn't matter to them; what they hear are songs of being-in-love. This is a first lesson in the artistic justification of insincerity. However, if there was something false, or inauthentic, or self-deceiving, in the emotion from which the song came, then that may have rubbed off on the lyrics. In which case (and not because things didn't turn out the way you hoped) it might be time to perform a salvage operation. Rather than scrap the song altogether, go back and rescue the lyric. This, after all, is the age of recycling! Sometimes it is a matter of adjusting a few words and phrases but keeping the overall situation.

At its most drastic, salvaging a song from a bad or immature lyric means throwing away the original words and starting again. This is easier said than done, because you have to find a new words, maybe a new theme, for music which will, initially, constantly remind you of the old words. The process may even make you change the music itself. Some odd things happen in this creative territory – the way the emotion from the old scrapped lyric can hang over into the new one with no apparent sign of where it comes from. Sometimes the change is about adjusting the emotional balance in a lyric, being fairer to the subject, covering your tracks, making things less personal, or less obscure.

As an insight into revising and re-writing a lyric, you could search out John Lennon's revision of 'Child Of Nature' into 'Jealous Guy', George Harrison's rejected stanza from 'While My Guitar Gently Weeps', or the two versions of Bruce Springsteen's 'Stolen Car'. This haunting song was originally released on *The River*, but the 4-CD box-set *Tracks* has an earlier version with a lyric twice as long. If you look on www.leonardcohen.com, you can even see original drafts of songs such as 'Suzanne' and 'Joan Of Arc' in Cohen's own handwriting and with all his crossings-out.

David Crosby

Interviewed by Sid Griffin

As a founder member of The Byrds, and a constant around which various permutations of Graham Nash, Neil Young and Steven Stills still form, David Crosby is one of rock's key figures. His songwriting fuses folk, pop, jazz, and Indian influences, with his lyrics encompassing the personal and social in equal measure.

Do you have a particular routine to get into when you know you want to sit down to write lyrics?
No, but that's an interesting item there. I have always wished I could write the way Bob Dylan writes where he gets up in the morning and starts writing on his typewriter and here come the lyrics. He's done this his whole life and I have never been able to do this and wish I was able to.

What I have found is that very often when I am going to sleep there is the period where the verbal crystallization level which is talking to you right now starts to slow down and go to sleep and another level which is more like an imaginative, intuitive level that is capable of making longer leaps of connection … that level gets a shot at the steering wheel for a minute and I will be almost asleep and suddenly words will start to come and I will have to wake up, turn on the light and start to madly scribble on something next to me.

And I remember asking a science fiction author that I love, William Gibson, if he had ever experienced that and he said "Yeah, all writers know this . . . we call it 'The Elves Take Over The Workshop' and that's why all good writers have a pad and pen next to their bed." I didn't know that. Yet sometimes the entire song will come out in one blurb: words, music, title, and it definitely happens to me. Sometimes it is just the words and if I don't have a musical inclination with it I will call James [Raymond, his son, the R of CPR] or Nash [Graham] or one of other people I write with. Mostly James these days.

We work together quite a bit on all the CPR music. The result has been a bunch of good music, some of the best I have ever written.

Paul Simon is notorious for rewriting and rewriting his lyrics to get them perfect. Other writers largely stick with what they were inspired to write the first time. Where do you stand on this?
I do much more than I did when I started. When I started I would just scribble it down and that was it, that was pretty much it. Then sometimes, you know, somebody would suggest something which would improve it, Nash in particular here; but generally I used to go with what I got start off the bat.

Then when I started using a computer all of a sudden I found I was a much better editor of my own work because I could take this out, put it up here, take that out, put it down there, move that up to here as the facility a computer gives you to work with your lyrics is tremendous. I did a whole lot more editing, polishing, experimenting and crafting after I started putting down my lyrics on computer.

How old were you when you started writing songs? Were you playing the coffee houses back in LA?
Yes, I started writing when I was maybe 19 or 20 years old, something like that. The first song I ever wrote was called, I think, 'Across The Plains', and it was not very good. I'm glad my early efforts happened but … the first song I ever wrote which was a decent song was probably 'Everybody's Been Burned' which The Byrds did [*Younger Than Yesterday* 1967].

What about 'I See You' by the Byrds? You're not keen on some of your other earlier songs?
Nah, I think 'Everybody's Been Burned' was probably the first really good one. It was kind of a torch ballad but it was jazzy and you could do a lot of things with it.

Which of your lyrics are you most proud of and why?
Hmmm, this is a tough question. You know I like the lyrics to 'Wooden Ships' quite a bit, I like the lyrics to 'Guinnevere' [*Crosby, Stills and Nash* 1969] quite a bit, I like the lyrics to 'Déjà Vu' [Crosby, Stills, Nash and Young, *Déjà Vu* 1970], but probably the ones I really like would be later ones from CPR: say 'Somehow She Knew' [*CPR* 1998]. 'In My Dreams' [Crosby, Stills And Nash, *CSN* 1977] is one of my best sets of lyrics. 'Dream For Him' [Crosby, Stills, Nash And Young, *Looking Forward* 1999] is good, I think 'At The Edge' [CPR 1998] is probably one of my very best sets of words. You have to read that last one; I just think they are really good words and the same for 'Angel Dream' [*Just Like Gravity* 2001]. I think 'Angel Dream' is one of my very, very best sets of words.

When writing a lyric sometimes you are telling a story and sometimes you clearly have a message you want to get across. What is the difference between the two?
The difference is I feel the 'telling the tale' songs have served me better. I wish that when I had a message to deliver I could be more circumspect and do it in a story form. I think that generally is more effective. You look at some of the story ones and they seem to do the job better, like 'Monkey And The Underdog' (*Just Like Gravity*) and when I just talk directly to you sometimes it is just not as effective. Let me put it this way: I wish I could write more story songs. Like 'Cowboy Movie' (*If I Could Only Remember My Name* 1971).

Do you find certain themes or interests in songwriting that you feel comfortable returning to?
I find with great regularity I wind up talking about dreams. I am not sure how this happens but they seem to loom very large in my lexicon of subject matter. To put it in a broader scope I write mostly about love. I write about love found, love lost, love explored, love unrequited, love treasured … that's really what I write about most.

One theme of yours I like is the sea and sailing.
That's quite natural. They say "write from what you know" and obviously it has been a huge part of my life. The sea and sailing are just fantastic metaphors for situations in real life. I've sailed since I was 11 so that means I have been sailing for 53 years!

At what stage in the songwriting process do your lyrics form? Are you a title first guy like Pete Townshend usually is or does it take a guitar riff first or what?
There is no set way with me. It happens every which way. Very often for me it is the words first as they are the hardest part but many times it has been words and music at the same time and a few times it has been music first. And some of those latter times it has been music I have developed over years, literally years.

There are a number of cases where I have had a theme where I have played it on the guitar a very long time before it finally gels into a song. There then is obviously co-writing. I love to co-write with other writers because you spark each other and you wind up going someplace you would not have gone. Look at 'Yvette In English,' [*Thousand Roads* 1993] which I wrote with Joni [Mitchell], a song which definitely came out a way I would never have had it go… look at 'Hero' [*Thousand Roads*] with Phil Collins or all of the stuff I have written with James. I really love writing with somebody else, it is probably my most favorite way.

Are you like Dylan in the lyrics are most important or are you, with your unusual guitar tunings and sophisticated harmonies, more of a melody man when writing songs?
That's a tough question. It varies from song to song. Some songs the lyrics are definitely more important. You get a song like 'They Want It All,' (*Crosby And Nash* 2005) the whole thing is in the story I am telling you about Enron as the music doesn't really matter at all other than as a canvas to paint on. In general, though, the music is so important in being the context, which allows you to deliver the words and deliver the emotion and the emotional context the words need. Although I think it is harder to write memorable words than it is to write memorable music. Good, memorable lyrics anyway.

Is there any way you know you can find inspiration or it is waiting for the moment when it comes to you?

Other people can just do it. The only thing I can do is make a space for it. Pick up an instrument … I keep a couple of guitars right next to my bed, I am looking at 'em right now, and I play them to sort of tickle the old muse button and see if there happens to be a muse flying by. So at least you are making a space for it to happen. I have always wished I could write on demand. *[Adopts silly voice]* "Hey, write a song about the Eiffel Tower!" *[Sings in music hall voice]* "It's big and built in a hole and it's tall and it's GREEAAATTTT!" I can't, though. I have never been able to write songs on demand.

Are there popular music clichéd images or themes you try and avoid yourself? You know, references or metaphors you cringe from when you hear them?

I try not to think about that. Because it will cripple you as a writer from going for the very heart or throat of something good or bad when you want all your emotional avenues open. You shouldn't say "Gee, Paul Simon already used that image." I don't want to think like that, I want to go to the heart of the thing I am trying to communicate and not worry about someone saying there has already been a tune with horses in a rainstorm in it. I don't really care. Because all of this has been said before and all of it has been played before. The best melody I ever came up with no doubt some poor South American peasant with a flute played 4,000 years ago. There is no really new stuff, so why worry? Go for the heart of the thing anyway and don't worry about anybody else having used it.

You are unique as a songwriter with your use of modal tunings, science fiction images, sophisticated church and jazz harmonies, your shying away from repeating a big anthemic chorus every verse . . . has this uniqueness helped or hurt you?

Good question! In general I think it helps to have a willingness to push the envelope and try to do new things. It generally helps you, though every once in a while you can get a little far out and you shock the people around you. I remember when I was in The Byrds and I did 'Mind Gardens' (*Younger Than Yesterday*) and the people around me thought I had surely skipped a beat and were sure I was gonna go completely bonkers any second. 'Cos that was pretty strange. But I liked it. And I liked the fact it did two or three brand new things that other people weren't doing. Same for 'Critical Mass' or some songs on my first solo album, *If I Could Only Remember My Name*, like 'Tamalpais High (At About Three)' or 'Song With No Words (Tree With No Leaves)'.

In terms of the business and the music industry do you feel you get respect from your fellow writers?

Fellow writers respect, yes. The industry's respect, no. What the music industry wants is a clone of whatever is top of the charts. The last thing they want is innovation, they couldn't give a fuck less about that. Cause they are like a school of fish in that they are all following each other and they don't want to do something new. It scares them; anything new totally befuddles them and scares them. That is the music industry. They are absolutely not okay with art or trying to do new art; it has nothing to do with what they want to do.

My peers, on the other hand, yes. People will come up to me and say, "Man, that one tune such-and-such … how did you DO *that*?" So I tell them what it was I did or played to get the song as they heard it. The strange guitar tunings helped me out a tremendous bit here. I learned a tremendous amount from Joni and a tremendous amount from Michael Hedges. I think Michael Hedges just about split my skull open when I heard him. Also a Bulgarian folk music LP from the 1950s, that really had a huge influence on me. I heard that when I was in The Byrds. I got turned onto that and Ravi Shankar bang, bang, right in a row and that screwed with my mind a great deal.

When you are writing a song how important is the title to you? You've had some offbeat titles to your tunes.

Yeah, 'Tamalpais High (At About 3)' is one. Just the album

title *If I Could Only Remember My Name* is one. I was told that was too long a title. I don't think titles are too important, I think the content is the deal though sure, I have fun with titles just like other writers do.

How important is the first line of a song in drawing the listener in?
Oh, crucial. The first couple of lines are the entry point for the journey you want to take the listeners on; this is where you get them to step on the train in the first place. They are crucial.

Would you spend more time on the opening of a song just to get them on the train?
Not usually. The opening lines of the song are frequently the first piece of inspiration that comes to the writer, and they usually come pretty fast. The place where it takes more honing and crafting is later on in the song when the writer is trying to sustain that level of inspiration and craft which flowed so effortlessly at the top of the song. You have to have a sensible journey to the song with a beginning, middle and an end. The ends of songs are very critical too.

How do you feel about rhyming? Some of your songs scan very well as poetry and some are free verse.
'Mind Gardens' certainly didn't rhyme! I like rhyming and generally my songs rhyme but sometimes I toss it to the winds and don't bother.

When you do rhyme do you stay with it until you feel your rhymes are perfect?
Nothing's perfect. Rhyming is a sub-art form in itself, a really strong part of great songwriting. It is fun to be clever with it and fun to do it. What I really like is making the rhyme happen before the end of the line. Do two lines which scan out, the second line rhymes and ends then there would be a tag and end of two or four or six more words after that. I like that. Then there is internal rhyming within the line of the song.

Now, many times I will do as in the song 'Games' (*Graham Nash/David Crosby* 1972). The word "more" rhymes with the word "war" at the end of a line, and then I sing "don't you know that" which is just a tag after the line of the song. And I like doing that.

When you are writing songs are there traps to avoid which you have fallen into before?
Yes. Yes. And I think probably the biggest one for me is preaching. Sort of pontificating. I don't like it when I catch myself doing it. It drives me bats. What I want to do is tell you a little story that has the truth which I am trying to get across buried in it, but sometimes I am so pissed off I talk right to you. And that would be 'They Want It All' [*Crosby And Nash* 2004] or that kind of a song. Which is, you know, less sophisticated and is kind of a punch in the jaw; but sometimes that is how you feel.

Can the popular song lyric deal with any particular subject?
Yes. There are absolutely no rules.

Have you tried to push the envelope out here as well?
Yeah, I mean as I said I mostly write about love but you can write about anything. 'Just Like Gravity' [CPR, *Just Like Gravity* 2001] is a good example. It is literally a song about gravity. Literally, seriously, about gravity. It is not about something else.

Which other songwriters do you admire today?
Let me give you a list. Joni Mitchell. Bob Dylan. Randy Newman, Jackson Browne, Neil Young, Graham Nash, Bonnie Raitt, Nickel Creek, James Taylor. Michael Hedges' songs on *Watching My Life Go By* stunned me, they were such beautiful songs … and Shawn Colvin almost above everybody except Joni. Shawn Colvin just knocks my dick in the dirt. She is a brilliant writer and I wish to God I was as good as her.

Section 4

the magic of titles

A strong title can do wonders for a song, whether providing its initial inspiration or summing up its theme and mood. It can even help you structure your writing.

"The songs have titles that read like paperback novels." (*Melody Maker* review of Procol Harum's *A Salty Dog*, July 1969)

"So I'm like anybody else with the title. I purely wrote whatever I got out of it. I didn't have any problems with thinking it was, like, gay men or anything. I just loved the metre, I just loved the shapes of the words." (Jim Capaldi of Traffic on 'The Low Spark Of High-Heeled Boys')[57]

For many songwriters the beginning of a lyric inspiration is the title. In my own songwriting, I've always reserved a page in each notebook purely for writing down titles. I thought this was a personal bias, but researching this book, I have been struck by how many other songwriters say they also value titles, and therefore what a significant role the title takes in lyric writing.

So many writers use a title as the seed from which to 'grow' a song-lyric. US band Fountains of Wayne wrote three songs for a debut album in 1995 and then spent a week in a New York bar making lists of titles to see if they could turn them into songs. There are very good reasons for valuing titles:

- Never underestimate the power of a good title. It can inspire you to write a lyric. Keep a list of potential titles for songs.

- A title can stabilise the theme and mood of a song until you get around to writing the whole lyric and music.

- A title can inspire your audience. If you're writing a batch of songs for an album imagine picking up the finished CD and glancing at the titles. This is what people are going to do in a music store or surfing the web. A title may influence someone to listen to, or download, a track out of sheer curiosity.

- Titles are the first point of contact with your music for artist management and record companies when they see your demo. Before they've heard a note of music they see the title. What effect will the titles have?

- Have your titles been used before? Led Zeppelin were not the first songwriters to title a song 'Stairway To Heaven'. Neil Sedaka released a single of that name in 1960. But let's face it, no-one else is going to write a better 'Stairway To Heaven' than Led Zep's, so discretion suggests you leave that title alone.

- If they were someone else's songs would the titles make you curious to hear the music?

- Do your titles have character? Do they stir your imagination? Consider 'Baby I Want Your Love', 'Another Day' or 'Blue Sky'. Such, and similar, titles have been used many times; they're not exactly inspiring. An unimaginative title may indicate unimaginative music.

- Be clever, be memorable, be relevant to your lyric.
- Unless you are writing a concept album, don't have too many similar titles on an album, and make sure two that are similar don't go next to each other in the running order. Roy Orbison's album *In Dreams* (1963) had 'In Dreams', 'Dreams', 'All I Have To Do Is Dream', and 'Beautiful Dreamer'. Maybe that's too many 'dream' titles in close proximity.

Having a good title early on when writing a lyric matters, because *where* it comes in the lyric has a significant effect on the structure. A title may determine what is the first line of the song, the last line of a verse, or the shape of the chorus. The strongest position is in the chorus where it functions as the hook of the song. As such, it is likely to be sung quite a few times during the song and will therefore stick in listeners' minds. It can also go at the beginning of the verse, or the end of the verse, or at the end of alternating lines if you want to use it as a refrain. Sometimes it will end up elsewhere. Commenting on his lyric for 'I Say A Little Prayer', Hal David noted that the title would ordinarily fall in the chorus, but that he chose to put it in a "less obvious place", the middle of the verse. The danger, though, is that people will think that the chorus hook is the title.

A witty title which isn't very singable won't make a good chorus. Think about where in the lyric you want to put the title, or even if it is going to be there at all. 'Desperado', 'Eight Miles High', and 'Everybody's Talkin' At Me', are three songs with the title as the first phrase of the lyric. If the title isn't anywhere in the song, listeners would have to remember the title not from the song performance but from the DJ saying afterwards, "That was 'Amber Sunlight Days' by The Fire Department". The title is the label by which people remember your song. If you make it catchy it helps the song lodge in their minds.

Choosing a title

The title should indicate what the song is about, its mood or emotion, or something about the central event or story. Occasionally you may want to title a song by a phrase that isn't in the song itself but describes what the song is about. Otherwise, if the title isn't obvious, look through your lyric and either choose a phrase that would make a good title or think of one that encapsulates the song. The incompleteness of a title can itself be a deliberate hook.

Some song titles use brackets to add information, which means the song can be known by long and short form. You can develop a personal style of song title, as Bob Dylan did when in the mid-1960s he wrote titles like 'Queen Jane Approximately' and 'Positively Fourth Street'. These stood out at the time because of the unusual placement of words like "approximately" and "positively". They gave the titles ambiguity and energy. How much less interesting would be Bob Dylan's 'Queen Jane' and 'Fourth Street'!

Finally, try not to over-amplify. This does for our sensibilities what sticking your head in a PA stack does for your ears. Take Curtis Lee's title 'Pretty Little Angel Eyes'. OK, we get it – she's cute and you like her a lot. Still, those eyes don't have to be pretty AND little AND angelic!

Types of title

Here is a selection of *styles* of title. This is not an exhaustive catalogue, and some titles belong to more than one of the categories, but it provides valuable templates. If you have already written songs you may recognise a type you already use. These categories will help you see how to unpack the implications of a title, so that you understand how your own title ideas can set up a lyric. This assists the process of writing a sketch.

PRONOUNS

"Marvin [Gaye] was a sex symbol from the start. That gave me the idea to encourage the writers to create 'You' type songs where he could sing directly to the women. 'YOU're a wonderful one…', 'YOU are my pride and joy.' … He even recorded a song just called 'You'." (Berry Gordy)[58]

These are titles that have "I", "you", "he", "she", "they", and "our" in them, often with the word "love" there too. They are very popular, especially in commercial songwriting. They immediately establish the presence of persons and invite us to identify with them. We can imagine we are being addressed, or that the singer is speaking for us to someone else we wish to address. These titles often reveal what the dynamic is in the relationship(s) in the song. The Motown song-catalogue is full of them and there are many in the early songs of The Beatles. The most over-used of these is 'I Want You', which is the title of songs by Bob Dylan, Squeeze, Elvis Costello, Madonna, The Beatles, Basement Jaxx, Marvin Gaye, and more.

Motown songs: 'I Was Made To Love Her'; 'I Know I'm Losing You'; 'You Keep Me Hanging On'; 'I Heard It Through The Grapevine'; 'How Sweet It Is To Be Loved By You'; 'It's Wonderful (To Be Loved By You)'. The Beatles: 'She Loves You'; 'I Want To Hold Your Hand'; 'And I Love Her'; 'From Me To You'; 'I Saw Her Standing There'; 'You've Got To Hide Your Love Away'.

PERSONAL STATEMENT

A variation on the pronoun title is where it makes a specific statement about the speaker, the "I". This sets up the lyric as an explanation of this initial statement and its consequences. Consider a title like 'I'm Gonna Make You Love Me'. It prepares us for a lyric explaining *why* the speaker has to *make* the other person love him or her, how they intend to do it, what they hope will happen, and so on.

The Beatles: 'I Feel Fine'; 'I Call Your Name'; 'I Am The Walrus'; 'I Need You'; 'I'm Down'; 'I've Got A Feeling'; George Harrison 'If Not For You'; Bob Dylan 'It Ain't Me Babe'; The Who 'I Can See For Miles'; The Monkees 'I'm A Believer'; David Bowie 'John, I'm Only Dancing'; The Kaiser Chiefs 'Everyday I Love You Less And Less'.

CONDITIONAL

A 'conditional' song title adds a word or phrase which makes the statement depend on something else – a piece of information, an event, a cause or a fear. These titles exploit words like "if", "can", "can't", "don't", "just", "when", "then", "after", "ain't", "be", "because", "from", "here", "how", "keep", "let". They make the title dynamic because it functions like half of an equation, with the other half implied or stated in the lyric.

Hence Chicago's 'If You Leave Me Now' sets up an expectation of finding out the consequence posited by the title. Bruce Springsteen's 'Out In The Street' could have been titled (after what he sings in the chorus) '*When I'm* Out In The Street', which has a different emphasis.

The Beatles 'When I Get Home'; 'If I Fell'; Trini Lopez 'If I Had A Hammer'; Tim Hardin 'If I Were A Carpenter'; Jimi Hendrix 'If 6 Was 9'; Harold Melvin And The Blue Notes 'If You Don't Know Me By Now'; Elvis Presley 'I Just Can't Help Believing'; Temptations 'Just My Imagination'; Patti Smith 'Because The Night'; Percy Sledge 'When A Man Loves A Woman'; Fleetwood Mac 'Don't Stop'.

TITLES WITH VERBS

Since verbs denote action they give a title energy. This covers very general verbs like "come", "get", "give", "hold", and well as verbs like "run", as in Bryan Adams' 'Run To You'. In these titles the speaker, or another character, is doing something. The lyric can develop from this action, its cause and its consequence.

The Beatles 'Ask Me Why'; 'Carry That Weight'; 'Drive My Car'; 'Fixing A Hole'; The Supremes 'Come See About Me'; Billy Ocean 'Get Out Of My Dreams, Get Into My Car'; Spencer Davis Group 'Keep On Running'.

DESCRIPTIVE TITLES

Some titles are plain descriptions. They might be the name of a person, or a place, or a time, or an event. They are apt not to be as dynamic as other titles, though they are usually clear in meaning. To make them dynamic, or give a hint as to the theme, add a word that suggests a mood, action or event. The Beatles didn't write a song called 'Strawberry Fields', it was 'Strawberry Fields *Forever*'. That "forever" gives us a glimpse of the speaker's feelings towards the place. A traditional descriptive title might have the word "ballad" in it, as in 'The Ballad Of John And Yoko', to signify a lyric that tells a story.

The Beatles 'Birthday' (time); 'Christmas Time (Is Here Again)' (time); 'Penny Lane' (place); Small Faces 'Itchycoo Park' (place); Kinks 'Waterloo Sunset' (time and place); Crosby Stills Nash & Young 'Marrakesh Express' (journey and place); Bee Gees 'New York Mining Disaster 1941' (place and event); Ocean Colour Scene 'The Day We Caught The Train' (journey and time).

OPPOSITES

One potent form of title is that which has some kind of opposition. Such a title indicates the lyric may be about conflict, and the struggle to bridge the tension between the terms. Pushed far enough, this can lead to outright paradox rather than simple contrast (see below).

The Beach Boys 'Heroes And Villains'; Free 'Fire And Water'; James Taylor 'Fire And Rain'; The Faces 'Glad And Sorry'; McCartney and Wonder 'Ebony And Ivory'; Joni Mitchell 'Shadows And Light'; Corrs 'Love Gives Love Takes'; The Beatles 'Hello Goodbye'; 'Within You, Without You'; Johnny Cash 'I Forgot To Remember To Forget'; U2 'With Or Without You'.

PROPOSITION

A proposition title is one which sets out an idea, rather than an action or feeling. Such titles are often versions of proverbs, or catchphrases that express current opinion. They may be offered as a corrective or as a consolation.

Although the use of "you" suggests a speaker introducing the idea to an audience, the song might also be addressed to the self. The lyric should explain the proposition and why it is important to the speaker, usually describing an experience which led to its adoption.

The Doors 'People Are Strange'; The Yardbirds 'You Can't Judge A Book By The Cover'; The Rolling Stones 'You Can't Always Get What You Want'; Mary Wells 'Let Your Conscience Be Your Guide'; Marvin Gaye And Tammi Terell 'You Ain't Living Until You're Loving'; Temptations 'Everybody Needs Love'; Smokey Robinson And The Miracles 'I Don't Blame You At All'; Korgis 'Everybody's Got To Learn Sometime'; The Beatles 'All You Need Is Love'.

QUESTION/INTERROGATIVE FORM

A title can invite curiosity if it asks a question, makes a demand, or addresses someone.

The Beatles 'Do You Want To Know A Secret?', 'You Can't Do That'; Travis 'Why Does It Always Rain On Me?'; Buzzcocks 'Ever Fallen In Love With Someone'; The Clash 'Should I Stay Or Should I Go?'; Dire Straits 'Where Do You Think You're Going?'; The Beach Boys 'Wouldn't It Be Nice'; Jeff Buckley 'Lover, You Should've Come Over'; Moody Blues 'Go Now'.

REPETITION

Many titles use repetition, which helps the title/hook lodge in people's minds. Repetition is rhythmic and well-suited to a chorus; it can also intensify a word. The commonest repetition in a title is where words are repeated twice or three times. A pleasing variation is where a word is repeated in a modified form, as with Fleetwood Mac's 'Dreamin' The Dream', Hole's 'Softer, Softest', or Travis' 'The Last Laugh Of The Laughter'.

REPETITION BY TWO: The Beatles 'Cry Baby Cry', 'She Said, She Said'; Monkees 'A Little Bit Me, A Little Bit You'; Bob Dylan 'Lay Lady Lay'; Bob Marley 'No Woman No Cry'; Smashing Pumpkins 'Tonight Tonight'; David Bowie 'Rebel Rebel'; Undertones 'Really Really'; Genesis 'Follow Me, Follow You'; Abba 'Knowing Me, Knowing You'; The Youngbloods 'Darkness, Darkness'; Strokes 'The End Is The End'.

REPETITION BY THREE: The Who 'Run Run Run'; The Hollies 'Stop Stop Stop'; The Damned 'Neat Neat Neat'; Wings 'Hi Hi Hi'; The Beatles 'Long Long Long'; Teenage Fanclub 'Dumb Dumb Dumb'; James Brown 'It's A Man's Man's Man's World'; Johnny Cash and Bobby Bland 'Cry Cry Cry'; The Beach Boys 'Fun Fun Fun'; Paul McCartney 'Say Say Say'; White Stripes 'Take Take Take'; Abba 'I Do I Do I Do I Do'.

REPETITION BY FOUR: K.C. And The Sunshine Band '(Shake Shake Shake) Shake Your Booty'

ALLITERATION

Titles (such as the above) that repeat a word also feature alliteration. This is an effect caused when words start with similar consonants. Alliteration is a linguistic device valued in poetry because it stresses the sounds of words, thus bringing them closer to the condition of music. In moderation this can be appropriate for a lyric.

Stone Roses 'Sugar Spun Sister'; K.D. Lang 'Constant Craving'; The Who 'You Better You Bet'; 'Anyway, Anyhow, Anywhere'; Scott Walker 'Plastic Palace People'; 10,000 Maniacs 'Tension Makes A Tangle'; Jim Stafford 'Spiders and Snakes'; Zombies 'Sticks and Rolling Stones'; Smokey Robinson And The Miracles 'Darling Dear'; Gene 'Sick, Sober And Sorry'; Van Morrison 'Slim Slow Slider'; AC/DC 'Dirty Deeds Done Dirt Cheap'; Heaven 17 'Penthouse And Pavement'.

RHYMING TITLES

Another way of making a title memorable is to include a rhyme. This was popular in 1950s rock'n'roll songs.

The Beatles 'For You Blue', 'Helter Skelter'; The Smiths 'Frankly Mr Shankly'; Shorty Long 'Function At The Junction'; Bill Haley And The Comets 'See You Later Alligator', 'Razzle Dazzle'; Iron Maiden 'Bring Your Daughter To The Slaughter'; Little Richard 'Good Golly Miss Molly', 'Tutti Frutti'; Badfinger 'Name Of The Game'; Marshall Crenshaw 'Someday, Someway'.

WORDPLAY TITLES

Wordplay in a title takes many forms. Sometimes a lyric generates inadvertent wordplay by virtue of the fact that different words share the same sound and can only be told apart when read. So did the Moody Blues sing about *nights* or *knights* in white satin? Did the Hollies sing about someone "Gasoline Alley *bred*', or a foodstuff "Gasoline Alley *Bread*'? Why did Elvis want to return to Zenda?

Conscious wordplay in titles goes from puns, riddles, *non sequiturs*, double meanings, incomplete phrases, and variations on catchphrases, all the way to outright paradox. Use it to tease your audience. Meatloaf famously declaimed that he'd do *anything* for love but he wouldn't do *that*. This enticed listeners to concentrate to see if the lyric explained what "that" was. The Beach Boys' *Pet Sounds* album cover brought out a double meaning in the word "pet", which could mean "favourite", since the band were pictured feeding animals. Elvis Costello developed many early song lyrics by exploring double meanings, using phrases like 'High Fidelity' and 'Needle Time' from the world of recorded sound and applying them to relationships. Both Costello ('Love For Tender') and Louis XIV ('Illegal Tender') have played with the financial meaning of "tender". Here are examples of wordplay titles, taking paradox first.

PARADOX: These titles may not all be strict paradoxes but they provoke our curiosity by asking the question, how can that be? Look through the titles and see if you grasp what the paradox is in each case. In some it is easy to see that there is a drama lurking behind the title which instantly explains the lyric theme.

Simon And Garfunkel 'Sound Of Silence'; Stereophonics 'Hurry Up And Wait'; The Strokes 'Alone, Together'; Fleetwood Mac 'Before The Beginning'; Frank Sinatra 'Glad To Be Unhappy'; Joy Division 'Love Will Tear Us Apart';

Vanessa Williams 'Colors Of The Wind'; Fifth Dimension 'Wedding Bell Blues'; David Byrne 'Tiny Apocalypse'; Beautiful South 'I Love You But You're Boring'; The Kendalls 'Heaven's Just A Sin Away'.

AMBIGUITY: These titles arouse our curiosity because they don't tell us all we need to know to make sense of them.

Undisputed Truth 'Smiling Faces Sometimes'; Love 'Seven and Seven Is'; Love 'Alone Again Or'; The Beatles 'Love You To', 'And I Love Her', 'And Your Bird Can Sing', 'That Means A Lot'; Buffalo Springfield 'For What It's Worth'; The Wallflowers 'The Beautiful Side Of Somewhere'.

WORDPLAY WITH COMMON PHRASES: Most of these work because the listener recognises the title is playing with a well-known phrase. Billy Ocean's 'When The Going Gets Tough The Tough Get Going' is a popular saying where the first "tough" is an adjective, but the second a noun referring to a group of people; the first "going" is a noun describing a set of conditions but the second is a verb. He didn't have to change anything; the word-play was in the phrase to begin with.

The Beatles 'Eight Days A Week'; Stevie Wonder 'Yester-me, Yester-you, Yesterday'; Smokey Robinson And The Miracles 'I Second That Emotion'; Brian Eno 'Seven Deadly Finns'; Electric Prunes 'I Had Too Much To Dream (Last Night)', 'Get Me To The World On Time'; Suede 'Animal Nitrate'; Def Leppard 'Armageddon It'; Robbie Williams 'Ego A Go Go'; Joan Armatrading 'Me Myself I'.

IMAGERY

A title might also be based around an image. This could be visual (in which case it is another example of a descriptive title) or a simile or metaphor, and could have a symbolic meaning. It might take the entire lyric to explain what the image means. Motown hit 'The Onion Song', credited to Marvin Gaye and Tammi Terrell, compares the world to an onion, whereas in The Beatles' 'Glass Onion' the same image is a satire on misguided interpretations of their songs. The image in a title can have its roots in the songwriter's desire to conceal the autobiographical roots of a song, as was the case with The Beatles' 'Norwegian Wood', about which John Lennon said, "I was trying to write about an affair without letting my wife know I was writing about an affair, so it was very gobbledegook. I was sort of writing from my experiences, girls' flats, things like that.'[59]

Cream 'Sunshine Of Your Love'; The Supremes 'Up The Ladder To The Roof'; 'Reflections'; Martha Reeves And The Vandellas 'Live Wire'; The Drifters 'Up On The Roof'; Bob Dylan 'Tangled Up In Blue'; David Bowie 'Always Crashing In The Same Car'; Captain Beefheart 'A Carrot Is As Close As A Rabbit Gets To A Diamond'; Supergrass 'Sofa (Of My Lethargy)'; The Marvelettes 'The Hunter Gets Captured By The Game'.

SIMILES

Similes by their very nature are propositional. A simile in a title asserts that [x] is like [y] and the presumption is that the lyric will explain this. As the following titles show, one of the most popular terms to feature as [x] is "love". Songwriters have created many similes for love, and will continue to do so.

Gene Vincent 'Love Is A Bird'; Martha Reeves And The Vandellas '(Love Is Like A) Heat Wave'; Pat Benatar 'Love Is A Battlefield'; Magnetic Fields 'Love Is Like a Bottle Of Gin'; Bob Dylan 'Like A Rolling Stone', 'Like A Hurricane'; The Verve 'Life's An Ocean'; The Supremes 'Happy (Is A Bumpy Road)'; Johnny Cash 'Dark As A Dungeon'; 10cc 'Life Is A Minestrone'; 10,000 Maniacs 'Like The Weather'.

SLANG

One fast method to signal your 'hipness' to the audience is to use slang (as long as it's this year's slang and not that from forty years ago, daddy-o). This wins you brownie points with a sector of the market, but runs the risk of alienating others, and might limit the number of artists who would feel comfortable covering the song. All street slang dates quickly. To be fashionable today is to be a hostage to posterity – but since popular songs are often seen as ephemeral maybe this doesn't matter. Current (2006) slang titles include deliberate mis-spelling ('-er' endings become 'a', as in 'flava') and substituting numbers for words in text-message form (you becomes 'U').

Laura Nyro 'Stoned Soul Picnic'; Squeeze 'Cool For Cats'; Wayne Fontana 'Groovy Kind Of Love'; T.Rex 'Life's A Gas'; James Brown 'Papa's Got A Brand New Bag'; Mel and Kim 'Uptown Top Rankin''; The Beach Boys 'I'm Bugged At My Ol' Man'; The Prodigy 'Serial Thrilla'; Love 'Bummer In The Summer'; The Offspring 'Pretty Fly (For A White Guy)'; Extreme 'Get The Funk Out'.

THE NO-TITLE TITLE

Sometimes it seems songwriters can't think of what to call a song, and don't find one before the deadline. The result is titles like this:

Elton John 'This Song Has No Title'; Robert Plant 'Mystery Title'; Status Quo 'Mystery Song'; Heaven 17 'Song With No Name'; Blur 'Song #2'; Smashing Pumpkins (and others) 'Untitled'.

VARIATIONS ON 'STRAWBERRY FIELDS FOREVER'

To illustrate the contrasting effects of title styles, here is a set of variations on the title of The Beatles 1967 classic, to illustrate how the same image could be presented in a variety of ways to match the title categories described in the preceding pages. The original title could be classified as a proposition and has alliteration:

'I Love Strawberry Fields' (pronoun); 'Strawberry Fields' (descriptive name); 'The Ballad Of Strawberry Fields' (narrative); 'Strawberry Fields Forever Fields of Strawberry' (inversion); 'Funky Strawberry Fields' (buzz-word); 'Like A Strawberry Field' (simile); 'Strawberry Fields of Uncertainty' (metaphor); 'Strawberry Fields Possibly' (grammar wordplay); '(Shall We Go To) Strawberry Fields?' (question); Strawberry Fields And Stone Pavements' (opposites).

CLICHÉ SONG TITLES

A cliché is an expression that no longer (to use a cliché) cuts the mustard. Once it was evocative, but no longer. Clichés are phrases that are like dead spots on an instrument: they lack resonance. There are ways of rescuing a clichéd title. One is to take a word like "beautiful", which has occurred with positive associations in titles like 'Beautiful Stranger/Dreamer/Losers' and join it to something unexpected, as in 'Beautiful Screw-Up'.

Here is a list of over-used, maddeningly unimaginative song titles. If they ever meant anything, they don't now. Use them only if you're being funny or ironic. The track listing from hell would be any album that had more than a third of its tracks named with these titles. Do yourself a favour – avoid them.

'Love Song'; 'My Song'; 'Song For You'; 'This Song'; 'Alone Tonight'; 'Lonely Nights'; 'Money'; 'Fade Away'; 'Baby Blue'; 'Just Another Day'; 'Time'; 'Sea Of Love'; 'Love Is Here'; 'Blue Sky'; 'Behind The Lines'; 'Together Forever'; 'Shine On'; 'Wind Of Change'.

THE TRACK-LIST RECIPE

Cliché titles are so prevalent, there are many mainstream albums whose track-listings can be partially predicted using this list. Given 12 songs on an album try matching:

1. **A title with a number in it**
2. **A title with something plus "sunrise", "morning" or "sunset"**
3. **A title named after a street**
4. **A title featuring the word "day"**
5. **A title featuring the word "rock"**
6. **A title with a girl's name**
7. **A title with the word "heart" and/or "together"**
8. **A title with the word "fire"**
9. **A title with "rain" or "sun"**
10. **A title with the word "sky"**
11. **A title with the word "lonely"**
12. **A title with the word "fade"**

You can see this if you go into a shop and look at CDs from the mainstream rock/pop/soul areas. Music which belongs to a sub-genre will have a different set of title styles because sub-genres in popular music are partly differentiated from the mainstream by lyric themes and images. Heavy metal bands do not sing lyrics about loving their pet dogs; teenage pop stars do not sing songs about sacrificing goats. Genre-defining titles can be as predictable in their own way.

Nick Cave

Interviewed by Simon Smith

Nick Cave's favourite lyrical themes – death, violence, religion, love and a mythic view of the American South – have found expression backed by the abrasive art punk of The Birthday Party, and latterly the increasingly melodic Bad Seeds. Cave has also written a novel and several film scripts.

How important are song titles in terms of their connection with the lyric?

Hugely important. When there isn't an appropriate one we would end up quite deliberately using titles such as 'The Witness Song' or 'The Ship Song'. These have quite a resonance for me, in the same way as I've always like 'The Something Blues'. There's an immediate recognition to that. You know what you're getting.

And, talking of blues, John Lee Hooker is, to me, the greatest of the blues lyric writers. There's something incredibly subtle and deeply rooted. And it's improvised, and you can tell it's just come out of him sitting there and doing a free rant, but it goes to places that you wouldn't imagine. It's spine tingling. He gives himself a lot of space to create the whole picture. There's a whole trance, hypnotic thing both to the music and the lyrics. If you half listen to John Lee Hooker it can be kind of meaningless, but if you listen to what he's actually singing about, it's riveting.

He has probably influenced me more than any other lyricist. I mean, Bob Dylan hasn't really influenced me much, in the sense that he's just too good. If you try to write a song like Bob Dylan, it just sounds sub-Bob Dylan. Once you try to mimic it's a real sign of desperation.

Although, as you said earlier, you do start out trying to emulate stuff that you like.

Well you carry on doing that to certain a degree. It's been difficult recently because I've been trying to get words together, and you just get snatches of something, like a half idea for a song. This can spiral into a feeling that you have nothing to say. I was looking through a lyric book for the last album, and it was interesting to see that some of these very successful songs started out of the most inane thoughts.

Wasn't 'There She Goes, My Beautiful World' [from* Abattoir Blues*] about having lost your muse?

Yeah. Exactly.

When did you first start to write lyrics?

Well, I'd always written poetry, for as far back as I can remember. It was kind of a private vice, and I didn't really tell anybody about it. I grew up in a country town in Australia, and it wasn't something that you shouted from the rooftops.

Not a manly pursuit?

No, you didn't indulge in that kind of behaviour. Incredibly suspect. I can still remember some of it, not the actual words but what they were about. Love stuff – so nothing's really changed. When I joined a band later [Boys Next Door] we did a lot of covers – initially Sensational Alex Harvey Band and Alice Cooper – then we started creeping in a few of our own songs. I think I was mostly just interested in words.

So the words came first?

Yes. I mean, I had nothing to say. I was trying to cling on to anything that half resembled a song. Most of the efforts aren't worth spending any time on. What you initially try to do is find a voice for yourself. You try to do anything you possibly can, and the only way you can judge it is if it resembles something else that you like. And after a while you begin to find your voice and you try to work on that. It's about finding an authentic voice and developing that from record to record, and that never stops.

You seem to have reached a point where you are recognisably yourself. There is, after all, a school of Nick Cave.

I guess. However, the difficulty is to continue to find that authentic voice, but one that is sufficiently developed from the last record. I'm really in that process at the moment, in the early stages of writing a new record, and I'm sitting around not having written any songs for a year with absolutely nothing in my head whatsoever. The difficulty isn't actually in writing the lyrics themselves it's in finding the voice again, but one that doesn't sound like the one that you had on the last record

Taking that further, over your career you have employed themes that have gone across a number of albums. For instance in The Birthday Party and earlier days of The Bad Seeds there was the more obviously Southern Gothic-influenced material and the prison songs. This all seems to have changed dramatically after* Murder Ballads *(1996) when you released* The Boatman's Call *(1997), which introduced a more obviously autobiographical element to your lyrics – in particular people latched on to the PJ Harvey element [Harvey and Cave had had a relationship around this time] – and there was less character play in the songs.

Yeah. Well, I wouldn't do that kind of earlier material now. Things did change, and I'm really pleased that they did. I think there's a dividing line there. A lot of people who liked my music prior to that change possibly didn't like it so much after. There's a more confessional element that I dabbled in on *Boatman's Call*, but over the next couple of records that dropped off, because it's kind of a dead-end street. I mean, to rely totally on what's happening in your life is not always the best food for songs, particularly when day after day life is pretty much the same.

What I felt really happy about with the last record [*Abattoir Blues/The Lyre of Orpheus,* 2004] was that it achieved a balance, in that I felt that wasn't writing anything that wasn't true to myself, but at the same time it was an artistic statement as opposed to a list of grievances.

Who would you say has influenced you most over the years?

I'd have to say they aren't songwriters for the most part. There are a few poets – Ted Hughes, WH Auden, Robert Lowell, Philip Larkin, Thomas Hardy – and they've had a general influence on me. As for the lyric writers that I rate, I'd say Bob Dylan, Leonard Cohen, Mark E Smith, John Lee Hooker, early-mid-period Van Morrison, Shane MacGowan, people who I feel are really great with words.

***You had a novel published [*And The Ass Saw The Angel, *1989] and have written film scripts [*The Proposition, *2005], including an unused script for* Gladiator II.**

Which was f***ing brilliant.

Is there any parity with what you do with lyrics and prose and scriptwriting?

Only that I find other forms of writing far easier than lyrics. Lyric writing is really hard, the hardest thing that I do. It's really f***ing hard and writing a script is really f***ing easy.

Some of the problems with lyric writing must come down to how traditional a route you want to take – whether to use rhyme, for instance.

All the poets I'm really affected by use rhyme. I've never been able to get into a lot of American post-war poetry, which just sounds like endless ravings and witterings.

So you're not a Ginsberg fan?

No, although he's probably better than some of the others. He uses more formal structure than some of those guys. The more it breaks down and the more those rules are thrown away, the less affecting it is for me. I'm not really interested in people's opinions or ideas – I'm certainly not interested in my own – rather the problem of putting what you want to say into some kind of formal structure.

How about having your lyrics printed on album sleeves, so people can read them as pieces in their

own right? Not every songwriter is happy to do that, but you always have.

It probably would've been better if I hadn't, perhaps. But there was a certain tradition, in the days of progressive music – and I grew up with that – where part of listening to music was poring over the lyrics, no matter how f***ing stupid they were. The cover and all its elements were an important part of the experience, and this is lost now. You don't even know song titles any more: track 6.

Is there any influence of place on your writing?

Your habits change from place to place and the influences of other people on you change. But I wasn't swapping countries for inspiration.

And what about the religious element in your work?

I always found the idea of God interesting and mysterious, linked very strongly to my creative side, so it seemed something I could place in my work. But I probably wouldn't do it any more.

And you've always had a great line in swearing. It always sounds natural, not as if you're doing it to shock.

Yeah. Well, I'm pretty foul mouthed. I'm quite conscious of it, though. I mean, it just seems to work.

There's a lot fear and violence in your lyrics, and characters who create fear around them. 'Deep In The Woods' [*The Bad Seed EP *by The Birthday Party, 1983] is a case in point, where a woman is murdered and then you in character come out with the line "I took her from rags right through to stitches." Hilarious.

Well, I would of thought that most of that stuff was comic to begin with, and I hope it was seen that way. I guess it's the comic element that I'm most interested in, because it's the stuff that feels really good to write, though you can't always say it. It sits in your notebook for a while, and you kind of warm to it a bit and you slot it in. These things, the outrageously comic lines, are the ones I end up enjoying most.

Like Leonard Cohen. Those who write him off as a bedsit miserablist aren't hearing the humour. And it's always been there, even in the early stuff.

Yeah. Have you listened to any of those albums recently? They're so dark, particularly *Songs Of Love And Hate*. But there's a humorous element, and I really like that record – but I wouldn't like all records to be like that. Such sustained cruelty. "There's a funeral in the mirror / And it's stopping at your face …"

That's funny.

lyric with them. The rhymes need not be in the same order but you could retain the shape of the verse and chorus (and bridge, if there is one).

- Start a sketch by choosing a few interesting rhymes from a rhyming dictionary and write phrases to fit them.
- Don't rely on spelling alone – some words rhyme even though they are spelt differently: jokes/coax, slip/barbiturate (imperfect).
- Keep rhyme schemes simple. Use alternate rhymes, where every other line is rhymed, in a verse and bridge; save couplet rhyming, where each pair of lines rhyme, for a chorus or the end of a verse.
- Don't try to fight your way out of a rhyming problem by mangling tenses, as Bob Dylan once did when he used "knowed" instead of "knew", and Neil Diamond when he devised "brang" instead of "brought" to rhyme with "sang".
- Verses do not have to have identical rhyme schemes. Two four-line verses might sound okay with lines two and four rhymed, with a third verse rhymed ABAB – an increase of rhyme to give the third verse added weight.
- A special version of this technique is to insert an internal rhyme in a lyric where there hadn't been one before, as in the line: *At the Ball their hearts in thrall to a smile like a disease*. For examples of multiple rhymes in a single line see Bruce Springsteen's debut album (especially 'Blinded By The Light'). Used sparingly internal rhyme can be handy to end a chorus, as Travis did with ' Driftwood' when they rhymed "find/bind/grind" in a single line.

Multiple rhymes on the same sound create an impression of artifice. This works fine in certain types of song, such as comic numbers (where the artifice becomes funny) or satires (where it feels like hard-edged sarcasm). See Barry McGuire's 'Eve Of Destruction', Bob Dylan's 'Like A Rolling Stone', 'Just Like A Woman' with its chorus of "aches/makes/fakes/breaks', and U2's 'Bad'. In 'While My Guitar Gently Weeps' repeated multi-syllabic rhymes make the statements portentous.

PERFECT VERSUS IMPERFECT RHYME

In the past some songwriters believed rhymes should be perfect (*strong/along/wrong*). In practice, few songwriters now worry about this, and there is one obvious reason why imperfect rhymes may not matter. Most vocalists are not especially clear in their enunciation (hence comical mis-hearings of lyrics, known as 'mondegreens', in books like Gavin Edwards' *Scuse Me While Kiss This Guy* and *When A Man Loves A Walnut*). Often, the last syllable of a word is hardly audible. So rhyming "mind' with "time' in a lyric is perfectly okay, because the vowel sound 'i' counts more than the words' terminations. That means imprecise rhymes are frequently met with in lyrics:

alone/home; stones/cloned; rage/days; name/rain; down/shout; line/time; sign/time; young/fun; gained/ remain; tree/need; free/succeed; nursed/worse; hate/cake/ache.

These shouldn't be confused with 'half-rhymes' like "powder/hunger", where only the final syllable rhymes. Imprecise rhyming makes possible something like Sting's ingenious "cough/Nabokov" rhyme in the last verse of 'Don't Stand So Close To Me'. Rhymes can also be squeezed out of mis-pronunciations and colloquial words, such as "warn yer" with "corner", and "do yer" with "hallelujah". In 'Big Yellow Taxi' Joni Mitchell rhymed "museum" with "see 'em", and The Ramones put "tell 'em" with "cerebellum". Such contractions once looked crude, but in some contexts as a change of register they can be playful and expressive.

Most rhymes are 'masculine' – that is, stressed and single-syllable. The 'feminine' rhyme involves a two-syllable word, the second syllable of which is unstressed, as in "flowing/growing'. A single or two-syllable word can complete a two- or three-syllable rhyme and vice versa: *tambourine/cream; suspicion/exhibition; action/satisfaction; ended/suspended; perpetually/spectacularly*. There are many of these in Tony Christie's 'Amarillo' (dawning/morning, pillow/willow, ringing/singing), no doubt because the title lends itself to double-syllable rhyme.

Parallel phrasing

Having looked at verse, chorus, and bridge structures, here's another useful structuring device. One lazy way of generating a lyric is to use parallel phrasing. This kind of lyric involves minimal creative output to get it started and then it almost writes itself. I wouldn't advise using this technique often (it easily becomes tediously predictable) but it is okay occasionally. The technique involves writing a phrase and then retaining its structure, repeating the phrase with a variation. Roy Orbison's 'Pretty Woman' does this to some degree with phrases built on the title. Here's an example: "Some days are full of promise, / Some days never leave the ground; / Some days are like an echo chamber, / Some days don't have a sound."

The technical name for this (when it happens in poetry) is 'anaphora' – phrases that parallel each other. This is an easy technique since the part of the phrase which stays the same from line to line nudges you to the next idea, and if you introduce alternate rhyming the search for a rhyme often suggests the next line. The longer you keep such a phrase going the more it draws attention to itself – which may be undesirable. Imagine a song with three eight-line verses: 24 lines all commencing "some days"! It would be too repetitious. One way of avoiding this is to break with the pattern, either by confining the repeated phrase to alternate lines or leaving it after four statements.

If it doesn't figure anywhere else in the lyric, parallel phrasing is very effective in a chorus, where you want an increase of tension and focus. Clearly repeating a phrase with small variations can provide that.

Songs which use parallel phrasing include Pink Floyd's 'Another Brick In The Wall', 'Eclipse', The Police's 'Every Breath You Take', Sam Cooke's 'What A Wonderful World', The Byrds' 'Turn Turn Turn', Velvet Underground's 'Who Loves The Sun', Ian Dury's 'Reasons To Be Cheerful, Part 3' and 'What A Waste', Coldplay's 'Fix You', and Noel Harrison's infamous simile-fest 'Windmills Of Your Mind'.

The list lyric

A song which is a list by *content* doesn't necessarily have the same exact syntactical parallels, though some do. The list-driven lyric has an actual list of related objects, persons, or events. List songs include The Kinks' 'Village Green Preservation Society', The Stranglers' 'No More Heroes', The Plastic Ono Band's 'Give Peace A Chance', Madonna's 'Vogue', Ian Dury And The Blockheads' 'Hit Me With Your Rhythm Stick' and 'Reasons To Be Cheerful', The Beach Boys' 'Surfin' USA', Cornershop's 'Brimful Of Asha', and The Beatles' 'Dig It'. There is also R.E.M.'s 'It's The End Of The World As We Know It', which Michael Stipe said came from a dream in which he was the only person at a party whose initials were not LB. (The other guests included Lenny Bruce, Leonid Brezhnev, and Leonard Bernstein.)

Nick Cave and The Bad Seeds' 'There She Goes, My Beautiful World' namechecks St John of the Cross, Karl Marx, Johnny Thunders, Dylan Thomas, and Philip Larkin. In the musical field, Van Morrison's 'Cleaning Windows' refers to Leadbelly, Blind Lemon Jefferson, Sonny Terry, Brownie McGhee, and Muddy Waters, and Arthur Conley's 'Sweet Soul Music' lyric is structured as a list of 1960s soul stars including Otis Redding, Wilson Pickett, and James Brown.

The refrain

One special form of repetition in a lyric is the refrain. A refrain would normally be the title of the song. A refrain that isn't the title might lead listeners to think it *was* the title. A refrain can come anywhere in a lyric, though the normal location is at the end of a verse. The refrain could be a line that comments on and explains what would otherwise be puzzling images. The Police's 'King Of Pain' enigmatically has only descriptive images in each verse, including a flag, a dead salmon, a black spot on the sun, a hunted fox, and in each case the backing vocals deliver the explanatory refrain stating that each image stands for the singer's soul. Without it we would not know the significance of the images. Another example would be the function of the title of 'I Say A Little Prayer' as a refrain in the verse. Interestingly, it does not feature in the chorus. It is also possible to make a refrain change its meaning throughout a song. If you want to explore this further the best thing to do is to read poems which have refrains and note how they work.

One of the most obsessional instances of a refrain is Elvis Costello's 'I Want You', in which almost every other line is punctuated by the title functioning as a refrain (the song lasts for six minutes). The repetition is psychologically justified because it expresses the obsessional nature of the person in the song (though I can't avoid feeling that the songwriter enjoys the whole scenario with a perverse aesthetic pleasure).

Hyperbole and under-statement

Hyperbole (exaggeration) is a stylistic feature of many lyrics. The more romantic the lyric the more likely it will contain hyperbole. You can spot hyperbole because it involves statements which are not literally true, as in the phrase "What kept you? I've been here a century at least." It may have been put there consciously or unconsciously. It naturally arises in love songs as a way of describing extreme feelings, is melodramatic, and certainly eye-catching. It is so much the natural currency of popular music that an anti-hyperbole title like The Housemartins' 'Five Get Over-Excited' is positively revolutionary – no-one in the pumped-up sensationalist world of pop, where everything is bigger than life, admits to getting over-excited about anything.

Here are some song-titles or lyrics which use hyperbole. None of these statements is literally true:

Walker Brothers 'The Sun Ain't Gonna Shine Anymore'; David Ruffin 'My Whole World Ended (The Moment You Left Me)'; Four Tops 'I'll Turn To Stone'; The Only Ones 'Another Girl, Another Planet'; Jesus and Mary Chain 'Nine Million Rainy Days'; Stevie Wonder 'Drown In My Own Tears'; Evanessence 'Bring Me To Life'; The Gap Band 'You Dropped A Bomb On Me'; Roberta Flack 'Killing Me Softly With His Song'; Blue Oyster Cult 'Cities On Fire With Rock And Roll'.

Under-statement is much less common in lyrics. Where hyperbole operates on a principle of "more is more", under-statement in romantic lyrics is the equivalent of "less is more". A lyric can be set up so that even a relatively moderate statement of affection could become very moving. Don't forget you have the power of the music itself to generate emotion, and the more emotional the music the more you can afford to restrain the lyric's overt declarations. The title of Paul McCartney's 'Maybe I'm Amazed' is great under-statement, provoking us to ask, what do you mean, *maybe*? If you are amazed, how could you be unsure? The purpose of the under-statement is to communicate the singer's feeling of having stumbled onto something magical.

Bruce Springsteen's 'Night' is a thunderous rock song whose lyric states the intent to find one true love somewhere in the big wide world. Dire Straits' reflective 'On Every Street' has the same theme, but couldn't be more of a contrast in its under-statement, lyrically and musically. They're both fine songs. But we hear more hyperbolic anthems than we do reflective, understated songs (a quiet song can also be full of hyperbole). So a good rule of thumb is: the more emotive your subject the more understated, even indirect, you can afford to be.

Irony

Irony is a sophisticated writing technique. An ironic statement is intended to have the opposite meaning to its apparent one. Irony requires an active, alert, intelligent listener who will consciously reverse the apparent meaning of a ironic statement. If you think you have such listeners, writing and performing ironic songs is an option.

The bigger your audience, the greater the percentage who take your songs at face value. They will think you mean what you appear to say. This is dangerous territory, so proceed with caution. Ironic songs could get two reactions, neither of which you want. If the irony is missed (and there are many, including in the media, who are very good at missing it, who will shoot first and ask questions later, if at all), many will take your lyric literally, making you a proponent of the very views you are attacking, winning you mistaken friends and enemies.

Irony is also used to be cynical with the audience. For many bands (whether intentional or not) irony ends up as a "have your cake and eat it" strategy. Imagine writing a deliberately over-the-top arena rock number called 'Gonna Rock You All Nite' as a send-up along the lines of Spinal Tap. Play it mega-loud in an arena of beer-swilling headbangers. Half the audience takes the lyric at face value and misses the irony (allowing the band to feel patronisingly cleverer and 'subversive', even as it takes the money). The other half of the audience gets the irony, has a laugh and feels 'in' on the act. The band wins either way. The career of The Sex Pistols offers many examples of this.

Acronyms and anacrostic lyrics

In their pure form these are pattern lyrics where a word is spelt out letter by letter, often in a chorus. Ian Brown's 'F.E.A.R' has a lyric of phrases whose first letters spell out the title word. In The Four Tops' 'Still Water (Peace)' each letter of the word 'peace' is taken as the first letter of the words Privilege, Ease, Absence, Calm and Everlasting. Cream turned the phrase "she walks like a bearded rainbow" into the acronym 'SWLABR'. Other examples of spelling out words include Ottawan's 'D.I.S.C.O', Tammy Wynette's 'D.I.V.O.R.C.E.', Al Green's 'L.O.V.E.', John Cougar Mellencamp's 'R.O.C.K. in the U.S.A.', Rhythm Syndicate's 'P.A.S.S.I.O.N.', and Pulp's 'F.E.E.L.I.N.G.C.A.L.L.E.D.L.O.V.E'. Songs that use other well-known formulae include Jackson 5's 'ABC', and Manfred Mann's '5-4-3-2-1'.

Wordplay

One of the ways of making your lyrics more entertaining is to introduce an element of wordplay. We have already seen how wordplay can be used in a title. Wordplay comes in many guises – repetition, puns, catchphrases, the deliberate distortion of clichés and proverbs, drawing attention to similar sounding words, and so on. The common factor is a momentary heightened increase of interest in the properties of language itself. That's why a lot of wordplay in certain types of lyric will make them sound insincere, as though the singer is more focused on getting off a good line than expressing an emotion. However, insofar as a sense of humour is not incompatible with deep emotions or maturity of outlook, a little wordplay can give a lyric sophistication.

Try working with two meanings of the same expression, such as "When he drove into her life he drove her out of his mind." The first "drove" means driving a car (literal meaning) but the second, to drive someone out of their mind, is a metaphor. Another example would be the phrase "market towns and forces" which links in a levelling phrase two things which are not of the same order. A market town is a real place you can visit; a market force is an abstraction. The levelling out is meant to be suspicious. It draws attention to the fact that these things do not belong to the same levels of reality, and that to treat them as though they were (this is the implied protest) is damaging to people's lives. This shows how wordplay can carry a punch in a political song.

Wordplay becomes important in comic and satirical songs, but of itself is not always funny. In a song about beaches and surfing the phrase "pipelines and pipe dreams" connects two quite different things – a pipeline is a type of wave, a pipe dream is a dream that stands little chance of coming true. Think of the repetition of the word "absolute" in Bowie's 'Absolute Beginners', which is a form of wordplay, or the cumulative, rhythmic force of the 13 uses of "nothing" in the chorus of Gilbert O'Sullivan's 'Nothing Rhymed'.

The ability to generate wordplay in your lyrics is comparable to the discovery that you can write songs about other lives and experiences than your own. With wordplay you are no longer stuck in a framework of literal meaning. However, once this animal is off the leash it is easy to get dragged all over the place. The result can be a lyric full of clever wordplay which is incoherent. Try to make sure wordplay serves the theme, not the other way round.

Cliché

"I love the music but what the f*ing hell are you singing about? You want to be writing lyrics that a 16-year-old girl putting her make-up on can sing." (Producer Steve Lipsom, allegedly, to XTC's Andy Partridge)[63]**

A cliché is a phrase which has been used so many times before that it has lost its original force. Clichéd images, metaphors and similes are so worn they are invisible; they no longer function as comparisons.

The good news about clichés is that, unlike in poetry, where a cliché used unconsciously signals incompetence and poor technique, you can get away with clichés in commercial songwriting. This is partly because lyrics are often so banal that noticing the cliché is like looking for white ink on white paper – it has faded into the background – and the magic of music can make a cliché seem unimportant. Your songwriting peers may notice clichés, but then they're not providing your royalty cheques. So how careful you are depends on what sort of level of craftsmanship you aspire to and what sort of audience you're going after.

Unfortunately clichés can take the form not only of words, phrases or images, but also stereotypical situations, characters and emotions. The traditional blues lyric that commences "woke up this morning' has become for many simply funny. We have a strong sense that we know exactly the situation and the sentiment that will follow. It's too predictable.

It takes time to become sufficiently knowledgeable about a breadth of song history to be able to spot if you are simply recreating a stereotypical song lyric. Avoiding specific phrases is easier. A cliché can be rescued if you use it ironically or deliberately foreground it in some way. Aerosmith did this when they took the phrase "falling in love" and used it as a song title 'Falling In Love (Is Hard On The Knees)'. Giving a clichéd metaphor a comically literal meaning is a sure way to rescue it, if temporarily. Using such romantic language but not really meaning it makes the singer look rakishly witty and lyrically aware.

Here is a list of clichés in lyrics that should be avoided. Much of the objection to this language is that it is imprecise and generalised:

no matter what they say, this cold world, cold as ice, cuts like a knife, backs against the wall, down the line, make a stand, sands of time, my heart beats like a hammer/drum, share my load, set me free, fantasy/reality, like a moth to a flame, love tears us apart, little miss, pretty, down on my knees (usually beggin' you please), walking down the street, tonight, make you mine, blue as can be, broken heart, these four walls, looking for some action, sun and rain, catch you when you fall, guess I'm ...

Unusual vocabulary

"We should be on the look-out in our reading and conversation for that unfamiliar word with an intriguing sound, the one whose meaning we have always guessed at but about which we are not certain." (Jimmy Webb)[64]

Generally speaking, the vocabulary you employ in a lyric has to be pretty straightforward. The more commercial your ambitions the truer this is. There are a number of reasons for this:

- Polysyllabic words can be awkward to sing.
- They can be hard to hear, especially at a gig.
- Using words unfamiliar to your audience might obscure the theme of your song.
- It might cause them to think that you're 'too clever' or bookish.
- Complex words might not fit in the genre of your music.
- Abstractions can make a lyric seem insufficiently grounded.

You are on safe ground if you include current colloquial expressions. This is one way to bond with a young audience, provided you're roughly the same age as they are. Different youth sub-groups have their own slang.

It is true that occasionally songwriters use a rare word, as in these titles: The Monkees 'Propinquity (I've Just Begun To Care)', Clifford T. Ward 'Wherewithal', Oasis 'Acquiesce', Family 'Burlesque', Canned Heat 'Parthenogenesis' and 'Nebulosity', Evanescence 'Tourniquet'. Sometimes an unassuming word in the right place creates a special tone, as with Madonna's 'I'd Be Surprisingly Good For You'. The use of a foreign word or two can lend an air of sophistication. In the case of the Manic Street Preachers 'Glasnost' it was the actual theme and there was no English equivalent. Badly Drawn Boy derived 'Donna And Blitzen' from the German phrase *donner und blitzen*.

Songwriters have also entertained themselves and us by inventing words. Here is a selection, including a couple of ten-ton monster compound words:

Phil Collins 'Sussudio' (a word to represent a drum fill); R.E.M. 'Ignoreland'; T.Rex 'Jeepster'; Donovan 'Barabajagal'; Iron Butterfly 'In-A-Gadda-Da-Vida'; Lisa Germano 'Tomorrowing'; Jethro Tull 'Aqualung'; The Beach Boys 'Cabinessence'; Roxy Music 'Pyjamarama'; David Bowie 'Moonage Daydream'; Bluetones 'Autophilia'; Muse 'Screenager'; Megadeth 'Youthanasia'; Marillion 'Assassing'; Little Richard 'Tutti Frutti' 'Awopbopaloobopalopbamboom'); Isaac Hayes 'Hyperboliesyllaciscequelalymistic'; Parliament 'Supergroovalisticprosifunkstication'; Sly And The Family Stone 'Thank You (Falettinme Be Mice Elf Agin)'.

Nonsense

There are moments when nothing but pure nonsense will do the trick. And if you've been accused of writing lyrics that are nonsense why not go the whole hog? Nonsense syllables form part of the jazz 'scat-singing' tradition, where a singer imitates the improvisatory freedom of an instrumental soloist. They also feature in more organised patterns in doo-wop and harmony singing. They tend to suit more light-hearted songs. Sometimes you might end up with a nonsense refrain left over from an early draft of a lyric, originally put there to fill a gap in a verse when you were working on a melody. Such refrains are good for audience participation – it's easy to sing along with a song when you don't have words to learn, as Mungo Jerry's 'In The Summertime', T.Rex's 'Hot Love', and Neil Sedaka's 'Breaking Up Is Hard To Do' ("come-a, come-a, down dooby-do down down") demonstrate. As Frank Zappa once pointed out, everyone in the world understands "la la la". At one time the Eurovision Song Contest was full of songs with choruses that seemed to all go "bong-cheedle-cheedle-bong-doo-dee". Nonsense … international language, you see …

The Beatles 'Ob-La-Di-Ob-La-Da' (and the long fade on 'Hey Jude'); Manfred Mann 'Doo Wah Diddy Diddy'; The Police 'De Doo Doo Doo, De Dah Dah Dah'; Lulu 'Boom Bang-a-Bang'; Stevie Wonder 'Shoo- bedoo-bedoo-day-day'; Madonna 'Shoo-Be-Doo'; The Kaiser Chiefs 'Na Na Na Na Naa'; The Crystals 'Da Doo Ron Ron (When He Walked Me Home)'; The Rivingtons 'Papa-oom-mow-mow'; Major Lance 'Um Um Um Um Um Um'; Roy Orbison 'Ooby Dooby'.

Proverbs and catchphrases

Proverbs, quotations and catchphrases can contribute to a lyric. Dip into books of them and you will be amazed at how many you know without realising it, and how many can be adapted as lyric themes, titles or first lines. Even if you don't reproduce them straight, you can give them a twist by changing a word, introducing a pun, inverting their terms, or taking a term literally that was meant as a metaphor – as Billy Bragg did when he turned the phrase "milk of human kindness" into milkman of human kindness and promised to leave an extra pint. This is funny and touching at the same time. The point about these phrases is that they belong to everyone.

PROVERBS

Proverbs have been around for generations. The trick with a proverb is to find a way of twisting it or deducing something from it that wouldn't normally follow, or write an ironic continuation, or even splice two incompatible proverbs together.

Take the proverbs "like the cat with the cream' and "dog in the manger". If we reverse the terms we get the unsettling potential of "She's the cat in the manger, the dog with the cream". The proverb "too many cooks spoil the broth" is about people getting in each other's way. Reversing it produces "too many broths spoil the cook", which could mean that if you have to do the same thing over and over eventually it gets to you. Or how about, "you can lead a horse to water but you can't make it think (or sink)", instead of the expected "drink".

The Temptations 'Beauty Is Only Skin Deep'; Billy Joel 'Only The Good Die Young'; The Velvelettes ''Needle In A Haystack'; The Only Ones 'No Peace For The Wicked'; Jimmy Cliff 'The Bigger They Are, The Harder They Fall'; Thomas Dolby 'She Blinded Me With Science'; Four Tops 'Still Waters Run Deep'; Badfinger 'Storm In A Teacup'; Bryan Adams 'Where Angels Fear To Tread'; David Gray 'Silver Lining'; Bo Diddley 'You Can't Judge A Book By The

Cover'; The Fantastics 'Something Old Something New'; Ian Hunter And Mick Ronson 'Once Bitten Twice Shy'; Frankie Goes To Hollywood 'The World Is My Oyster'.

CATCHPHRASES

Catchphrases are coined all the time by comedians and advertising agencies, TV commercials and posters, etc. Both make excellent titles and sometimes first lines (but don't infringe copyright). Keep an ear and eye out for memorable slang phrases. Take the phrase "mission creep", which was popularised in the 1990s. In it, "creep" is a verb – to move forward slowly but inexorably – but "creep" is also slang for a person who makes you feel uncomfortable ("he's a creep"), as in the famous Radiohead song. Seeing those meanings gives you the basis for developing a song about a person on a mission.

Sometimes bringing stock phrases together is enough to wake them up. Combining "cold light of dawn" with "harsh light of day" is more interesting than using them separately.

Up-to-date catchphrases can make your song seem contemporary and street-wise, especially if you do something original with them. Some catchphrases are connected with drama or storytelling, like "meanwhile back at the ranch" or the traditional "Once Upon A Time' (a song title by many, including Donna Summer and Simple Minds). If I used this as a title I would seek an unexpected word or image to substitute for "time" – like "once upon a look". Another group are just ordinary phrases taken from everyday life, sometimes instructions or warnings, that have potential metaphorical meanings, like the Manic Street Preachers' 'Everything Must Go', Black Grape's 'Shake Well Before Opening', and Whitesnake's 'Slippery When Wet'. Turning these phrases into songs seems to sometimes release energy in them.

Jethro Tull 'Later That Same Evening'; Sparks 'This Town Ain't Big Enough For The Both Of Us'; Joss Stone 'Less Is More'; Donna Summer 'If You've Got It Flaunt It'; Aerosmith 'Don't Get Mad Get Even'; Nick Lowe 'Cruel To Be Kind'; David Gray 'Dead In The Water'; Everything But The Girl 'Come Hell Or Highwater'; Radiohead 'Everything In Its Right Place', Manic Street Preachers 'There By The Grace Of God'; Meatloaf 'You Took The Words Right Out Of My Mouth'; Elvis Costello 'Accidents Will Happen'; Coldplay 'A Rush Of Blood To The Head'.

Having discussed many precise techniques and devices for lyrics in this section, our next step is to turn to the world of imagery.

Andy Partridge

Interviewed by Todd Bernhardt

XTC first came to attention as part of the British new wave of the late 1970s. Their meandering, interrupted career hasn't bought great wealth or fame. It has, though, produced much fine pop music, the lion's share of it written by the band's guitarist/singer Andy Partridge – a man usually characterized as an English eccentric in the Ray Davies mould.

Your lyrics give the impression of being highly crafted, and work on several different levels. How much of this is intentional, and how much is 'happy accident'?

Lyrically, I love word games. I love them in literature, in poetry, and in song lyrics. I love the fact that the same bunch of words can mean so many different things, through a different inflection, or another way of looking at it. I never look at anything straight-on – I also look at it from the back, then from above, then from underneath, then I want to slice it open and see what's inside.

That said, I don't think there are 'happy accidents' with the lyrics, because I sweat blood to get them! They are by far the toughest things to feel happy about. The music is a lot easier.

I'm constantly wrestling with my 'editor'. I never had an editor at one time, but I've grown one over the years, and he's become too important. I have to find ways of killing him off, or putting him to sleep until I need him.

Are there any tricks you've come up with?

[Sighs] It's tough, because the older he gets, the more ornery he gets, and the more aware he is of ploys to put him to sleep. It's really useful having an editor, because it's great for shaping up raw material, but I find the editor's getting so strong, he's not letting raw material be born. To make raw material, you have to be a bit stupid and have no restrictions, so you can grab anything and use it. The 'idiot creative you' might say, "If I stick and this together, that could make one of those!" But the editor says, "You're never going to use that piece, put it down."

Or, "You or other people have said this before"?

Oh, that's the hat he wears: "You've done this before. You've said this before." That's the death of inspiration. I *hate* the idea of repeating myself.

Do you remember writing your first song, and if so, what was it?

I do. I must have been about 14, and it was truly awful. It was called 'Please Help Me', and was obviously a cry from my anguished teenaged soul. It went something like *[in whiny teenage voice]*, "Please help me / I'm drowning in a sea / Please help me."

Something like that is the first mark you make in the exercise book of life. You know you're going to go wrong, that it's going to be surpassed immediately, so it's best to get it out of the way. It was my –is it called meconium? You know, baby's first turd? My musical meconium [laughs].

Lyrics or music first? Is there a pattern?

No, there is no pattern. Sometimes I mess around with chords, and they suggest something, like the sea, or clouds, or a box – anything. I'm a bit synaesthetic when it comes to that – I can hear sounds, and think, "That's just like fog, or a wet day in November." Often, the lyrics come because I'm trying to explain the synaesthetic nature of chords –the picture that they're painting.

"Easter Theatre" [*Apple Venus Volume 1* 1999] was like that. Very brown, muddy, ascending chords that made me think, "This sounds like something pushing up through the ground –like new buds, ooh, it's Easter." And before I knew it, I'd vomited up the *reason* for a song. The tone of an instrument also can suggest things, like on 'Chalkhills and Children.' [*Oranges and Lemons* 1989]. There's the little melodic figure at the beginning, which I thought sounded medieval and earthy, combined with placid, droning high keyboard chords, which sound like you're floating – so it suggested floating over a land. The lyric came out of my efforts to mentally grasp what this piece of music was about.

Sometimes it's the other way around. I'll write a poem or a piece of prose, and then think, "Gosh, that wouldn't make a bad song." 'Summer's Cauldron' [*Skylarking* 1986] was like that. So is a song that's coming out on my latest *Fuzzy Warbles* disc, '2 Rainbeau Melt'. It started as a poem, then I improvised music around the poem. But it's rarer, doing it that way.

Except for a very few songs –such as 'Your Dictionary'* [Apple Venus Volume 1 *1999] –you don't seem to be a confessional lyric writer. Is this intentional?

I think I am confessional, but I dress up in masks. When I say "she" or "he" or "those", I probably mean me. When I say "them", I might mean me and her, or when I say "you", I might even mean me! You play all the characters in the little production yourself, and you supply their voices, but so it doesn't look wrong, you give them masks of other people. Because you've got a mask on, you can be more truthful.

Does this enable you to learn things about yourself that you might not otherwise have known? For example, if you look at the lyrics on* Nonsuch*, it's interesting that that it was recorded before your divorce.

I know – it's *impending*. I do that quite a lot. I like looking back at lyrics where I can go, "Oh, my goodness, look what you've said! You didn't realise it at the time." I recently wrote something called, 'I Gave My Suitcase Away.' Although I wrote it intending it to be for someone else – a woman who wanted songs on the subject of coming back to live in England and not going away again – I realised a few weeks later that it's *totally* my sentiment. It's good to surprise yourself.

Does your writing change when you write for someone else?

Yeah, because you're freer. You can grab any old rubbish, thinking, "I haven't got to sing this!" It's a way to discover stuff you might not look at for yourself – I suppose it's another way of fooling the editor. You might come away with something really good, and really truthful, about yourself and your opinions.

Who would you say were your biggest influences lyrically?

Probably Ray Davies, and Lennon & McCartney. They're the top three. Ray Davies just because – I mean, look at the lyrics to 'Autumn Almanac', one of my favourite-ever songs. It's this weird, disjointed look at English life through one of those lenses that shatters it up into lots of little pictures. I love the woodiness of it, and the creakiness of it, dusty and dank – much like England.

He and you, actually, are often cited as deliberately English lyricists.

I don't try to be English. I guess because I am, it comes out English. But I don't sit down and think *[affects terrible Dick Van Dyke-style English accent]* "Cor blimey, can I put a Union Jack and a beefeater's outfit on, Mary?"

But it sounds like it's not anything you've ever run away from, while some people, who might have been reaching for wider acceptance, might have said, "Maybe I shouldn't use this word because people in the U.S. or Japan might not know what it means."

No, I think it's important to be who you are. That's the strongest asset you can have.

How do you feel about rhyming? Is that important to you?

I think lyrics are best when they have an internal tempo, and little internal rhymes. I always try to create a push/pull tension with internal rhymes. Not necessarily at the end – you might put a lazy or fake red-herring type rhyme at the end, but all the tension is internal. It's quite a ballet, if you get it right.

I love the old Hollywood, 'Wizard of Oz' thing, where they bend things to fit, fantastically, clumsily. I find that really exciting. "What if it was an elephant? I'd wrap him up in cellophant! What if it was a rhinoceros? Imposseros!" *[laughing]* It's not even a real word, but you know what he's going for. I like bending the English language until it screams.

So, Broadway musicals and things like that also influenced you?

Oh yeah. As a kid, there were two good things on the radio. There were show songs, or novelty songs – Spike Jones, or stuff like The Playmates' 'Beep Beep,' or 'The Mole in the Hole' by The Southlanders, or 'Big John' [by Jimmy Dean, 1961] – anything with sped-up voices, too much reverb, weird sound effects. That's what I was bombarded with until Beatles songs started creeping on to the radio.

Is anything off-limits for you, lyrically?

Well, I like sex. Everyone in the world likes sex! So why are there no songs that talk directly about sex? The ones that do are just laughably awful. "I want to sex you up" is pretty banal. I wish I could write about sex in a direct way. I do write about sex a lot, but it's so heavily metaphorised that you might not know what the hell I was talking about.

Are there clichéd images or themes that you think are particularly horrible?

"Baby." If I use "baby" – which I don't think I have at all – it would have to be very ironic. I also don't use the word "guy," so if that goes into a song, it's probably for a certain effect. I don't mind "old Englishisms" though, because I actually use them occasionally.

Do you think that you have, lyrically, a "voice"? Is there such a thing as an Andy Partridge lyric, or do you try to avoid that?

That's an odd one, because I still don't know what it is! I like to think I might be achieving it, but maybe that's a little pomposity, because I'm dealing with the English language and a finite amount of words, and it's probably been said so much better by people like Shakespeare, Arthur Miller, Kurt Vonnegut, and other greats.

I do like the idea that with most of my lyrics –not all of them –you could sit and read them, and they'd feel good as a spoken thing. That's important to me. I want the lyric to be able to be stripped away from anything that is interdependent with it, and still work. Like a really nice watch – if you took the watch apart, each piece would still be beautifully made.

Metaphor

Like a simile, a metaphor is a comparison between two things, but done in such a way that it is implicit, not explicit. The two things are brought closer together, almost identified with each other. This can be handy in a lyric where space is at a premium, but metaphor is also not as immediately clear as a simile. "The soldiers went into battle like a herd of sheep" is a clichéd simile. "As sheep, the soldiers went into battle" is slightly shorter but still a simile. "The soldiers were herded into battle" is a metaphor. They have been identified with the animals simply by the verb "herded". Some verbs are connected so often with certain things the verb alone will evoke the object. Farmers herd sheep and cattle – creatures whose lives are not self-governed. This means we don't need to spell out the comparison between the soldiers and the animals; "herded" does it alone. Similarly, we could write "Your absence is like a wolf / hanging around my door" (simile) or, using a metaphor, "The wolves of your absence are hanging round my door".

It takes time to develop an awareness of metaphors working through verbs, since it comes more obvious to think of them as nouns. Take the line "sun melts the frost off each whitened roof and fence". This has two problems: "whitened' is awkward to sing and "melts' is a predictable verb. Better is "sun smokes the frost off each roof and fence".

The simile "the sun evaporates the frost like smoke" is compressed into the verb "smokes'. A literal and a metaphorical meaning hinging on a single word can be pressed into a single line. In "when he drove into her life he drove her out of her mind", the first "drove" is literal, the second makes driving a metaphor for making someone feel unbalanced.

Imagine two ex-lovers who meet again out of curiosity and re-kindle (there's a metaphor!) a relationship: "Thinking it was safe to meet / And play with fire". To play with fire is a metaphor for taking a risk. A rock critic writing about Janis Joplin reaches for a metaphor to describe her husky vocals: "Hers was a voice flecked with rust." Both similes and metaphors can be momentary details, but they can also be extended to occupy a whole verse.

A metaphor can be a 'local event' in a lyric, whose meaning does not extend further than about a line. In the line "At night radar wipes its tired eye" such a metaphor is a momentary decoration. Radar is naturally associated with an eye because it is a means of looking. The "wipe" is the sweeping beam which travels 360 degrees round the circular display panel.

By contrast, a 'thematic' metaphor is a comparison that dominates an entire song. In fact, it is possible to write a song-lyric entirely within a thematic metaphor (say, a civil war) and never say what the metaphor relates to. Thematic metaphors can unify a lyric, giving an over-arching plan of reference. They can stiffen the emotion and stop certain subjects (like love songs) becoming sentimental or too plain. Such grand metaphors disguise personal themes yet keep the drama open to the audience who can place their own dramas in the metaphor.

Like similes, over-ingenious metaphors can work in a comic situation. On the other hand, over-elaborated metaphors can turn into the sort of allegory which is unintentionally funny.

Simile and metaphors are particular examples of imagery in songs. The following pages provide a catalogue of the most common types of imagery.

A catalogue of imagery

THE WEATHER

"*A butterfly caught up in a hurricane* – the image suddenly came to me. I put the words in the song. I heard distant thunder, smelled the air just before the rain, saw lightning streak across the sky, felt the winds blow. Soft winds ... warm breeze ... a power source ... a tender force ... quiet storm ... blowing through my life ... I finally had the musical concept I'd been seeking since hearing [Marvin Gaye's] *What's Going On*. I also had a device for moving from one tune to another: the wind. I saw seven songs carried on the back of a breeze, blowing through the record from start to finish." (Smokey Robinson on the genesis of his album *Quiet Storm*).[67]

On Planet Pop the weather is always a main topic of lyric conversation. The forecast is for heavy and persistent rainfall with outbreaks of thunder, but we should see sunshine later. Writing about the weather can be a way to avoid writing anything specific in a lyric at all. Nothing beats weather imagery for implying meanings in a vague, metaphorical way. If you reach for it, avoid creating a homily with this imagery – we don't need to be told "every winter must turn to spring", as though it has only just struck you that one follows the other, followed by a rhyme on "sing". Promising to shelter someone from the rain or the storm is sheer cliché, so those images need a touch of the unexpected to make them tolerable. No-one should ever write another song called 'Wind Of Change'. Buddy Guy's 'Change In The Weather' and 'Feels Like Rain' are examples of weather imagery lyrics. Jamie Blunt's 'Tears And Rain' is a daft title because it's almost a tautology in the lexicon of pop. We know that rain is like tears, so it doesn't need to be spelt out. Similarly, Willie Nelson's 'Blue Eyes Crying In The Rain' is too much. Refresh weather imagery by reversing its usual metaphorical associations. Passion and desire are normally associated with fire, but you could connect them with snow and ice.

Here's a breakdown of the metaphorical weather on Planet Pop, with its associated meanings.

RAIN (love, life, redemption, tears, unhappiness, suffering, being happy regardless of what life throws at you):

> **The Beatles 'Rain'; R.E.M. 'I'll Take The Rain'; Ann Peebles 'I Can't Stand The Rain'; B.J. Thomas 'Raindrops Keep Falling On My Head'; Gordon Lightfoot 'Early Morning Rain'; Tom Waits 'Diamonds On My Windshield'; Gene Kelly 'Singing In The Rain'; Temptations 'I Wish It Would Rain'; Carole King 'It Might As Well Rain Until September'; James Taylor 'Fire And Rain'; Garbage 'Only Happy When It Rains'; Turin Brakes 'Painkiller (Summer Rain)'; Bob Dylan 'Hard Rain's A-Gonna Fall'; Travis 'Why Does It Always Rain On Me?'; The Move 'Flowers In The Rain'.**

RAINBOW traditionally a symbol of hope, biblically a sign of God's covenant with humanity after the flood. Rainbows tend to appear after rain):

> **Marmalade 'Rainbow'; Mountain 'Sitting On A Rainbow'; Richard and Linda Thompson 'The End Of The Rainbow'; Robbie Robertson 'Sign Of The Rainbow'; Laura Nyro 'Broken Rainbow'; Judy Garland 'Over the Rainbow'; Kate and Anna McGarrigle 'Rainbow Ride'; The Rolling Stones 'She's a Rainbow'; Bill Nelson 'The Gold At The End Of My Rainbow'; Dennis Wilson 'Rainbows'.**

SUNSHINE (happiness, love, joy, morning, summer, emotional warmth):

The Beatles 'Here Comes The Sun', Stevie Wonder 'You Are The Sunshine Of My Life'; Donovan 'Sunshine Superman'; The Beach Boys 'The Warmth Of The Sun'; Isley Bros 'Summer Breeze'; Traffic 'Paper Sun'; Bill Withers 'Ain't No Sunshine'; Cream 'Sunshine Of Your Love'; Katrina And The Waves 'Walking On Sunshine'; Velvet Underground 'Who Loves The Sun'; The Supremes 'Automatically Sunshine'; Elton John 'Don't Let The Sun Go Down On Me'.

WIND (difficulties, adversity, change, resistance, natural force tending to motion):

Van Morrison 'Full Force Gale'; Rod Stewart 'Mandolin Wind'; Scorpions 'Wind Of Change'; Bob Dylan 'Idiot Wind', 'Blowin' In The Wind'; The Byrds 'Hickory Wind'; Donovan 'Catch The Wind'; Neil Young 'Like A Hurricane'; Joni Mitchell 'Let The Wind Carry Me'; Nick Heyward 'Whistle Down The Wind'; Richard Thompson 'Mystery Wind'; Robert Plant And The Strange Sensations 'Let The Four Winds Blow'; Jimi Hendrix 'The Wind Cries Mary'.

CLOUDS/FOG (mystery, not being able to see, confusion, getting lost):

Joni Mitchell 'Both Sides Now'; Kate Bush 'Cloud-busting', 'The Fog'; All About Eve 'In The Clouds'; Mercury Rev 'Nite and Fog'; Lindisfarne 'Fog On The Tyne'; Judy Garland 'A Foggy Day'; Kristin Hersh 'Fog'; Paul Weller 'Above The Clouds'; The Rolling Stones 'Get Off Of My Cloud'; The Temptations 'Cloud 9'.

STORM/FLOOD (overwhelming emotions, dramatic events, conflict, loss):

Bob Dylan 'Shelter From The Storm'; Howlin' Wolf 'Smokestack Lightning'; Fleetwood Mac 'Storms'; The Doors 'Riders On The Storm'; Jimi Hendrix 'In From The Storm', Doves 'The Storm'; The Verve 'Stormy Clouds'; Led Zeppelin 'When The Levee Breaks'; Madonna 'Drowned World'; Bruce Springsteen 'Lost In The Flood'; Stevie Ray Vaughan 'Texas Flood'.

SNOW/ICE (purity, burial, danger, skating on thin ice, emotional coldness):

Kings Of Leon 'Velvet Snow'; Madonna 'Frozen'; Van Morrison 'Snow In San Anselmo'; Haircut 100 'Snow Girl'; Genesis 'Snowbound'; And Also The Trees 'From The Silver Frost'; Lorrie Morgan 'Blue Snowfall'; Josh Ritter 'Snow Is Gone'; Emmylou Harris 'Roses In The Snow'; Everything But The Girl 'Frost And Fire'.

TOPOGRAPHY

"Hank Williams, Woody Guthrie... everybody has that landscape inside them, doesn't matter if you live in the city, it's a mythical landscape that everybody carries with them." (Bruce Springsteen 1992)[68]

" ... initially I get just a natural image like sky, sea, sun, earth and then something very domestic like washing. The juxtaposition of those things is endlessly interesting." (Neil Finn of Crowded House)[69]

"It sort of expressed to us the intensity [of] the feelings ... It sang well and it painted a nice image." (Ellie Greenwich, co-writer, on the title of 'River Deep Mountain High')[70]

Topography covers imagery connected with the features of the physical world. This excludes specific, named places. Traditional folk songs belong to societies and times where a landscape's terrain and features were greater obstacles than now. Such difficulties express psychological struggles, as in Rodgers & Hammerstein's 'Climb Every Mountain'. People still use the cliché of the urban jungle for the city. Dido uses the metaphor of land as emotional territory and relationship in her song 'This Land Is Mine', with perhaps a nod to Woody Guthrie's 'This Land Is Your Land' where the land image is not metaphorical but literal.

Along with landscape imagery go song-lyrics that refer to maps and charts, such as R.E.M's 'Maps And Legends' and Wire's 'Map Reference 41 Degrees N 93 Degrees W'. These tend to be more artistically successful than yet another lyric about rivers that run (as proverbially they do) to the sea. Probably the greatest extended use of oceanic/water imagery in rock is throughout The Who's concept album *Quadrophenia*.

MOUNTAINS (aspiration, determination to overcome great odds, a place where you get a much broader perspective. They are often part of the hyperbole of love songs. When they fall into the sea this denotes the end of time, which is when he can finally stop loving her):

Diana Ross 'Ain't No Mountain High Enough'; Ike And Tina Turner 'River Deep Mountain High'; Kate Bush 'King Of The Mountain', Led Zeppelin 'Misty Mountain Hop'; U2 'One Tree Hill'; Aimee Mann 'Crawling Up A Hill'; David Bowie 'Up The Hill Backwards'; The Beatles 'Fool On The Hill'; Fats Domino 'Blueberry Hill'; Neil Young 'Sugar Mountain'; Goldfrapp 'Felt Mountain'; The Byrds 'Wild Mountain Thyme'.

RIVERS (change, the flow of time, an obstacle, redemption, benign waters of life, on a more human scale than the sea.

Fountains, springs and waterfalls are related images. They can also imply the journey through death to the afterlife):

Bruce Springsteen 'The River'; Al Green 'Take Me To The River'; Doves 'Caught By The River'; Neil Young 'Down By The River'; R.E.M. 'Green Grow The Rushes', 'Find The River'; Johnny Cash 'Big River'; Fats Domino 'Going To The River'; Fleetwood Mac 'Silver Springs' ; Jimmy Cliff 'Many Rivers To Cross'; Tony Christie 'Yellow River'; Creedence Clearwater Revival 'Green River'; Travis 'Driftwood'; Henry Mancini 'Moon River'; The Band 'Up On Cripple Creek'.

FIELDS (freedom, the wide open outdoors, places of seduction, the fruitfulness of nature at times of harvest, battles if a war context):

Gary Moore 'Out In The Fields'; Sting 'Fields Of Gold'; The Beach Boys 'Cotton Fields'; R.E.M. 'West Of The Fields'; Big Country 'Fields of Fire'; Nanci Griffiths 'Fields Of Summer'; Lenny Kravitz 'Fields Of Joy'; Garnet Rogers 'Golden Fields'; Dreamtale 'Green Fields'.

DESERTS AND PLAINS (a barren place, emotional aridity, hardship, a tough journey, occasionally the exotic and/or the erotic):

Maria Muldaur 'Midnight At The Oasis'; David Bowie, Martha Reeves And The Vandellas 'Quicksand'; Smokey Robinson And The Miracles 'The Love I Saw In You Was Just A Mirage'; America 'Horse With No Name'; The Coral 'Arabian Sand'; Screaming Trees 'Gray Diamond Desert'; Led Zeppelin 'Kashmir'; Nirvana 'On A Plain'; Rory Gallagher 'Out On The Western Plains'.

WOODS (a tangled situation, being lost and far from civilization, magical encounters. Note the expression "we're not out of the woods yet". A jungle is a more brutal version of this meaning as in the cliché of the "urban jungle"):

> **The Cure 'A Forest'; Paul Weller 'Wild Wood'; Tyrannosaurus Rex 'Find A Little Wood'; Robbie Robertson 'Go Back To Your Woods'; Don McLean 'Winter Woods'; Jethro Tull 'Songs From The Wood'; Mercury Rev 'Black Forest (Lorelei)'; Johnny Burnette 'Setting The Woods On Fire'; Bruce Springsteen 'Jungleland'; Simple Minds 'Oh Jungleland'; Guns'n'Roses 'Welcome To The Jungle'.**

ISLANDS/BEACHES (isolation, being cast away, solitude, escape, holiday, hot beaches, paradise. Castles made of sand are the best example of sand as representing all things transient. "Sands of time" is another cliché, connected to an hour-glass):

> **The Springfields 'Island Of Dreams'; Madonna 'La Isla Bonita'; Weezer 'Island In The Sun'; Elton John 'Island Girl'; Billy Bragg 'Island Of No Return'; The Police 'Message In A Bottle'; CSN&Y 'Lady Of The Island'; Kenny Loggins and Dolly Parton 'Islands In The Steam'; Jimi Hendrix 'Castles Made Of Sand'; Stevie Wonder 'Castles In The Sand'; Ramones 'Rockaway Beach'; The Shangri-Las 'Walking In The Sand'.**

SEA (hyperbolic imagery of romanticism. The metaphor of drowning is very popular. The sea can be of love (as it is in Fleetwood Mac's 'Sara') or depression or eternity. Ships and sailing also figure for the journey of life):

> **Rod Stewart 'Sailing'; Pearl Jam 'Oceans'; Led Zeppelin 'Down By The Seaside'; Roxy Music 'Grey Lagoon', 'Sea Breezes'; Robert Plant 'Down To The Sea'; U2 'Drowned'; The Who 'Sea and Sand', 'Drowned', 'I Am The Sea', 'Water'; The Beach Boys 'Wreck of the Marie Celeste', 'Surfin' USA', 'Surfin' Safari', 'Catch A Wave', 'Surfer Girl'; Manic Street Preachers 'Ocean Spray'.**

THE HEAVENS: SUN, SKY, MOON, STARS

After the features of the earth, lyricists turn their attention to the sky. The sun tends to be treated as the source of sunshine (i.e. as weather), rather than as a cosmic body, and symbolically is anything you shouldn't look at directly. It also represents hope and is the symbol of better times if it has temporarily set or gone behind a cloud.

> **Thin Lizzy 'The Sun Goes Down'; Elton John 'Don't Let The Sun Go Down On Me'; Walker Brothers 'The Sun Ain't Gonna Shine Anymore'; Gordon Lightfoot 'Sundown'; Eric Clapton 'Behind The Sun'; Bob Marley 'Sun Is Shining'; The Cult 'Sun King'; Stackridge 'To The Sun And The Moon'; Nanci Griffith 'The Sun, Moon and Stars'.**

The stars signify eternity, devotion, unfathomable laws, fate, destiny, and in a more mundane way, celebrity.

> **Nina, Madonna 'Little Star'; Radiohead 'Black Star'; Rose Royce 'Wishing On A Star'; Madonna 'Lucky Star'; Lee Marvin 'Wanderin' Star; Portishead 'Wandering Star'; Albert King 'Born Under A Bad Sign'; Perry Como 'Catch A Falling Star'.**

The sky itself is often symbolic of freedom and flying, and sunset and dawn have a special appeal for lyricists (see the entry on 24 hours in **Section Nine**).

The Allman Brothers, Patty Griffin, Ring Of Fire (and others) 'Blue Sky'; Jeff Buckley 'The Sky Is A Landfill'; Kate Bush 'The Big Sky'; Bob Dylan 'Under the Red Sky'; The Platters 'Red Sails in the Sunset'; Pink Floyd 'Goodbye Blue Sky'; ELO 'Mr. Blue Sky'; David Wilcox 'Blue Horizon'.

The moon as silver moonlight is the perfect setting for romance, but as a body it is mysterious, 'witchy', haunting. Under certain atmospheric conditions the moon will appear in other colours than silvery-white. It has been described in song-lyrics as silver, yellow, red, blue and black.

Television 'Marquee Moon'; Elvis Presley 'Blue Moon of Kentucky', Tyrannosaurus Rex 'By The Light Of A Magical Moon'; Waterboys 'The Whole Of The Moon'; Echo And The Bunnymen 'The Killing Moon'; Van Morrison 'Moondance'; Henry Mancini 'Moon River'; Matt Monroe 'Fly Me To The Moon'; The Rolling Stones 'Moonlight Mile'; Creedence Clearwater Revival 'Bad Moon Rising'; Janis Joplin 'Half Moon'; Ray Noble 'By The Light Of The Silvery Moon'.

THE LYRICIST'S ZOO

Animals provide a ready supply of images and metaphors for human life. They often have symbolic qualities granted to them, some of which are already folklore, and some of which are grounded in observation of their behaviour. There are many proverbial sayings that encapsulate the symbolic meanings given to animals, such as "cry wolf" and "black sheep of the family". This is also fertile territory for out-of-hand misanthropic attitudes and satire, notoriously in The Beatles' 'Piggies'. The majority of songs that use animal imagery are not actually about the animals themselves; rare exceptions include Michael Jackson's 'Ben' (about a pet rat) and The Who's comic 'Boris The Spider'.

BIRDS: In the lexicon of popular song there are probably more lyrics that mention birds than there are about any other creature. Traditionally associated with freedom (hence the proverbial "free as a bird"), the bird belongs to the sky, not the earth, and thus signifies the soul, or a free-living spirit. Bird imagery expresses the romantic desire for transcendence – think of 'One Day I'll Fly Away' or 'Love Lifts Us Up' with its mention of eagles. By virtue of its wings, the bird is symbolically related to the angels. Songs nominally about birds, therefore, are usually about freedom, innocence and escape.

The Beatles 'Free As A Bird', 'And Your Bird Can Sing'; Supertramp 'Free As A Bird'; Elton John 'High Flying Bird'; The The 'Sweet Bird Of Truth'; It's A Beautiful Day 'White Bird'; Jimi Hendrix 'Night Bird Flying', 'Little Wing'; Snowy White 'Bird Of Paradise'; Siouxsie And The Banshees 'Painted Bird'; Neil Young 'Birds'.

Songbirds such as nightingales, blackbirds, larks and others are an easy metaphor for a woman singing (think of Eva Cassidy's *Songbird*) or the power of music itself, as in Norah Jones's 'Nightingale', Carly Simon and James Taylor's 'Mockingbird', Fleetwood Mac's 'Songbird', Joe Cocker's 'Bye Bye Blackbird', and The Beatles' 'Blackbird'. As singers, birds represent the romantic ideal of organic creativity – instantaneous, unreflecting, ever-renewing, and apparently effortless – as evoked across Kate Bush's album *Aerial*. In the act of singing, what a bird *is* and what it *does* are one. In human experience only rarely do we achieve states of consciousness where doing and being are blissfully one.

Swans are supposed to sing most expressively before their death, hence the phrase "swan song" when something is on its way out. The mockingbird comes a close second to the songbirds in lyric mentions because it can satirise or imitate someone. Doves have their traditional Biblical meaning of peace. The seagull is linked with the freedom of the sea, owls represent wisdom, night and far-seeing, and roosters carry a sexual connotation.

Buffalo Springfield 'Blue Bird'; R.E.M. 'Swan Swan Hummingbird'; Seals and Crofts 'Hummingbird'; Anne Murray 'Snowbird'; Prince 'When Doves Cry'; Kristin Hersh 'Cuckoo'; Joni Mitchell 'Black Crow'; Elton John 'Skyline Pigeon'; Bebop Deluxe 'Sister Seagull'; Canned Heat 'An Owl Song'; Steve Miller Band 'Fly Like An Eagle'; The Police 'Canary In A Coal Mine'; Donovan 'Three Kingfishers'; Manfred Mann 'Pretty Flamingo'; Willie Dixon 'Little Red Rooster'.

BUTTERFLIES: Next to birds in the lyric menagerie come butterflies. Butterflies symbolise something beautiful, fragile and ephemeral. There is a recognition that any attempt to capture and hold onto this living beauty is doomed to fail. The Mission's 'Butterfly On A Wheel' alluded by title to an editorial in *The Times* of London in June 1967, following the drug trial of Mick Jagger and Keith Richards, though the song itself is about a young woman damaged by a love affair. The Muse song listed refers to chaos theory – that a butterfly on one side of the world is part of a sequence of effects linked to hurricanes on the other:

Four Tops 'Elusive Butterfly'; Mission 'Butterfly On A Wheel'; The Verve 'Catching The Butterfly'; Jam 'The Butterfly Collector'; Paul Weller 'Amongst Butterflies'; Lloyd Cole 'Butterfly'; Heart 'Dog and Butterfly'; Lenny Kravitz 'Butterfly'; Muse 'Butterflies and Hurricanes'.

ANIMALS: Symbolically, dogs are loyal but downtrodden, except in folksongs if they are sheep-dogs; if they are black they can symbolise depression (though not Led Zep's black pooch).

Led Zeppelin 'Black Dog'; Nick Drake 'Black-Eyed Dog'; Robert Johnson 'Hellhound On My Trail'; The Stooges 'I Wanna Be Your Dog'; David Bowie 'Diamond Dogs'; Elvis Presley 'Hound Dog'; Monkees 'Gonna Buy Me A Dog'; The Rolling Stones 'Walking The Dog'; The Everly Brothers 'Bird Dog'; Tom Waits 'Rain Dogs'; Aerosmith 'Sick As A Dog'; The Beatles 'Hey Bulldog'; Cat Stevens' 'I Love My Dog'.

CATS: Cats are feline, independent, and sexy, and associated with women. "Cat" can also be slang for a person of either sex who is a happy-go-lucky, hip person.

The Beatles 'Leave My Kitten Alone'; The Cure 'The Love Cats'; Harry Chapin 'Cat's In The Cradle'; The Stray Cats 'Stray Cat Strut'; Kinks 'Phenomenal Cat'; The Rolling Stones 'Stray Cat Blues'; Elton John 'Honky Cat'; David Bowie 'Cat People'; Ted Nugent 'Cat Scratch Fever'.

HORSES: Horses are powerful and sexy; donkeys represent the easily exploited – as in the colloquial "donkey-work". There is a strand of sexual innuendo to do with riding animals such as ponies, horses and even a camel (in Maria Muldaur's 'Midnight At The Oasis'), for instance in The Rolling Stones ' 'Beast Of Burden'; and another in the milking of cows, hence lyrics like 'Milk Cow Blues' and the allure of the dairy-maid in ribald folk songs.

America 'Horse With No Name'; The Byrds 'Chestnut Mare'; P.J. Harvey 'Horses In My Dreams'; Free 'Ride On A Pony'; Racing Cars 'They Shoot Horses Don't They'; U2 'Who's Gonna Ride Your Wild Horses'; The Rolling Stones

'Wild Horses'; The Beatles 'Dig A Pony'; Lee Dorsey 'Ride Your Pony'; Canned Heat 'Pony Blues'; Sleepy John Estes 'Milk Cow Blues'; Sandy Denny 'One-Way Donkey Ride'; Paul McCartney 'Ram'; Rainbow 'Black Sheep of the Family'.

FOXES: Foxes are traditionally cunning, and the adjective "foxy" means sexually alluring and independent, as in Jimi Hendrix 'Foxy Lady', Manfred Mann 'Fox On The Run', and Thin Lizzy 'Johnny The Fox'. Hard rock and heavy metal groups are lyrically fond of anything that will give you a nasty bite or sting, such as snakes, scorpions, tigers, lions, wolves, etc. Predatory animals signify power, energy, and self-determination. Spiders are almost invariably mentioned in terms of their webs – an image for the laying of a trap in which someone might be caught, as in Coldplay's 'Trouble' or Dream Theater's 'Caught In A Web'.

Survivor 'Eye Of The Tiger'; The Tokens 'The Lion Sleeps Tonight'; Beck 'Paper Tiger'; Metallica 'Of Wolf And Man'; Duran Duran 'Hungry Like The Wolf'; Joni Mitchell 'Coyote'; Red Hot Chili Peppers 'True Men Don't Kill Coyotes'; Leadbelly 'Black Snake Moan'; Heart 'Barracuda'; Accept 'Fast As A Shark'.

THE HEART – THE EMOTIONAL SELF

One of the hardest cliché metaphors to deal with is the word "heart". This is the universal term for referring to the seat of the emotions, and there isn't really a substitute. There are many phrases which reinforce it: don't take it to heart, he broke my heart, lift up your hearts, heart-felt, hearts and minds, from the heart, heartache, being hard-hearted, that was a heartless thing to do, etc. To deliver something "straight from the heart" (a title used by Bryan Adams) is to speak with sincerity. The nearest might be "soul" but that has religious connotations. As the symbol of romantic love it is hardly surprising that popular music is full of songs with hearts in them. Avoid a cliché like "heart of stone" (which has been used by The Rolling Stones, Springsteen and many others), and don't fall into the trap of over-egging the image of the heart. The phrase "two hearts" is lyric shorthand for two lovers.

Use "heart" by all means, but if you want to be a cut above the average find something new you can do it. In 'Lines written a few miles above Tintern Abbey', the English poet William Wordsworth (1777-1850) wrote of sensations felt "along the heart". We don't think of the heart as having an "along"; it's a great image.

Cilla Black 'Anyone Who Had A Heart'; Blondie 'Heart Of Glass'; Neil Young 'Heart Of Gold'; Isley Brothers 'This Old Heart Of Mine'; Bonnie Tyler 'Total Eclipse of the Heart'; Captain Beefheart and His Magic Band 'Ashtray Heart'; Kate and Anna McGarrigle 'Heart Like A Wheel'; Magnetic Field 'Cactus Where Your Heart Should Be'; Yes 'Owner Of A Lonely Heart'; Eagles 'Heartache Tonight'; Elvis Presley 'Heartbreak Hotel'; Gene Pitney 'Something Got A Hold Of My Heart'.

ROSES

When it comes to flowers in lyrics, roses have special status. They stand first for beauty; secondly, the price paid for beauty, because they have thorns (thus an association between red roses, blood, and problems in love); thirdly, this is a beauty that will not last; fourthly, a rose-garden is an image for a place of content and paradise, a place where nothing goes wrong – hence the proverbial "bed of roses". They are probably the first flower that springs to mind when a songwriter goes looking for a comparison to say how beautiful is his love, some way ahead of the foxglove or lesser-spotted meadowsweet. In this respect song-lyrics follow in the wake of centuries of poets.

Elvis Costello pointed up the rose as a symbol with his album title *Mighty Like A Rose* – an interesting title as it invites us to re-consider what concept of strength is being used to support the simile (roses are not "mighty" in any conventional sense). Wings titled an album *Red Rose Speedway*, comparing the petals to a racing track.

Lynn Andersen 'I Never Promised You A Rose Garden'; The Damned 'New Rose'; Marv Johnston 'I'll Pick A Rose For My Rose'; Bobbie Vinton 'Red Roses For A Blue Lady'; Joni Mitchell 'For The Roses'; The Jam 'English Rose'; Mary Black 'The Thorn Upon The Rose'; Poison 'Every Rose Has Its Thorn'; Bon Jovi 'Bed Of Roses'; Eurythmics 'Thorn In My Side'; Thin Lizzy 'Black Rose'; Aretha Franklin 'A Rose Is Still A Rose'; Seal 'Kiss From A Rose'.

GAMES OF CHANCE

Games of chance, gambling, form a popular set of metaphors for song-lyrics. The assumption that underpins much of this imagery is that life is a game of chance, and risks have to be taken, so gambling expresses something about the human condition. Since popular music loves an outsider, a gambler can be the subject of a lyric, as well as a metaphor. Gambling metaphors are especially popular with hard rock and heavy metal bands, possibly because bands who tour a lot kill time by (amongst other things) playing cards and betting. The figure of the gambler is romanticised in popular culture. Gamblers are mostly portrayed as getting away with the risks they take.

A roulette wheel is associated with the idea of a wheel of fortune. Dice-throwing is a common lyric image, as in the cliché "the die is cast". Playing cards offer ready-made characters, since a pack contains court figures of jack, queen, king. The suits have symbolic meanings – hearts relates to emotions, diamonds to money and gemstones, spades to power and death because the suit is black. K. C. And The Sunshine Band punned a disco hit title with 'Queen Of Clubs'. There is the expression 'poker-faced', meaning to conceal your feelings.

A more sophisticated version of the card lyric refers to chess, which implies thoughtful strategy and the gradual conquest of another, as well as symbolic figures such as pawns, knights, kings, and queens (see the white queen/black queen mythology on the second Queen album). The pawn image is a cliché of protest lyrics.

Bob Dylan 'Queen Of Hearts'; Motorhead 'Ace Of Spades'; Ned Miller 'From A Jack To A King'; Wink Martindale Deck Of Cards'; The Rolling Stones 'Tumbling Dice'; Neil Sedaka 'Solitaire'; The Cramps 'Domino'; Robbie Robertson 'American Roulette'; The Faces 'Pool Hall Richard'; Penetration 'Life's A Gamble'; Wayne Fontana 'The Game Of Love'; Chris Isaacs 'Wicked Game'.

FIRE

The Prodigy, Sly And Robbie, U2, Scooter, Jimi Hendrix, and The Pointer Sisters are just a few of the artists who have recorded songs called 'Fire'. Michael Stipe drew attention to the fact that there is fire imagery throughout R.E.M.'s *Document* album. The other elements (air, water, earth) tend to be subsumed in weather or topographical imagery. Fire imagery is tied up with desire, passion, sex, and the erotic. Someone you fall in love with was once colloquially known as your "flame". The image acknowledges the transience of romantic love, as a flame can only burn for as long as it has adequate fuel. Fire can also represent a trial or a test that may be purifying. In Christian myth it is associated with purgatory or the sufferings of hell.

Bruce Springsteen 'I'm On Fire'; Crazy World Of Arthur Brown 'Fire'; Elvis Presley 'His Latest Flame'; Free 'Fire And Water'; The Move 'Fire Brigade'; James Taylor 'Fire And Rain'; Billy Joel 'We Didn't Start The Fire'; Super Furry Animals 'Fire In My Heart'; Deep Purple 'Fireball'; Prodigy 'Firestarter'; Cheap Trick 'The Flame'; Bangles 'Eternal Flame'.

COLOUR

The appeal of colour imagery is that it is strongly visual. Colours have important psychological effects – which is why we think carefully about the colours in our homes and public spaces. Colours already carry associations that relate to moods and states of mind. A colour in a title can give the listener half an idea of what the song is about immediately. Looked at in a more pragmatic way, it also provides an instant starting point for the marketing of your song through any visual medium: adverts, record sleeves, posters, live performance and stage lighting, videos. Imagine writing a song called 'Flame So Blue'; your lighting technician has half the job done for that song straight off (notice how in concert bands use blue lighting for slower songs). Consider the role red and white play in the career of The White Stripes.

Before surveying individual colours, remember that the word "colour", singular or plural, often crops up in song titles. Donovan wrote 'Colours' by leading each verse off with a different colour. Other generic 'colour' songs are 'Colour My World' (Petula Clark, Chicago), Cyndi Lauper 'True Colors', 'Colours' (Phil Collins, The Sisters of Mercy), 'Forbidden Colours', (David Sylvian and Ryuichi Sakamoto), 'She Comes In Colours' (Love), 'Love Is A Wonderful Colour' (The Icicle Works), 'The Colour Field' (by The Colour Field), 'The Colour Of Love' (Billy Ocean), 'Colours Fly Away' (The Men They Couldn't Hang), and 'Colours Fly Away' (Teardrop Explodes). Sometimes it isn't always obvious what the colour in a title refers to, as with The Band's debut *Music From Big Pink* (it was in fact a house).

An obvious type of colour symbolism is based on a flag. Burning Spear's 'Red, Gold and Green' alludes to the colours of Rastafarianism, and anything with red, white and blue could be the US or the UK. Red and blue also have left/right political connotations. In The Who's 'Blue, Red and Grey' the colours represent dusk. (The multi-coloured rainbow can be found under weather imagery). Here are individual colours and a selection of songs.

WHITE: The associations of white are purity, innocence, snow ("white as the driven snow"); "white lies", which are forgivable; weddings; a white flag (surrender, as in Elvis Costello's 'Wave A White Flag'), peace; the white man; a whitewash is a cover-up; a whited sepulchre is hypocrisy; illness; death.

Procol Harum 'Whiter Shade Of Pale'; Tomorrow 'My White Bicycle'; Billy Idol 'White Wedding'; Bing Crosby 'White Christmas'; Foreigner 'White Lie'; Velvet Underground 'White Light White Heat'; Big Star 'Life Is White'; Paul Kantner and Grace Slick 'White Boy'; Texas 'White On Blonde'; Meredith Willson 'My White Knight'; Billy Idol 'White Wedding'; Clannad 'White Fool'; Sunscreem 'White Skies'.

BLACK: The associations of black are, on the positive side, power, authority, mystery, sexual allure; on the negative side, tragedy, grief and mourning, hate, loss, death, and depression. The word is also a term of imprecise racial description. A number of artists have recorded "black" albums, including Prince and Metallica. Probably the most used song title with this colour is 'Fade To Black' (see Dire Straits and Metallica, to name two), closely followed by 'Black And Blue', a title used by Suede, Dio, Pearl Jam,

Sevendust, and Rancid. In the gloomier corners of popular music (Goth, grunge, HM) black is *always* the new black. To see things "in black and white" is to see them in polarized and simplistic terms, as implied by a title like Costello's 'Black And White World'.

The Rolling Stones 'Paint It Black'; Santana 'Black Magic Woman'; Soundgarden 'Fell On Black Days'; Stephen Stills 'Black Queen'; Doobie Brothers 'Black Water'; Paul Weller 'Black Is The Colour'; Suede 'Black Or Blue'; Kiss 'Black Diamond'; Deep Purple 'Black Night'; Screaming Trees 'Black Sun Morning'; Janis Ian 'Black and White'; Big Bill Broonzy 'Black; Brown and White'.

GREY: The associations of grey are more negative than the other colours. Black may be negative but it always has a thrill with it; grey commits the ultimate pop sin of being plain dull. Grey has associations of boredom, mediocrity, conforming, uniformity, being suppressed, and overcast (of a sky). Of hair it means the dreaded first sign of ageing (this can be dignified by describing it as silver).

Madness 'Grey Day'; 10,000 Maniacs 'Grey Victory'; Family 'Mellowing Grey'; Richard Thompson 'Grey Wall'; Gene Pitney 'Blue Turns to Grey'; Visage 'Fade to Grey'; The Monkees 'Shades Of Grey'; Grateful Dead 'Touch of Grey'; Pretty Things 'Defecting Grey'; XTC 'Wrapped In Grey'; Caravan 'In The Land Of Grey and Pink'; Joni Mitchell 'Two Grey Rooms'.

SILVER: The associations of silver are primarily something of value, money, something metallic, moonlight, age (silver hair, which in turn could represent wisdom). If metallic, silver can represent the future, since in TV commercials and sci-fi films the future is often depicted as a world made up of grey and silver surfaces. There is also the proverb that every cloud has a silver lining, and to have a 'silver tongue' is to be a persuasive speaker.

Echo And The Bunnymen 'Silver'; Mountain 'Silver Paper'; Hawkwind 'Silver Machine'; Jeff Beck 'Hi Ho Silver Lining'; The Rolling Stones 'You Got The Silver'; The Beatles 'Maxwell's Silver Hammer'; Genesis 'Silver Rainbow'; Sonic Youth 'Silver Rocket'; Andrew Kerr 'Silver Suitcases'; The Rolling Stones 'Silver Train'; Fleetwood Mac 'Silver Springs'.

GOLD: Like silver, gold represents value, money, wealth, and wedding rings. It can also be a colour of hair, the best of something (a "golden" age), the wisdom of a rule that should not be broken, and the fields at harvest time. Spiritually, it is something or someone who is dependable – as in Neil Young's 'Heart Of Gold'. Proverbially, silence is golden, and there is a pot of gold waiting at the end of every rainbow.

The unwary in popular lyrics are left with "fool's gold" (a popular lyric title used by Thin Lizzy and Stone Roses). Mythically, the figure most likely to spring to mind in connection with gold is King Midas, who was granted a wish to turn everything he touched into gold, then found this turned out to be a curse.

David Bowie 'Golden Years'; Sting 'Fields Of Gold'; The Tremoloes 'Silence Is Golden'; Shirley Bassey 'Goldfinger'; The Beatles 'Golden Slumbers'; U2 'Silver And Gold'; Syd Barratt 'Golden Hair'; Freda Payne 'Band Of Gold'; Fleetwood Mac 'Gold Dust Woman'; Dire Straits 'Love Over Gold'; Dio 'Golden Rules'; Razor Light 'Golden Touch'; Tina Turner 'Golden Eye'; Richard Thompson 'Gold Kisses'; Stevie Wonder 'Golden Lady'.

BROWN: Like grey, brown is a colour without especially strong or attractive associations. It implies conformity, dullness, paper bags, and the colour of earth. It is most attractive for songwriters when used as an eye or hair colour (for which brunette might also be used) or linked to something else.

The Stranglers 'Golden Brown'; The Rolling Stones 'Brown Sugar'; June Tabor 'Shallow Brown'; James Brown 'Shades Of Brown'; Lynn Miles 'Big Brown City'; Boney M 'Brown Girl In The Ring'; Roni Size & Reprazent 'Brown Paper Bag'; Billy Bragg 'Greetings To The New Brunette'.

RED: Along with blue, red is the most likely colour to turn up in a song lyric. Blue and red symbolise the two key emotional states in lyrics: passion and misery. They are linked with fire and water. The connotations of red are passion, blood (possibly murder), the heart, the emotions, sex, and wine. To be angry is to "see red". Infra-red is one end of the visible light spectrum. We speak of a "red-light district" and in The Police's Roxanne the young woman plied her trade by switching on a red light. To be a "scarlet" woman is to be a sexual predator. Overnight flights are catching the "red-eye"; otherwise, to have red eyes may indicate crying. (Red rose songs are listed under roses, red clothing and shoes are under clothing in **Section Nine**).

A little red book is understood to contain addresses and phone numbers of lovers, past and present. To see things through rose-tinted glasses is to idealise a situation. A red herring is a piece of information that leads away from the direction you should take. In a recording studio a red light indicates the necessity for quiet because a session is in progress. A "red letter day" is a special day on which something great has happened.

Spirit 'Red Light Roll On'; Jimi Hendrix 'Red House'; Nena '99 Red Balloons'; Love 'My Little Red Book'; Split Enz 'I See Red'; The White Stripes 'Red Rain'; Neil Diamond 'Red Red Wine'; Robin Williamson 'Red Eye Blues'; The Incredible String Band 'Red Hair'; Kris Delmhorst 'Red Herring'; U2 'Red Light'; Limp Bizkit 'Red Light – Green Light'; Robert Johnson 'They're Red Hot'.

Variations on red include ruby and scarlet, which are intensifications of red. Pink is a toning-down, less active, feminine colour – a more luxurious and less everyday version of red; also a skin-colour, and a colour of the sky at dawn and twilight.

All About Eve 'Scarlet'; Mercury Rev 'Vermilion'; Tommy James And The Shondells 'Crimson And Clover'; The Misfits 'Crimson Ghost'; Alan Dale 'Cherry Pink and Apple Blossom White'; Aerosmith 'Pink'; The Cure 'Pink'; Nick Drake 'Pink Moon'; Psychedelic Furs 'Pretty In Pink'; Cherry Poppin' Daddies 'Pink Elephant'; AC/DC 'Sink the Pink' ; Bruce Springsteen 'Pink Cadillac'; They Might Be Giants 'Stormy Pinkness'.

ORANGE: Orange is a rare colour in song-lyrics. It is notoriously hard to find a suitable rhyme for it if you end up with it at the end of a line (although "syringe" is not bad); this may have discouraged people from putting it in a title. It tends to appear either in protest songs about the deployment of the defoliant Agent Orange in the Vietnam war (see R.E.M. 'Orange Crush'), or as part of a riot of colour in a psychedelic song.

Dandy Warhols 'Orange'; Depeche Mode, Kate Wolf 'Agent Orange'; Love 'Orange Skies'; Natalie Cole 'Orange Colored Sky'; Johnny Cash 'Orange Blossom Special'; Van Dyke Parks 'Orange Crate Art'; Cocteau Twins 'Pink Orange Red'.

YELLOW : This colour is primarily associated with sunshine and summer, blonde hair, corn, the Far East (as in Springsteen's reference to the "yellow man" in 'Born In The USA'), and is a favourite colour for psychedelic songs. Try applying it to something that isn't usually yellow to get this playful effect (this goes back to The Beatles' 'Yellow Submarine'); yellow is bright, child-like, innocent, frivolous, so painting a submarine yellow is not something the military would go in for. Sometimes the word lemon is used as a substitute for yellow.

Coldplay 'Yellow'; Donovan 'Mellow Yellow'; The Beatles 'Yellow Submarine'; Joni Mitchell 'Big Yellow Taxi'; Phil Lynott 'Yellow Pearl'; Jackson C. Frank 'Yellow Walls'; Christie 'Yellow River'; Mitch Miller 'The Yellow Rose Of Texas'; Haircut 100 'Lemon Firebrigade'; Dawn 'Tie A Yellow Ribbon Round The Old Oak Tree'; The Leaves 'Lemon Princess'; Randy Newman 'Yellow Man'; Sonia Nordenstam 'Keen Yellow Planet'.

GREEN: The associations of green fall into quite distinct areas: it is the colour of nature, of grass, the environment and the politics thereof; it also stands for money ("greenbacks"); for envy or jealousy (the green-eyed monster), and inexperience (to be green in judgement). To get the "green light" is to be able to go ahead with a project. Ireland is described as the "Emerald isle". Something "evergreen" (see Barbara Streisand's song of this title) can weather all seasons. To have "green fingers" is to have a talent for gardening.

New Order 'Everything's Gone Green'; Johnny Cash 'Forty Shades Of Green'; Siouxsie And The Banshees 'Green Fingers'; Fleetwood Mac 'The Green Manalishi (With The Two-Pronged Crown)'; Nelly Furtado 'The Grass is Green'; Tom Jones 'Green, Green Grass of Home'; The Jam 'Pretty Green'; Lemon Pipers 'Green Tambourine'; Dinosaur Jnr 'Green Mind'; Bonnie Raitt 'Green Lights'; Donovan 'Turquoise'; Mr Big 'Green Tinted Sixties Mind'.

BLUE: Along with red, blue is the most likely colour to find in a song-lyric. When the popular song-lyric isn't passionate, it's sad ... *blue*. So "blue" is shorthand for a whole gamut of emotions that run from mild sadness to outright depression, until, as The Foo Fighters put it, 'The Deepest Blues Are Black'. Blue is the colour of sky and ocean, of water, which have positive meanings, and of smoke. Blue lights are associated with the police and emergency services such as ambulances. Something that comes out of the blue is a complete surprise. Blue can signify electricity, and there is a generic character called "Baby Blue" who crops up in many songs. I have not included titles where "blues" implies a style of music.

Bob Dylan 'It's All Over Now; Baby Blue'; 'Tangled Up In Blue'; Prince 'Blue Light','Computer Blue'; Nick Drake ' Way To Blue'; Janis Joplin 'Little Girl Blue'; Joni Mitchell 'Blue'; Madonna 'True Blue'; Tommy James and Shondells 'Crystal Blue Persuasion'; Marillion 'Lavender Blue'; White Stripes 'Blue Orchid'; Kate Campbell 'Fade to Blue'; Paul Mauriat 'Love Is Blue'; Laura Nyro 'Mr Blue'; R.E.M. 'Electron Blue'; Ella Fitzgerald 'Born To Be Blue'.

PURPLE: This colour does not feature often in lyrics because it is not an everyday colour. Purple is associated with royalty and wealth, and can function as a colour of twilight. Related colours are violet and indigo. Ultra-violet is the opposite extreme of the visible spectrum of light to infra-red. Purple's most famous recent use in popular music is Prince's song and film *Purple Rain*. This title has a psychedelic tone that was set by Hendrix's 'Purple Haze' in 1967. Perhaps too Hendrix was responsible for inspiring Robert Plant of Led Zeppelin to give their 'Living Loving Maid' a purple umbrella.

Stone Temple Pilots 'Purple'; Van Morrison 'Purple Heather'; Sheb Wooley 'Purple People Eater'; Tempo and April Stevens 'Deep Purple'; Marvin Gaye 'Purple Snowflakes'; Joni Mitchell 'Turbulent Indigo'; Frank Sinatra 'Mood Indigo'; Babes In Toyland 'Bruise Violet'; Peter Gabriel 'Indigo'; U2 'Ultra Violet (Light My Way)'; Dire Straits 'Under a Violet Moon'; Stevie Nicks 'Violet and Blue'.

EYES

We speak of "making eye contact", of seeing eye to eye, of eyes as the "windows" of the soul, and of lovers who gaze into each others' eyes. So it's not surprising that many song titles have "eyes" in the title. Occasionally, it's not just love that gets in the eyes. Jackson Browne wrote his 1970s hit 'Doctor My Eyes' when he had an eye infection, The Platters lamented that 'Smoke Gets In Your Eyes', Richie Havens offered 'Eyesight To The Blind', and Sam Cooke even dared to say 'I'd Rather Go Blind'. In proverbial usage, to be "green-eyed" is to be jealous (hence Less Than Jake's 'Green Eyed Monster'), and to be "wide-eyed" is to be surprised and/or innocent. Combining eyes and colour is a favourite song-title ploy. The most popular eye colour is blue, with brown and green close behind. Blue also allows for a play on the meaning "sad", hence Crystal Gayle's 'Don't It Make My Brown Eyes Blue'.

Art Garfunkel 'Bright Eyes'; Roxy Music 'Angel Eyes'; The Eagles 'Lyin' Eyes'; Dusty Springfield 'I Close My Eyes and Count To Ten'; The Supremes 'When The Lovelight Starts Shining Through His Eyes'; The Who 'Behind Blue Eyes'; Coldplay 'Green Eyes'; Fleetwood Mac 'Emerald Eyes'; Chuck Berry 'Brown-eyed Handsome Man'; Crystal Gayle 'Don't It Make My Brown Eyes Blue'; Everly Brothers 'Ebony Eyes'.

For lyrical ingenuity about eyes, consider the phrase "luggage eyes" which occurs in T.Rex's 'One Inch Rock'. Marc Bolan explained: "At first I was thinking she had eyes with bags beneath them ... then I thought – why not 'luggage eyes'?".[71]

This survey of popular lyric imagery is by no means exhaustive, but it will make you think about well-used images and how they relate to your own lyrics. Have a look at your writing for common images that you use repeatedly. If they are obvious or clichéd ones, consider giving them a rest and developing your own. If you are a more experienced songwriter, look for images that are distinctly yours. These may be part of your finger-print as a songwriter, but it is worth checking to make sure they aren't over-used to the point of becoming repetitive. Neil Finn of Crowded House: "There's a point in every writer's life where they've got to look hard and long at the stock images they use.'[72]

Paul Buchanan

Interviewed by David Sheppard

The Blue Nile are the thinking fan's cult group. By delivering just four albums of poised electro white soul in more than 20 years, the band have created a mystique around themselves. At their heart is singer/ songwriter Paul Buchanan, whose evocative impressions of the strangeness and beauty of ordinary things account for much of the band's enduring appeal.

You are obviously concerned with imagery. But are there any clichéd images or themes that make you cringe when you hear them in other people's writing, or traps you try to avoid when writing lyrics?

I never cringe at other people's lyrics. Clichéd images and themes are one thing, but I hope that I hear the lyrics with the correct intent, so if something is throwaway, I accept it as such. I really cannot think of one howler that sticks in my craw. I truly don't think like that. A popular song lyric can be about anything – I think they are.

There are obvious traps with songwriting – I don't feel a rhyme has to be perfect, for example. It's more important to avoid self-parody and just being contrived in any way.

How old were you when you wrote your first song and why did you write it?

I was about 15 when I wrote my first song, in my room, sitting on the edge of the bed after the dishes were done. For a while songwriting meant simply re-arranging the chords from whichever song I had just learned and making up a new song from there. There was no one thing that inspired me to write songs, it was more a case of 'them' not 'it'. I probably only realized that I had some facility for songwriting about the time I lost it!

Songwriting has never really been a diary for me, more a kind of memory. I do look back over the songs and recognize the narrator – though I think that's more to do with us [The Blue Nile] being stringent about the tone of voice we used in recording the vocals. Certain themes, situations and motifs do recur in my songs, however: conversations between men and women; the city; buildings; lights; night-time and day-time; hope; the countryside outside the city ... I think they're just my favourite ideas, though I wonder increasingly about their legitimacy.

Do you have a routine for writing lyrics?

I don't really have a routine for songwriting at all. I write too many things down. Inevitably, the best ones chose their moments and are simple. I do redraft and revise things, but only a little.

The Blue Nile albums always take a while to make but some songs are written quickly, often in one sitting. In fact there are quite a few that were written like that. 'Because Of Toledo,' or 'The Days Of Our Lives' are two from the last album [*High*], but I can think of a few others. Often I write 80 per cent of the song in one go and enjoy doing the rest later; sometimes I write a verse or so too much.

I've read what Tom Waits once wrote about songwriting being like trying to carry water in your hands and I'm aware of this idea that songs pre-exist on some metaphysical plain and songwriters are merely the conduits through which the muse flows. I do sort of believe in it. It seems too grand to lay claim to songs as an abstract currency in my own case, but I can assure you my job has been mainly staying out the way if something passable occurs.

At what stage in the songwriting process does the lyric form?

For me, the various elements of a song form at approximately the same time. The lyrics, the chords and melody and most importantly the rhythm of the phrasing, those things have to be working in unison for me for it to be a song.

How important do you think lyrics are in songwriting?

Lyrics will always have a considerable primacy on one level for me, but then I'm very vain! Lyrics aren't always the main thing. Obviously, for Bob Dylan and his ilk the words are pretty central – I guess in some hip hop too. But in a lot of pop music lyrics aren't really that important at all.

I don't think a good lyric outweighs the music that frames it. There must be synergy between words and music. I actually think phrasing, as it varies from singer to singer, is crucial to how a song works. Sometimes, of course, the words must take precedence. Even the sound of the words or the way you can make them feel with your voice might be more important than the melody in a particular part of the song. I like it to be cumulative. Words and music should serve each other.

Is a great lyric the combination of the personal and the universal? Perhaps, though I think forthrightness is the real key. A wonderful line is "What's it all about, Alfie?" I'm throwing that in. The next line is also a winner: "Is it just for the moment we live?" [from Burt Bacharach and Hal David's 'Alfie']. I like the line "All the stars that never were/ are parking cars and pumping gas" [from Burt Bacharach and Hal David's 'Do You Know The Way To San Jose'] – it's just good, isn't it? I like to draw out observations of everyday life. Mind you, I will never express a fraction of what I see every time I go out for a walk. I suppose I do file images away then and re-evoke them later in songs. My efforts are so trivial I won't expound further!

I don't think it's the writer's job to stand outside life and merely observe it. The standing to one side bit I'm really not sure of: perhaps it's part of the process but I'm not convinced that it's a good thing. I think that inhibits the writer's ability to empathize with and express to his fellow citizen. Maybe he's just projecting his own illusions onto people? As a writer, I'm really not trying to alienate or misinterpret anyone. I want to be popular for God's sake!

I am influenced by lyricists and authors – too many to go into detail, really. Honestly, everybody and everything is an influence. People I hear on the subway; a letter from the eighteenth century; the lettering on an old book; anything ...

How much importance do you attach to a title?

Song titles are important, but they're not always obvious from the start. 'Tinseltown In The Rain' [from *A Walk Across The Rooftops*] was just a line in a song I'd written. It was Robert [Bell, Blue Nile keyboardist] who saw it as a title. It's emphatic. I think first lines in songs are more important - I think good songs tend to have good first lines; it's not a very encouraging place to be stumbling.

Which of your lyrics are you most proud of?

A favourite lyric of mine would be this from 'Easter Parade' [*A Walk Across The Rooftops*]:

"In the bureau, typewriters quiet
Confetti falls from every window
Throwing hats up in the air,
A city perfect in every detail
Easter Parade."

I like the shape; I like the stillness that song was trying to evoke.

- What is their motivation? Why do they do what they do?
- What is the theme or point of this story? This arises from the relationship between the central characters and the end event.
- When did this story happen? Is it in the distant past, the recent past, or the present?

With these things decided you can fill in the details that you will need to round out the story. For example, where is this story happening? In what sort of society and landscape does it happen (this may have an important bearing on the content)? How much 'back-story' is needed, and what will be the first event in the lyric. Do you want to give the ending away at the beginning or keep it in reserve to keep the listener in suspense? Or is it a mystery where there is no final explanation for why something happened, as in the case of one of the greatest of all modern story songs, Bobbie Gentry's 'Ode To Billie Joe'. Did Billie Joe jump or was he pushed? What was the relationship between him and the young female narrator who can't eat her dinner? What was it that was thrown off the Tallahachie Bridge?

How to select a narrator

Another important decision is who is going to be the narrator – the one who tells the story? If you write from a detached third-person point of view, the narrator is not a part of the story, but an invisible presence in which the listener may have no interest. Another approach is to tell the story in the first person, from the central character's point of view. A third possibility is to write it in the first person, but to give your first person narrator an insight into other characters' points of view. Each of these is valid. The sequence of events can stay the same, but the meaning of the story might differ.

A narrative lyric can also be divided so it is multi-perspective, with more than one of the characters speaking. They could be given consecutive verses. This can be technically challenging to keep clear for the listener, but if the song is a duet with two singers (as in some of Meatloaf's songs, or the Elton John and Kiki Dee 'Don't Go Breaking My Heart') it becomes clear enough.

The narrative story has no time to be introspective and dwell on moods. The emotion of a character (and the atmosphere as a whole) must be sketched in a couple of lines, perhaps with imagery. Moods and implications are conveyed in many ways – sometimes through descriptive details, sometimes by choice of words. If a story lyric begins "He strolled down to the shining lake / Of calm and dappled blue" the imagery establishes a positive mood; if the same line were "He crept down to the sullen lake / Of cloudy gun-metal grey" there is a sense of foreboding. This is not simply because in one the lake is "shining" and in the other it's "grey". The verbs "strolled" and "crept" are important. "Strolled" suggests a carefree, relaxed movement; "crept" suggests something furtive, seeking concealment. Many lyricists seek to convey mood through adjectives, their descriptive words, and underestimate the power of verbs to do this. Take a line like "The windy dark night blew your hair". Compare it with the more dynamic "Darkness drums and pulls your hair', where the verbs work harder.

This is where a thesaurus is as handy as a rhyming dictionary. A thesaurus provides synonyms for words so you can make this kind of fine adjustment in later drafts, replacing adjectives with verbs. Controlling verbs in a narrative lyric is doubly important because verbs are words of action – and a story is usually about actions. So choosing the correct verb is telling part of the story in itself.

Verses, choruses, and stories

So how does a narrative lyric fit the common verse/chorus/bridge song structure? There is a slight mismatch here because a story doesn't repeat sections but a chorus often has the same words on each repeat. The traditional folk ballad avoided this problem by

- Using a simple song form in which there are no choruses or bridges, just a sequence of verses.

- Attaching a short refrain – a single line – to the end of each verse. This refrain is sometimes nonsense syllables (the stereotypical "fol-de'rol'de-day' type, with which people can join in), or a phrase or image that alludes to the song title, the central event, and may comment on its mood. So, "The lake was dark that day, that day / The lake was dark that day" is rhythmic, and could be a symbolic running commentary on each verse as the story advances.

- Add interest by changing a single word of the refrain from verse to verse – in this case lake could be replaced by "the sky', or even "his face', or "her thoughts were".

A refrain tacked on to the end of a verse provides one solution to the challenge of writing a narrative lyric in verse/chorus form. The chorus doesn't advance the story, it comments on it, indicates the theme; the verses convey the events. The bridge (if there is one) can either handle the critical moment in the story, in which case the last verse (if there is a verse after the bridge) describes the fall-out and consequences, or the change of heart that pushes the events to their climax.

Imagine a story lyric where a young man is offered the prospect of fame and fortune but has to leave his home town and his girlfriend behind. She is not happy and gives him an ultimatum: it's her or the road. Verse one could describe their relationship and usual life; verse two his career ambitions and his first opportunity which he turns down, then a chorus. In verse three he gets another opportunity and this time he feels he should take it. In the bridge his woman lays down the law, he changes his mind for an instant, and then realises it's no good. In the final chorus the words can then be altered to indicate he has made up his mind.

The love triangle

The narrative lyric can relate many different stories. One of the classic story lines in popular song involves a murder stemming from a love triangle, whose motive is jealousy, and which leads to revenge, death, imprisonment, or escape. In the lyric of 'Hey Joe', a song made famous by Jimi Hendrix, there's a dialogue. It isn't narrated by the murderer Joe. The events break down:

- A friend asks where he is going with a gun in his hand.
- Joe replies that he's going to shoot his woman because she's been "messing round town" with another man. This is before the deed is carried out.
- In a later verse Joe tells his friend that he's done it.

- The friend asks where he's going to go now to escape the law, and the answer is Mexico (useful thing, Mexico, if you've just shot someone).
- There he can escape punishment and live a free man.

Similarly, in Tom Jones' melodrama 'Delilah' a jealous man kills his lover just before the police break down the door, even asking for her forgiveness as he does it. There are narrative lyrics that have stories told from jail by the murderer awaiting execution.

Dido's recent song 'Mary's In India' is a narrative about a love triangle with a happy ending:

- One half of a couple, Mary, goes off to India, leaving her partner behind.
- Having a good time there, she decides to end the relationship. Dido's refrain has the sun setting on the young man and rising metaphorically on Mary.
- The narrator takes pity on the poor chap and consoles him.
- Eventually the narrator and the jilted young man form a new relationship.
- Now the sun is rising on him and setting on Mary.

The nice twist on this traditional parallel between the motion of the sun and the waxing and waning of love is that the international time difference (albeit exaggerated) allows us to pretend that it could be literally as well as figuratively true.

In Kate Bush's 'Babooshka' the triangle is occupied by two people and a fantasy figure. The wife decides she wants to enliven her marriage, so she invents a Russian *femme fatale* character and sends letters to her husband to elicit from him the emotional response that he once gave her. The irony of the situation is that in responding eagerly to this fantasy figure he is actually responding to his wife. The Eagles' 'Lyin' Eyes' is interesting for the way it inserts the chorus into the story line. The story concerns a woman who seeks out an affair because of the emotional austerity in which she finds herself. The chorus comments through the image of the "lyin' eyes" that can't be hidden. Since she is addressed as you, it is difficult to see who is saying this – is it the man she lives with? Is it the voice of her conscience? Is it an accusation or is there some sympathy in it?

Dire Straits 'Romeo and Juliet' takes characters from a pre-existing narrative (Shakespeare's) which is so famous that we know what they represent (doomed young love). Elvis Costello's 'Watching The Detectives' takes imagery from detective pulp fiction but doesn't quite provide enough information for us to know exactly what is going on. Instead, we get a superbly-wrought cinematic style packed with unforgettable images, but which lacks the necessary information to let us put it into a logical sequence. That lyric has film-makers' vocabulary, with phrases like "long-shot", "cut to", "close-up", as if the lyric is being laid out like a film.

Not all love triangles need be unhappy. A great example of the relationship between a lyric's emotion and its perspective is The Beatles 'She Loves You', whose joy and energy partly depend on the fact that it's selfless. The song is spoken by a third-person go-between whose intention is to patch up a lovers' quarrel. It cast The Beatles as true peacemakers long before the less specific 'All You Need Is Love'.

Stories of a rise and fall

A well-known narrative lyric form describes a rise to stardom. Chuck Berry's 'Johnny B. Goode' tells of a country boy, illiterate but musically gifted, a great guitar player, who sits by the railroad making up rhythms that match those of the trains. The chorus simply exhorts Johnny to "go" – to play for all his worth and make a shot at the big time. His mother foresees that one day he will have his name in lights. Although this doesn't happen in the song, we never doubt that it will. David Bowie's 'Ziggy Stardust' is a song that is part of a five-song sequence on the *Ziggy Stardust* album but in itself relates how a rock'n'roll star is destroyed by success. Similarly, The Jam's 'To Be Someone' tells the rise and fall of a rock band from the point of view of one of the band members:

- He dreams of how great it would be to be someone famous, like a footballer, a rock singer or a film star.
- He dreams of having lots of fans, lots of girls, proving his manhood and getting rich.
- He achieves these things but starts taking drugs.
- He starts spending a lot of money.
- His money and fame shrink.
- He loses his guitar-shaped pool, the media lose interest in him, he can't afford drugs, and instead of taking taxis, has to walk everywhere.

The lyric ends with the return of the idea that to be someone "must be a wonderful thing". It is left ambiguous whether this means he is once more dreaming of climbing the ladder of success, or whether the whole thing was a daydream in which he correctly imagined both the positives and the negatives of fame. Julianne Regan's 'Miss World' (recorded under the band name Mice) does the same thing with a young woman who decides to enter a beauty contest. It follows the same curve from poverty and obscurity to success and then back to anonymity. It's a lyric that repays careful reading.

Sometimes, stories don't have endings. It could be you don't know what the ending will be, or the characters leave off in the middle of something. We never know what becomes of the lovers in Bruce Springsteen's 'Incident On 57th Street'. In that song there is a family, two young lovers, and a death, all mixed up. It is interesting to consider a lyric like Bob Dylan's 'All Along The Watchtower', filled with dramatic events on a big scale, cryptic images, and buried connections. It ends with the two riders approaching the city. We never know what happens next. Handled well, the incomplete lyric invites the imagination of the listener to write what is left unwritten.

Point of view and voice

"I can't have every song, not necessarily just about me, but from my point of view – I always say, you must be a very big-headed person to write about yourself, or only from your own point of view. Why should you want to?' (Joan Armatrading)[76]

"On every album I adopt a different sort of character, and the character on this album [An Innocent Man) is sort of a sweet person who is in love and feeling good." (Billy Joel)[77]

Whether a lyric is a story or not, it does not have to be written from the first person: "I looked out this morning" could be "He/she/they looked out this morning". Think about who could speak your lyric? If you feel exposed writing from first person, get a new perspective on personal themes by addressing yourself as "you". Most listeners will think you are talking to someone else. The trick with this technique is to be careful not to mix this up with addressing someone as "you" elsewhere in the same lyric.

Shifting point of view is a way of changing the emotion of a song. I once sketched a lyric based on the phrase "closing down sale" which I'd seen in the window of a secondhand shop that offered house clearances. The many secondhand objects in the shop were taken from many lives. This made me think of endings, and then, metaphorically, of the end of a relationship as a closing down sale. I sketched the idea from the point of view of a couple breaking up. Then I considered how the imagery would work if it was the initiator of the split using it. The song would become a cruel put-down, selling off the other's affections ("You thought you were out of the woods / But now you're just secondhand goods"). Going on from that, I imagined a third person coming on the scene and falling in love with the rejected individual. For him/her the closing down sale brings incomparable good fortune. The person who was rejected is swept up by this new love. The closing down sale imagery turns into a song about happiness. It all depends on the perspective.

A different perspective could come from someone a different age to yourself. In his lyric book *Songs*, Bruce Springsteen wrote of *Nebraska*, "I often wrote from a child's point of view: 'Mansion On The Hill', 'Used Cars', 'My Father's House' – these were all stories that came directly out of my experience with my family."

Dramatic monologue

"I didn't want any more confessional songs, and I wanted to put myself in other scenarios. I can do that, I'm a craftsman. I don't have to just do one thing. It was a good release for me." (Sting on *Ten Summoner's Tales*)[78]

Half way between narrative and point-of-view, the dramatic monologue lyric gives the chance to speak in someone else's voice. Its essence is:

- Choose an interesting character and make this person the "I" who speaks.
- Try to find their tone of voice, manner of speaking, vocabulary.
- Let them describe their time, place, situation in life and disposition.
- Start with them at a critical moment in life, when something vital is about to happen to them, or when they are on the brink of an action or decision.
- Or describe the immediate aftermath of such an event or action.
- The more critical the moment, the more dramatic the monologue.
- This is a moment of self-revelation – the emphasis is on their state of mind, rather than on a sequence of events. The drama is an inner one.

A dramatic monologue can tell a story, but it can also imply what happened, and instead concentrate on creating an intriguing mood.

An excellent example of this type of lyric is Jimmy Webb's 'Wichita Lineman', which has the neatest of introductions, the first two lines telling us what he does for a living. From that point on his Lineman becomes a romantic, Everyman figure, whom we picture poised between the land and sky in all weathers. His solitude is both a pleasure and a curse, the solitude of being human. He is an existential symbol, yet so concretely realised that you never consciously think of this even as you are moved by it. Somewhere at the back of his dilemma, which is the dramatic bit, is a woman. He seems to have come to a realisation of how important this woman is to him. But we don't know what will happen or what needs to happen. The song retains its fascination. Jimmy Webb told Rob Chapman of *The Times* (4 November 2005),

A song like Wichita Lineman suggests the plains, the receding horizon, the loneliness of the lineman who's up this pole in the middle of nowhere. That's an actual image that I saw one day. I was driving along and saw this guy high up on a telegraph pole and I wondered to myself, "Gee I wonder who he's talking to and what he's talking about." There's a kind of tenacity, a blue-collar nobility to what he was doing … [Billy Joel] said what that song says is that inside any normal Joe you might see on the street there could be great thoughts and aspirations and just because a guy is working at some menial job it doesn't mean that inside of him there's not some great passion or great dream.[79]

It is a response worthy of the great American playwright Arthur Miller.

Another fine example, more obviously dramatic than 'Wichita Lineman', is Springsteen's 'Meeting Across The River' (from *Born To Run*). Producer Chuck Plotkin once said, "Bruce's gift is to locate the heart in some character's dilemma." The central character delivers a dramatic monologue talking not to us but to another character who is also part of the story. The result is an overheard conversation of unintended self-revelation. The "I" is attempting to put across a certain image to Eddie, but we form a different opinion. In this scenario a small-time crook talks to his friend about a "job", for which he needs to borrow money and get a lift through the tunnel to the other side of the city. He has a troubled relationship with a woman called Cherry, who is angry and threatening to leave him for selling her radio to a pawn shop. We never know what the "job" is, whether it worked or they got away with it. But the song leaves us feeling we know these people and something of their past and present. That in itself is a profoundly broadening experience.

Rodney Crowell

Interviewed by David Simons

Rodney Crowell spent the 1980s writing hits for the likes of the Oak Ridge Boys, Willie Nelson and ex-wife Rosanne Cash, while waiting patiently for his own solo career to take flight. That finally happened in 1988, when Crowell scored an unprecedented five straight Number One country hits, culled from his breakthrough release *Diamonds And Dirt*. Crowell continues to write stark, conversational, largely autobiographical songs of a kind that Nashville has long since abandoned.

Country music has a story-telling and narrative tradition, but many of your songs contain lyrics that are very personal and autobiographical, particularly the material from* The Houston Kid *(2001) onwards.

Everyone's always telling you, "Write what you know." For me, there's this poignant vividness about that early part of my life. With *The Houston Kid*, I just felt like I'd found a thread that had meaning – the perspective of the kid who's grown up and starts to take stock.

Do you consider how those types of song will come across on stage while you're putting them together?

Well there's no doubt that these songs really lend themselves to live solo performance –on the record, they're very dry and immediate. And the storytelling aspect is definitely something that you want to present stripped-down and austere – very much like Springsteen's *Nebraska*.

Though most of the material on* The Houston Kid *seems directly autobiographical, you also tell other people's stories, for instance in a song like 'Highway 17', about a father's criminal actions and his effect on his young children.

I think it's important to be able to take artistic liberties on occasion. Yet growing up I was surrounded by that kind of behaviour; it was just part of the lay of the land. I certainly never went to prison, but I knew plenty of kids who did. So I'd just grafted their experience into my own.

Though you've often worked with collaborators, you seem to avoid the writing-by-appointment style that's so prevalent in Nashville.

From time to time I've taken my chances and made a few songwriting appointments, but by and large they just don't work for me, because I don't really enjoy it. Whereas when I'm collaborating with a guy like Will Jennings, it's completely different. Will's an artist in the sense that he's a student first and foremost, he's very literate, and funny as well.

The same seems to hold true for another of your writing partners, Guy Clark.

Guy and I often get together and just sit around telling jokes, and if you can laugh with someone for the first 10 or 15 minutes before you start writing, then it really isn't like work.

For a lot of people, the sign of a great lyric is its ability to express a whole range of emotions.

'Stuff That Works', which I wrote with Guy, is like that. It works on so many different levels. On the one hand there are lines in there that are heartfelt serious—"Stuff you feel, stuff that's real." But then we were coming up with things like, "I've got a new used car that runs just like a top," and we were laughing over that.

I imagine that a good collaborator can act as 'editor' as the storyline evolves.

And that was really the case with that particular song. After we'd started it, Guy went home and I began putting together this whole laundry list of "stuff that works", just hundreds of things. And the next day Guy comes back and he starts going through this massive list of items, and he's like, "Nope … nope … not that one … I don't think so … forget it …" And he was able to whittle it down to the essentials.

The stuff that worked!

Right. You see, with Guy, there's so much gravity…if there's such a thing as a 'songwriter's songwriter' – and I've been called that on occasion – but for me, Guy's the one. He can just get all the shit out of the way and just distil it right down to the plop! *[laughs]* I always felt that way about Dylan, or Townes Van Zandt, and Springsteen as well. Those are the kinds of writers whose subject matter holds up under any circumstances – those words just speak for themselves.

A lot of songwriters, particularly in Nashville, tailor their subject matter to a specific individual.

I could work like that if I had to, but I really don't write that way. A lot of people write from the point of view of another person; their mindset is to simply provide material for a recording artist. Whereas I just don't think of myself as being outside of the song. The thing I've found is that when I successfully write for myself, it works for anybody.

Do words or ideas pop into your head spontaneously, or do you have to be in 'writing mode'?

You never know when a great idea is going to hit. This one particular time I was coming into LA from the airport, and I was in the back of a cab on the freeway, just me and my guitar. At one point this car bolts right by and cuts off our cab. And the cabby, who's pretty irate, just looks at the guy and blurts out, "Man, you give me the blues in the daytime!" And I'm like, "Um, you wouldn't happen to have a pen on you?" [laughs] There I am on this highway, and I start scribbling down the words to 'Blues in the Daytime' [*But What Will The Neighbours Think* 1980] – right onto the back of that guitar! I practically had the song finished by the time I got to the studio. When I got out, the cab driver looks over at me, smiles and says, "You will send me the check now, won't you?"

Lyrics and poems

"What happened was that I slowly began to cut the words down. Most poets do, you'll find. After a couple of years of writing flowery poetry – and I don't down that, but it's not really suited to rock'n'roll particularly – things I write now are just street poems. I do write stories which are probably like the old songs really, but I wanted to reach as many people as possible and I was beginning to think that wasn't the way to do it." (Marc Bolan of T.Rex)[80]

If writing lyrics involves being sensitive to words, does this make it basically the same as writing poems? This is a common but dangerous assumption, and for those who write poetry as well as lyrics it can cause problems. A far greater number of people write poetry than read it, as any poetry publisher or editor will tell you, and this is especially true when it comes to reading modern poetry. The average person's concept of poetry is based upon 19th century poetics and language. If you write poems or song lyrics from that position they will be stylistically out-of-date. So it is useful to understand the differences between writing poems and lyrics, because for the songwriter, it's the differences that matter most.

Lyrics are words whose full effect depends upon music. A lyric is a set of words intended to be sung, and to be supported by music. A lyric happens in time, so a listener cannot on first hearing ask the singer to stop and go back a line; reading a poem you could. Poems communicate ideas and feelings by word alone, straight off the page. This is crucial. Music is so potent it can lend banal and clichéd words an expressiveness they could never have in a poem. Delivered by Aretha Franklin, Levi Stubbs, Sam Cooke or Jeff Buckley, the most pedestrian phrases can still "work'. The music can compensate for the lack of style and substance in the lyric. Poetry has nothing to rescue it in the same way. The music can compensate for whatever profundity or style is missing from the words. Music can excuse or even temporarily revive clichéd words and images.

Music is so powerful it can also work against a lyric's content, instead of with it. Generally, we expect words and music to be congruent, ie, pointing in the same direction. The assumption is a happy song needs a happy lyric; a sad song needs a sad lyric. But this doesn't have to be so. Such are the subtle shades of meaning which music itself creates, the relationship between words and music can be more complex. An aware songwriter knows a lyric that appears to be a happy love story could be set in a minor key so that the song does not sound happy at all, and leaves us feeling that this happiness is a sham.

The mournful music of 10cc's 'I'm Not In Love' guarantees that we do not believe a word of what the singer is saying. He spends the lyric asserting that he isn't in love, yet we get the clear impression that he *is*, and, contrary to what he says, that it *does* all mean that much to him. Likewise, Elvis Costello's 'I'm Not Angry' is delivered with such musical punch and vocal venom that we know the singer is still very angry indeed. A similar effect results if a lyric of political satire is matched to a jolly up-tempo pop song. Likewise, the breezy, radio-friendly sound of Blue Oyster Cult's 'Don't Fear The Reaper' is at variance with its chilling death-wish lyrics. Bobbie Gentry's 'Ode To Billie Joe' is haunting because the troubling story of apparent suicide is related in a relaxed, laconic musical style. All the disturbance is under the surface. The Police's 'Every Breath You Take' has been sentimentalised as an elegy despite the fact that it is a horrible confection of possessiveness, and in Bob Dylan's 'Just Like A Woman' the music seems to be rebelling against the disdain of the lyric. Another special property of the song is that, with the use of backing vocals and counter-melodies, music allows for more than one line of words to be delivered simultaneously, which is impossible on the linear printed page.

So a lyric and a poem are different artistic entities. But it is true that some lyrics read well without the music, and can have a 'poetic' quality in terms of their imagery or phrasing, for instance the image-rich 'Across The Universe', which was one of Lennon's favourites. But even poetic qualities don't of themselves turn a lyric into a poem. The language of poetry is often too complex to set to music. Good poetry has less tolerance of cliché than song lyrics. There are images you can get away with in a lyric that could not be used in serious poetry. Poetry requires higher standards of grammar, control of syntax, and precision of language than lyrics, not to mention sensibility and intellectual content.

In practical terms, the good news for songwriters is that you can get away with a lot in a song lyric – things that would sink a poem without trace – and still have a hit record. I am not saying that the quality of a lyric doesn't matter, or that it doesn't mean that there aren't real differences of merit between lyrics. A song lyric can certainly achieve a degree of language and expression which deserves the adjective 'poetic' – yet it is still not a poem. But a song can be commercially successful even with a lyric that is formulaic and clichéd. In fact, a realist would opine that many are successful precisely because they *are* formulaic and clichéd.

Successful lyrics have to compress and streamline their ideas in ways in which poems do not. They must simplify their language and imagery to avoid things getting too complicated to follow. If you do write poetry, you can steal lines from your poems and insert them into lyrics, or re-write a poem as a lyric. Kurt Cobain used to put lyrics together by choosing lines from notebooks of his poems. The Lovin' Spoonful's 'Summer In The City', a Number One US hit in 1966, began life as a poem by John Sebastian's brother, Mark. Sometimes a poem by someone else might inspire you, as happened with Sheryl Crow when she was working on a song. She read a poem called 'Fun' in a volume called *The Country Of Here Below* by a writer called Wyn Cooper. Its first two lines run "All I want to do is have a little fun / Before I die, says the man next to me." She took that as the basis for a song, adding and deleting to make the words her own, but decided in the end that she could not match the spontaneity of the original. So she called the poet and agreed terms to use his work. The resultant song, to which she really only contributed the words of the chorus, became 'All I Wanna Do', a global hit.

On rare occasions, songwriters have incorporated actual poetic forms into their songs. The Verve's 'Sonnet' was not a sonnet, but Frank Black of The Pixies tacked a formally correct sonnet on the end of 'The Happening'. He also used the Japanese *haiku* form, which has lines of 5, 7 and 5 syllables, for the verses of 'Hang Wire'. Occasionally songwriters will put the word "ode" in a title to give a song an air of sophistication.

Another theme which underpins the relationship between poetry and lyrics is the assumption that lyrics matter anyway. Not all songwriters care equally about the words, and even those who do care are aware that part of the audience may not be bothered about the lyric. John Hughes, songwriting partner to Tasmin Archer, said, "Not everybody listens to lyrics. I read somewhere that the percentage of people who actually listen is five in every 100."[81] When Blur's album *13* was released, vocalist Damon Albarn commented, "I don't put my lyrics [on the inner sleeves] any more. I think you'll find that most people don't know what you're singing about until they look at the lyric sheet anyway. As long as the feeling is right, I don't care."[82]

Words as sound

"You see I'm always going for the sound of things. I have a hard time just writing things out, I have to hear them first. Sometimes I put it on a tape recorder, but then I transcribe it and it's lost its music." (Tom Waits)

"In 'Caroline, No', [Brian Wilson] talked about a young girl who has lost her innocence, but the specific words both in terms of rhyme and being less obvious – that's what I saw as my job. If there was a word he didn't like, I would change it. Or I would say, 'How does this sing?' So he would sing it. Words that have long vowel sounds are much easier to sing, so if it wasn't a word that you could 'hold out' we would try to find an alternative." (Tony Asher, lyricist for Brian Wilson for *Pet Sounds*)[83]

"Sometimes I would write a word that fit my conception of the phrase, and Burt would point out that it actually added a note. Or that there was a pick-up note where there shouldn't be, or some little detail like that, which would require me to find different words to say the same thing." (Elvis Costello on collaborating with Burt Bacharach.)[84]

Meanings are one thing, but don't forget the words of a lyric are for singing. You may have the right words for what you want to express, but you must also consider how good they sound when sung. Some perfectly good words and phrases are awkward to sing, some combinations of sounds are hard to vocalise clearly (because of the relation of vowels and consonants), some phrases might be grammatically correct but unrhythmic, and some styles of lyric don't go with a particular musical genre.

A song-lyric results in one type of rhythm (the words) being fitted to another (music). The words of a lyric have a rhythm before you put a melody to them. The English language naturally gives some words greater stress than others. In times past students studying poetry were required to mark which syllables were stressed and which were less stressed. One common 'metre', meaning a pattern of stresses, is 'ballad metre'. This has four stressed syllables in the first line, followed by three in the second, and so on. It is the metre used in many folk songs and hymns, for instance 'Amazing Grace'. The stressed syllables are underlined:

A<u>maz</u>ing <u>grace</u>! how <u>sweet</u> the <u>sound</u>
That <u>saved</u> a <u>wretch</u> like <u>me</u>!
I <u>once</u> was <u>lost</u>, but <u>now</u> am <u>found</u>,
Was <u>blind</u>, but <u>now</u> I <u>see</u>.

Whatever the pattern of stressed and unstressed syllables, it needs to fit with the beat of the music and the melody, so that unstressed syllables do not fall on moments in the music which carry emphasis. This is too complex an issue to discuss fully here, but here's a simple example.

If the first line of your lyric scans as "The sun comes up on a bright new day" just as a line of lyric, "the' should not end up on the first beat of the bar when you sing it. That would place too much emphasis on what is an unstressed word. "Sun' belongs on the first beat, and the melody will probably start with "the" on the last beat of the previous bar. It would also sound wrong if "The sun" was on beats three and four of a bar, so that "comes' falls on the strong first beat of the next bar. Most people avoid this problem by instinct, because it feels wrong, rather than by conscious intervention. As a general rule, if you find you are emphasising words like *the*, *of*, *a*, *at*, *to* by putting them on a strong beat, your setting of the lyric to a melody needs adjusting.

The effect of not matching syllabic rhythm to musical rhythm is clumsy, but in certain contexts intentionally playful, comic, even endearing. In The Darkness's song 'Friday Night' singer Justin Hawkins sings "badminton" as bad-min-ton, instead of the usual stress of bad-min-ton. Some singers even give words extra syllables for reasons of rhythm. In Catatonia's 'Londinium', singer Cerys Matthews amusingly turns the three-syllable "endlessly" into the four-syllable (and much easier to sing) "en – der – less – ly".

The songwriter, the lyric and the marketplace

"I don't have a record of writing hit after hit, the way Billy Joel or Paul Simon has, or Stevie Wonder had, – which I wish I had, but it isn't what I do. Even when I set out to try, it doesn't turn out that way … my taste does not correlate with the taste of the general public, for the most part." (Randy Newman)[85]

"When the song was over I said, 'Great, Norman – it was really great. But the words, you gotta change them. They just don't work. We can't put this record out. Not because it isn't a good song but because it sounds like you're promoting drugs.' 'No,' Norman protested, 'It's not drug-related. It's art.'" (Berry Gordy to producer Norman Whitfield about the Temptations 'Cloud 9')[86]

"Language consists almost entirely of fashionable slang these days; therefore when somebody says something very blunt lyrically it's the height of modern revolution." (Morrissey 1984)[87]

One of the basic questions for a songwriter is what do you want to write about? This is not merely a matter of self-expression. What you write affects whether you win an audience, how big that audience might be, who might cover your songs, and what commercial success your music might have. The default subject-matter for most people's lyrics is their own experience, especially universal experiences which move people most when they are young – relationships – searching for love, falling in love, winning it, holding onto it, losing it, finding it again. Most songwriters start by writing love songs, which is no bad thing since the majority of commercially successful songs fall in this territory, and that's because those lyric themes are what the greatest amount of people can relate to.

In terms of artistic freedom, the good news is that almost anything can be (and has been) a subject for lyrics. You can write about any subject in the world, within the legal limits of copyright and assorted laws of libel, obscenity, incitement to commit crimes, depending on the law of the land or religious oppression under which you live. If your songwriting remains a private concern between you, your guitar/piano, and your favourite technology for making demos, there isn't anything else to consider. You can be as naïve, as silly, as clever, as opinionated, as arch, as allusive, as low-brow, as high-brow, as complex, as simple, as obscure, or as clichéd, as you like. Songwriting is a hugely enjoyable pursuit even if you never intend to make a career out of it. Don't demean your music-making just because it isn't your profession, for it offers a fulfilment beyond the range of many hobbies.

However, when you seek an audience the game changes. Singing for other people is an act of communication. It entails awareness of who makes up your audience and who you would like in it. 'Audience' here includes the people who hear you busk in the street, the band members you want to play your songs, the audience who come to your gigs, the promoter you want to get bookings with, the manager you want to impress enough to take you on, the record company you want to sign you, the DJs you want to play your music, and then the wider public who buy CDs, downloads and concert tickets.

The bottom line is this: lyrics are a crucial part of the interface between your music and the audience. Music may have meanings of its own, but a lyric colours and channels those meanings. What a song means is almost always defined in the terms of what its lyric appears to be about. So how will the audience relate to your subject-matter? Will they understand it? What can they find in it for themselves? Some songwriters say they do not try to shape a song to an audience.

As some of the songwriter quotes above show, commercial issues can affect lyric content. The most obvious instance of this is when bands try to put swear words or obscene images in their lyrics. This used to cause songs to be banned. Sometimes there are conflicts between band and record label or producer about political or religious content. Sometimes songwriters pitching at an artist take into consideration how well-known the artist is. Here is songwriter Tony Macaulay:

"I spent hours sweating over the psychology of how the songs were put together. For example, if it was an unknown artist, we felt that if we started with a long, engaging verse, by the time they got to the chorus, the disc jockey would take it off and play another one, so if it was an unknown artist we'd start with a bit of the chorus just to tell them how good it was going to be. If it was a name artist, we could afford to start with a verse and then get that nice lift into the chorus so that you lulled them into the mood of the song, so when the chorus came it was a sort of big thrill."[88]

But commercial songs did not always have to suffer in quality. The artistry of Bacharach and David's classic 1960s hits is acknowledged everywhere. K.D. Lang contrasted the lyric style of "groove oriented pop' with a song like 'Walk On By': "It can be the most moving song and the most ambient song. The detail of those songs catches up with you later on. You can be as involved as you want because it's less intrusive. You lean towards it and the more you lean towards it the more vast it is inside.'[89]

Finding your themes: lyrics as identity

A songwriter who is also a performer forges an identity. This identity is comprised of many things, from a haircut and clothes to the size of your band (or whether you have one), the guitar you play, the way you sing, the style of your music. Some genres of music have a limited number of themes and you're not allowed to go outside them. The content of your lyrics is another element, as is how significant the lyrics are in relation to the music. With a band like Led Zeppelin the lyrics are less important to their reputation than lyrics are to the reputations of Bob Dylan, Bruce Springsteen, Leonard Cohen, Randy Newman, Joni Mitchell, Van Morrison, or Elvis Costello. In some cases musical content is second best to lyric content.

Among songwriters for whom lyrics are central, there are those who write more or less from experience and about themselves in the 'confessional' manner. In 1993 Loudon Wainwright III told *Mojo*, " ... I'm interested in me: I'm interested in what's happened to me and what went wrong with my folks' marriage and my erotic thing about my mother, all that interests me terribly. And I like to explore myself in song."[90] For others the art is in how you start with a personal experience or feeling but develop it. For Kristin Hersh there is the idea of not being completely self-centred:

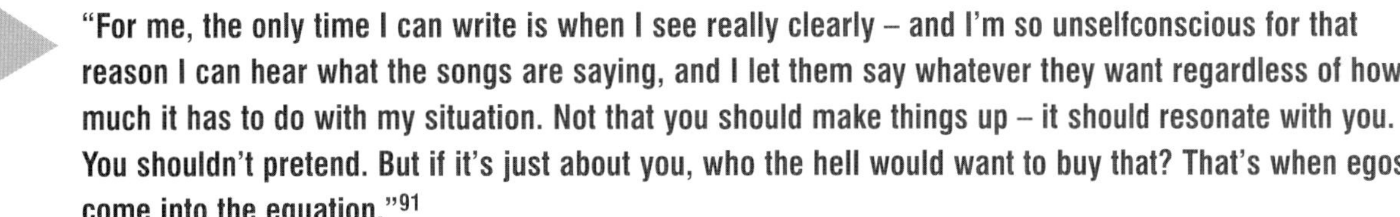

"For me, the only time I can write is when I see really clearly – and I'm so unselfconscious for that reason I can hear what the songs are saying, and I let them say whatever they want regardless of how much it has to do with my situation. Not that you should make things up – it should resonate with you. You shouldn't pretend. But if it's just about you, who the hell would want to buy that? That's when egos come into the equation."[91]

The notion of confessional lyrics leads to the assumption that what makes the song authentic is its being rooted in a personal experience. But songwriters know that the meaning of a song changes as time passes, even for the writer, as Joni Mitchell shrewdly observed:

"I know a song falls differently against your life many times. To keep it alive it has to – you're bringing new experience to it all the time, and it's not the experience you wrote it with, so it's open to interpretations ... The songs shift around – either it means something to you or it doesn't. And that's one reason why I resent the 'who is it about?' fixing it in time, 'It's about that over there...' No it isn't, it's a mirror – and it reflects you if you take the time to look as you pass it by."[92]

Many feel, with natural curiosity, that if they knew the origins of a song, its roots in the writer's personal experience, they would be closer to its meaning. This is one of the great misunderstandings about art and it is partly the consequence of a metaphor. Ever looked at a flower's roots and compared them to its petals in bloom? Which would you rather have on display in a vase on your table? Tom Waits provided an important insight when he said, "The stories behind most songs are less interesting than the songs themselves. So you say, 'Hey, this is about Jackie Kennedy.' And it's, 'Oh, wow." Then you say, "No, I was just kidding, it's about Nancy Reagan.' It's a different song now."[93]

Moving from writing about self to a wider frame of reference is something that has exercised Bruce Springsteen since the 1980s. It is obvious that when a songwriter wants to expand out from personal experience the lyrics can seem thinner and less convincing. In 2002 he said,

"The secret of the songwriting was to get personal first, then you sort of shade in universal feelings. That's what balances the songs. All experience is personal so you have to start there, and then if you

can connect in what's happening with everyone, the universality of an experience, then you're creating that alchemy where your audience is listening to it, they're hearing what they're feeling inside and they're also feeling 'I'm not alone.'"[94]

Songwriters also go through phases as to how they feel about this issue, because it is so fundamental. In 1984 Paul Weller declared that he had stopped writing about characters and situations, becoming more direct. But by 1995 he felt differently, stating he was wary of autobiographical songs, and that although they might start from personal experience he would develop the lyric away from it.

UK group Siouxsie and the Banshees were notorious for avoiding anything that could be construed as a mainstream lyric theme. Instead, they ploughed a Gothic furrow of songs about split personality, voodoo, darkness, suffering, perversity, S&M imagery, and so on. For bass player Steve Severin in 1978 it was a case of taking apart traditional rock lyrics and putting them back together in a different way. There's no doubt that this was one factor that prevented the band reaching a bigger audience (and that's okay – not everyone wants a big audience, or the compromises that go with it.) Nothing could be further from the subject-matter of Roy Harper, Richard Thompson, John Martyn, or Cat Stevens, singer-songwriters influenced by the late 1960s counter-culture, or Springsteen's meditations on blue collar life in America. In 1985 he explained:

"When I sit down to write, I try to write something that feels real to me. Like, what does it feel like to be thirty-five or something right now, at this point in time, living in America? It's not much more conscious than that. I generally try to write songs that are about real life, not fantasy material. I try to reflect people's lives back to them in some fashion."[95]

Some key questions about lyric intention

- Do you want people to understand your songs on first hearing?
- Do you want them to read and re-read them and discuss the meanings? Do you want to invite them to construct their own meanings?
- Do you want to be ambiguous or plain speaking?
- Do you want to sing about your own experience and take the route of naked autobiography? Do you want to write about your experience but veil it to some degree?
- Do you want to write about other people or general situations? Do you want to imagine characters and tell stories?
- Are you going to write about common everyday things that feature in most lives or do you want to offer a set of lyrics which are the door to an imaginary world (which might be truth in its own way)?
- Do you want to be playfully serious or seriously playful?
- Do you want to be direct and outspoken, funny, satirical, ironic, witty?
- Do you want to make your audience feel like you're Everyman (or Everywoman), muddling along like everyone else, writing songs about what "we" all feel?
- Or do you want to play Prophet with a Message, someone who wishes to expose the complacency and corruption of governments, media and consumers?

How you position yourself with regard to these choices has a bearing on the kind of lyrics you want or need to write. It is a big factor in commercial success, especially in the realm of the hit single and in chart 'popular music', where the range of subject-matter and its treatment is often staggeringly shallow. The commercial viability of a song can be reduced by lyrics which, by style or content, do not conform to some very prescriptive limitations. The challenge is to be original within the formulae.

Writing songs for other singers

If you are a songwriter pitching songs to famous acts who do not write their own, the lyric has to be one that the artist in question can sing. What is deeply meaningful to you may be a closed book to someone else. You may have to discipline your lyric style to be transparent and direct. Obscurity, hinting at meanings, is often mistaken for profundity. It is often symptomatic of fear, or not being sure what it is you're saying. Depending on your habits, there may be a need to avoid being obscure, and to be more restrained with imagery, to write less of what Randy Newman amusingly called "crystal explosions in the eventide" lyrics.

Not only style but subject-matter is a significant factor in who could cover your song. The melody and music might be great, but unfortunately the lyric might break the deal. Emmylou Harris said, "It's always the lyric that I look to first. It's always about the emotions. I've always been drawn to songs that deal with our vulnerability but also our undercurrent of strength …"[96] This is a major aspect of the discipline of writing songs for other people. Some themes will just be inappropriate. Middle of the road balladeers are not going to cover songs about the CIA, torture, or corrupt business deals. Conversely, can you imagine Britney Spears singing a death metal lyric? Or Nirvana singing a lyric about the joys of disco dancing? Or Norah Jones singing a witty but miserable Morrissey lyric? Or Travis doing a Rolling Stones lyric ode to debauchery?

English rocker Marc Bolan of T.Rex was one of rock's most original lyricists. He thought other people were unlikely to cover his songs because of the words. In 1972, he said:

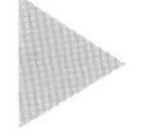

"It's like nobody really covered the Stones songs. It's like, well, I feel the lyrics are maybe too artistically camp for say [fictional stereotypical pop act] Twitch Younger And The Rockabeads to get away with, even though the melody might get them, but they'd look weird saying some of the words. I don't see people, apart from friends, covering my songs."[97]

In fact, since Bolan's early death in 1977 there have been many covers of T.Rex songs by bands on the margins of pop history, but not by mainstream artists, unless you count The Power Station's 'Get It On'. And there remains a sense that such covers are really acts of homage to the original, rather than convincing re-statements of the songs. No-one can cover 'Children Of The Revolution' without seeming to be acting out Bolan's part, because only he could put across its camp lyrics about driving a Rolls-Royce. The world of his songs is too *lyrically* idiosyncratic, despite the continuing appeal of his riffs. To take another example, you can imagine a soul singer covering U2's 'One' with a gospel slant and genuinely making the song their own. It wouldn't sound like someone pointing at U2. That's because the lyric doesn't put up any impediments. Likewise Jimi Hendrix's 'All Along The Watchtower' does not sound like someone pretending to be Bob Dylan, even though Hendrix's vocal has a Dylanesque slur, but most covers of 'Purple Haze' or 'Voodoo

Chile' sound like homages to Hendrix because no-one else can convincingly inhabit that lyric. We suffer from working weeks, tired limbs, broken hearts and relationship disputes, but not purple hazes, nor do we tend to chop down mountains with the edge of our hand.

Do you need to know what you mean?

"I can't necessarily interpret 'American Pie' any better than you can." (Don McLean, 1972)[98]

"The amateur songwriter's greatest single failing and one that is immediately obvious to the listener is that the writer does not know exactly where the song is going." (Jimmy Webb)[99]

Putting aside writing songs for other people, there is the question of how much control you can have over what your songs mean. Regardless of how good you are as a lyricist, if you perform songs and thus engage in communicating with the public, the audience may find things in your lyrics which you either didn't know were there, or didn't intend. Some writers are content with this, even encourage it. But the audience can wilfully misinterpret a lyric by not paying enough attention. People who radio request R.E.M.'s bitter put-down 'The One I Love', in the mistaken belief that it is a passionate love song, have failed to respond to the song's lyric beyond the first line. I have also heard some interpret 'Everybody Hurts' as a good song to commit self-harm or suicide to! This despite the fact that the lyric's whole point is to *dissuade* people from feeling that way by saying everybody has those moments and you have to hold on and keep going.

Another point is that a song does not necessarily mean what the author thinks it means, and sometimes the author doesn't have a conscious meaning. Kate Bush said that 'Love And Anger' "was an incredibly difficult song for me to write and when people ask me what it's about, I have to say I don't know because it's not really a thought-out thing."[100] Hendrix once confessed to changing his explanation of what his lyrics meant, when interviewed, because he wasn't sure of their meaning. For Gavin Rossdale of Bush, it's a case of "I just try to be as natural as possible. Sometimes I know what I'm going on about and other times I don't.'[101]

Sometimes the meaning of a song only comes to a songwriter much later. Working in the dark is sometimes part of the process, and can be exciting. The more personal the material the more likely this is to happen, because the unconscious may play a larger part. Skin of Skunk Anansie: "I think sometimes it doesn't hit you until later on what the song really means because you were probably hiding something from yourself – a couple of weeks later, you're a bit more honest and you realise what the lyric is about.'[102] Paul McCartney told *Mojo* in 2001, "I think 'Yesterday' was about the death of my mother … but it was only 20 years later when somebody made that suggestion, that I went, 'Yeah'." Pete Townshend of The Who observed, "The interesting thing is how a person's mind, my mind, becomes very one track at certain times. When I decided to put *Tommy* together as an 'opera', I simply amassed all the songs I had, and remarkably, about 80 per cent of them fit in somewhere. I seemed to have been unconsciously writing on a theme for almost a year without realising it."[103]

It is often the case that a songwriter doesn't have a clear lyric intention concerning the song they want to write. Bruce Cockburn claims almost never to write a song about a particular subject. Instead his songs come from imagery or odd lines and are built up from there.

Some songwriters are happy not to seek to define meanings. Neil Finn of Crowded House said, "The writing of a good song is enough of a mystery to me that I'm prepared to let things be unexplained and abstract even to me. If the words sound right, if they convey a certain depth or extremity of emotion, it doesn't matter if they don't relate to the line before, particularly.'[104]

Time and events will sometimes alter the meaning of some of your songs, whether you like it or not. Usually this is the result of natural changes in your life, but on rare occasions it can also happen when the imagery of a song accidentally lines up with a national event. In May 2005 I wrote a song which referred to London Underground tube stations. It started "I travelled far on the black Northern line" and had Edgware in the title. The second chorus began "City nights – they try to warn you." It was a love song, deliberately English in its imagery. Two months later, four bombs exploded in London, three of them in the Underground, one at Edgware and one on the Northern line. Suddenly, and unintentionally, the lyric had gained another level of meaning, whether I liked it or not. My love song had become an elegy. Which goes to show that the notion of what a song is 'about' and *how* songs can be 'about' things is complex and mysterious. And that is what keeps us writing lyrics and composing songs.

Several of my Backbeat songwriting books give hundreds of chord progressions that could be the basis for songs. I can't do the same with lyrics; it isn't possible to provide ready-made verses because that would involve taking decisions about meanings and themes, which only you can do. A guide to writing lyrics can't tell you *what* to write; that you must decide for yourself. It can't choose your themes, characters or stories. It must be your words on the page. But with this book close by, the words and lines will come easier than they did before.

Chuck D and Paris

Interview by Tamara Palmer

It takes a lot of trust for a world-renowned lyricist to perform an entire album written by another person, even if it's someone who is also an accomplished writer. But that's exactly what happened when hip-hop legend Chuck D, frontman of the multi-platinum selling group Public Enemy, challenged the controversial rapper/producer Paris to write an entire album project for him. The result, *Rebirth Of A Nation* by Public Enemy Featuring Paris (2006), retains the group's spectacularly bombastic beat style while preserving its lyrical stance.

Why is it important to you to know about so many of today's songwriters and to study them all closely?

Chuck D: I made very much a promise early on; whatever situation or craft or industry I had to be in, I was going to know it thoroughly. I wanted to go into the sports world as a sportscaster, and I knew everything it took about the sports that I happened to be into. But then on the music front, I made sure that I went into that with as much pomp and circumstance as I treated sports. I needed to know about the importance of musicians, the songwriters, the labels.

Reaching back into your earliest musical memories, who were the people that first made you pay attention to the lyrics?

CD: Well, number one, I'm a different aberration of sorts, because I grew up as a child of the '60s. It was like being in the right place at the right time at the right age. In the '60s, you grew up with the meshings of soul coming up out of rhythm and blues, and rock'n'roll formatting itself. When I grew up, the earliest part I can remember is Ray Charles, James Brown, and Motown on one end – and they felt like family members. And on the other you had the Beatles and 'I Wanna Hold Your Hand'. But by eight, nine, and ten years old, the lyrics happened to mean a lot more. Like Sly And The Family Stone, when they said 'Stand' or 'Thank You (Fa Lettin Me Be Mice Elf Again)', or 'Sing a Simple Song', or 'Everybody is a Star.' The titles meant volumes. And when I became a songwriter later on, I always made sure that I wrote from the title on down, because the title hooks you into a theme. But that was pretty much the promise that came out of a competition of songwriters that raised the standard in the craft to the point where I don't know if you can get a better time of songwriting than 1964-1974. Because it's when we had a war, we had assassinations, we had confusion. But the music clarified a lot of different things that weren't said in the news and in society itself.

Do you think we're going to see some of that spirit that over the next few years, as we're seeing musical reactions to events like the war in Iraq and Hurricane Katrina?

CD: The words spoke volumes back then because you didn't have the aspect of visuals. People weren't interacting with things as much then, and inside the words were a million stories. The words still mean so much today, but they add into anthems. It's the imagery that means so much more than the words or the song itself. So I don't know if it will go backwards. But I will tell you this much: when you attach the words to a visual, it takes on aspects that really defy comparison. Sometimes the pictures speak a thousand words, but if you have the words dictating the pictures, now that's something else.

The Public Enemy album, Rebirth of a Nation is quite a different approach for you on the songwriting front. Paris wrote 95 per cent of the lyrics, which is not something that people would expect of a hip-hop lyricist of your repute.

CD: I think, often, that the mistake made in rap music is that people feel that a vocalist should write their own lyrics. That's been a major, major mistake in hip-hop, because not everyone is equipped to be a lyricist and not everyone is equipped to be a vocalist. I don't think just because someone can write well that they can [perform well] on the microphone. I think if you don't have a voice that stands out and you don't have a style, you're better off writing for somebody else.

My knowledge of the history of songwriting says how the hell can you be in music, when the best songs of all-time were written by somebody else for a particular vocalist? I really pride myself on being a vocalist, so why can't I vocalise somebody else's writings? And then, I've got volumes of things that I've written myself. Of course, I can always push myself to write something I didn't write before, but you really can't change yourself, outside of yourself being yourself. Therefore I think a lot of artists could afford to have other people write for them and just put this rap ethic bullshit down that it's taboo.

A lot of people in the hip-hop community seem derisive of stuff that is ghostwritten, or written by someone else, like the collaborative effort can't be great work in itself.

CD: That's just bullshit. Isaac Hayes is one of the greatest songwriters of all time; he's in the Rock & Roll Hall of Fame because he's a songwriter. Isaac Hayes' songs as an artist are interpretations of Burt Bacharach and other great artists that made him shine to another level. Hayes was a great singer, a great artist and entertainer, *and* he wrote songs for Sam & Dave. Come on, if you write songs for Sam & Dave, you're more than capable of writing songs for yourself. But Isaac chose to do songs that were beautiful interpretations [of other's work]. It lessens the load, and extends the artistry. A lot of rappers could *definitely* afford to do this.

Paris: When we did *Rebirth of a Nation*, I basically had to become Chuck in order to understand his cadence, different intonations and things he had done before. His particular style really influenced me when I was first starting out, and I wanted to capture some of those classic Public Enemy elements on this project. I took my cues from previous tracks musically, and then there was a particular type of [vocal] flow that I took my cues from and certain techniques that I emulated.

How do you balance the desire to be entertaining with the need to be educational in your songs?

CD: A certain level of performance has to go into the words itself . . . the words can actually mean a lot just from the strength of the title. [James Brown's] 'This is a Man's World': Inside the fabric of the song itself, it gives you that little bit of an ironic twist. I don't think a lot of irony and wit is being played with as much, because you have a dependency on the visuals. When I tried to make videos in the beginning, I tried to make the video give you what the song *didn't* say. Hearing the song gives you a visual, but I'm not going to try to show you exactly what the song says; only what it doesn't say. But then, you have to be a twisted individual to try and fuck around with that in the first place! I always wanted to do something contrary and not the easy move. Matter of fact, I always wanted to make the difficult path in songwriting; not the obvious. I wanted to actually take people through twists, where sometimes there's booby-trapping and all of a sudden a song blows up on them, [like] "I didn't know it was about that!" I always wanted to do different things with songs, like almost put a timer on it and turn it and run and then people are dancing and then find out what the song is about. Or when you're able to do mirrors with it: it says one thing, but it mirrors another. And then there's *another* mirror that takes it into another realm that you didn't even figure out.

"Knowledge of and respect for the work of others is the first essential ingredient in the development of a truly effective technique." (Jimmy Webb)[105]

This section of *How To Write Lyrics* is a sourcebook of themes, created by categorising thousands of song titles into basic subjects. Many of the songs are famous, though the inventive titles of some less well-known songs demanded inclusion. If you do not know the song, or have a recording of it, try searching for it on the internet. Copyright restrictions make it very difficult to reproduce lyrics, or even sections of lyrics, in a book of this nature. Besides, this is a manual about *how* to write lyrics, not an analytic discussion of the merits and meanings of other people's.

Dip into this sourcebook if you can't think of anything to write, have a look at what others have done, and the catalogue of themes will get you going. This book has already quoted many songwriters, spelling out how important they find titles. If you find an intriguing title, search out the lyric in question to see how it handles the theme. The extent to which these titles engage with their ostensible subjects varies, and in some cases (such as the crime section) the groupings are intended to be not without humour. If there is more than one title using the same word or phrase, you have an opportunity to compare the lyrics if you seek them out (there are, for example, four titles mentioning San Francisco).

The sourcebook has the following categories (songs can belong in more than one of these, so don't think of them as watertight), covering the main themes of lyrics: love; sex and desire; names A-Z; clothing; rejection and put-downs; communication; media; dances and parties; living in the city; work; money; country/escape; amusement park and circus; geography: places in the USA; places in the UK; places in the rest of the world; journeys; homeward bound; transport – cars, trains, boats and planes; crime and punishment; time past; children and childhood; time present; divisions of the day; divisions of the week; the months and seasons; time future; smart answers; inspired by the arts; inspired by history; songs about music; politics and protest; fantasy; the supernatural; spirituality.

Every so often a songwriter composes some music, and then has to come up with some lyrics because none have immediately occurred to him or her. Thus looms the question, what to write about? The habit is to sketch from what has been happening to you or is currently on your mind, but not everyone wants to write 'confessional' lyrics, at least not all the time. Instead, find a new subject. The challenge is to make a connection between it and your feelings and interests. An element of identification or imaginative possession will help what you write ring true. This sourcebook will suggest many avenues to explore.

Happy songs and sad songs

"On the whole, sad is easier than cruel, as both cruel and happy are close to vain and foolish. They require qualification or totally unbridled joy (or relish in the case of cruel) ... There is just more sadness in the world." (Elvis Costello)[106]

At this point, consider the most basic emotional element of a lyric: is it (broadly speaking) happy or sad? If you have been writing songs for a while I wager there are more sad songs in your catalogue than happy ones. If this is true, you are in very good company – it's probably true of most songwriters. Why should this be? Simply put, from an inspirational point of view, when you're happy you feel full of life; you feel filled-full (the literal meaning of "fulfilment"). When you're unhappy there is a sense of emptiness, of something missing. At its most concrete this is the feeling expressed in thousands of songs about love unrequited or love lost. The songwriter tries to remedy that lack of fulfilment and emptiness by creating something ... ie, the song.

Chris Collingwood of Fountains Of Wayne once said, "I don't do happy. I do sad or angry or frustrated. My songs are obviously written with characters but typically they are not happy characters. Happy songs are hard."[107] For Stevie Nicks of Fleetwood Mac, whose mega-selling *Rumours* was born of emotional conflict in the personal lives of band members, it's a case of "they say great art comes out of tragedy and, unfortunately, I think it does. I like sad songs."[108] For Stephen Merritt of The Magnetic Fields the problem can be put thus: "What is there to say about a happy relationship? It's only interesting if it's a happy relationship in conflict with something else."[109] This sheds a light on why so many love songs involve the conceit of an unnamed, unspecified group of people who in some way frown upon the lovers or put obstacles in their way. Their presence is registered in clichés like "no matter what they say".

This may also explain why The Who's 'Happy Jack' is an unusually and genuinely happy song. Seen as something of a throwaway single, 'Happy Jack' is an eccentric lyric about a character who lives at the beach on the Isle Of Man, set to music which features typical mad Moon drumming, Townshend power-chording, and abrupt switches in volume. He is teased relentlessly by kids, who drop things on him and treat him as a donkey. Despite this-ill treatment, the kids cannot stop the waves, nor can they (as if there is some parallel between the two) stop Jack being happy. In the end, lyrically, the effect is convincing because of one key word: "prevent". His tormentors were unable to *prevent* Jack being happy. It implies that his happiness is as unstoppable as the ocean. This is funny and mysterious at the same time.

Genuinely happy songs are harder to write and make convincing. A sad song readily draws our sympathy (we've all been there); a happy song might draw our envy (because we don't spend as much time being happy as we'd like). "Bully for you ... ", we feel, listening to someone telling the world of their blistering new-found happiness which will last forever and ever, "... now get out of my face!" To make a happy song sympathetic you must avoid provoking a sceptical envy. Dance records pull it off better than most via their rhythmic energy. But finding happy songs that aren't driven by the lyric platitudes of the dance floor is harder.

Remember that whatever the emotion of your lyric, the emotion of the music is going to have a big effect on the final result – which is the most significant difference between writing lyrics and poetry (as was discussed in **Section Eight**).

Love

"We were always writing about the same subject and it's just a new way to say, 'I love you' ... (Jeff Barry)[110]

"When I was ten I was into ABBA. I was impressed by how adult they were. They had songs about divorce, people with kids breaking up ... ' (Stephen Merritt of The Magnetic Fields)[111]

As you know, love is the most popular topic for song-lyrics. There are innumerable angles and situations from which you can write as people go through all the various stages of falling in and out, and back in love. Here, the need is to strike a balance between the general and the specific, the personal and the universal. This central experience comes across more powerfully when the lyric evokes a specific time and place, as Dylan did to bitter-sweet effect with the Polaroid snapshot imagery of the lyric to 'Sara', and as Al Stewart did in 'Year of the Cat'.

EVERY STORY TELLS A PICTURE

Love songs often express an emotion or set of emotions around a conflict or crisis. The lyric may not tell us how this came about. One way to move away from always writing about feelings is to consciously tell a love story with a beginning, middle and end. This can grab the listener's attention through narrative interest – they want to know what is going to happen. There are songs like The Hollies' 'Bus Stop', Manfred Mann's 'Do Wah Diddy Diddy', or Squeeze's 'Up The Junction' that tell the whole story of a love affair.

Love songs tend to be defined as romantic, ie, between two adults, in the majority of cases a man and a woman. In the lyric chapter of *How To Write Songs On Guitar* there are several pages mapping the various existential positions people can take up towards one another in love lyrics. But love also manifests itself between friends, between siblings, between parents and children, and so on. Spiritual love is dealt with under 'spirituality' at the end of this section.

THE ARCHETYPAL LOVE-LYRIC SITUATIONS

SEARCHING FOR LOVE: This is about chasing and dreaming of an ideal.

> **The Eagles 'One Of These Nights'; Bruce Springsteen 'Dancing In The Dark', 'Night'; Dire Straits 'On Every Street'; Neil Young 'Heart Of Gold'.**

LOVE AT FIRST SIGHT: This can happen across a crowded room, at a party, on the street, in a café. There is an additional poignancy when it is someone in a crowd who you know you won't see again.

> **James Blunt 'You're Beautiful'; Roberta Flack 'The First Time Ever I Saw Your Face'; Monkees 'I'm A Believer'; The La's 'There She Goes'; Elvis Presley 'All Shook Up'; Tommy James 'Dizzy'; The Supremes 'The Happening'.**

LOVE REQUITED OR THAT'S HAD TIME TO INTENSIFY:

> **Moody Blues 'Nights In White Satin'; Eurythmics 'There Must Be An Angel'; The Searchers 'Every Time You Walk In The Room'; Stevie Wonder 'I Was Made To Love Her'; Dusty Springfield 'The Look Of Love'; The Beatles 'Eight Days A Week'; The Temptations 'My Girl'; Mary Wells 'My Guy'.**

LOVE IN PURSUIT: An intention is formed to pursue and to get noticed. This is a lyric where heroism is emphasised. There may be an obstacle to be overcome.

> **The Temptations And The Supremes 'I'm Gonna Make You Love Me'; The Pretenders 'Brass In Pocket', 'Talk Of The Town'; Bruce Springsteen 'She's The One'; Bob Dylan 'I Want You'; Elton John 'Your Song'; Spencer Davis Group 'Keep On Running'; Roy Orbison 'Pretty Woman'; The Ronettes 'Be My Baby'; The Beach Boys 'Wouldn't It Be Nice'; Madonna 'Cherish'.**

PROMISING TO BE THERE: Emotions are sublimated through a degree of selflessness. This also includes songs of friendship.

The Beatles 'From Me To You'; Jackson 5 'I'll Be There'; Four Tops 'Reach Out I'll Be There'; Cyndi Lauper 'Time After Time'; Queen 'You're My Best Friend'; (friendship) James Taylor 'You've Got A Friend'; Simon and Garfunkel 'Bridge Over Troubled Water'; Bill Withers 'Lean On Me'.

FINDING OUT YOU HAVE A RIVAL: This increases the emotional ante. The emotion might be expressed or not.

Elvis Presley 'The Girl Of My Best Friend'; Spin Doctors 'Two Princes'.

FINDING OUT YOUR FEELINGS ARE UNREQUITED:

Buzzcocks 'Ever Fallen In Love With Someone'; The Temptations 'Just My Imagination'; Elton John 'Sorry Seems To Be The Hardest Word'.

DENYING YOUR FEELINGS:

10cc 'I'm Not In Love'; Thin Lizzy 'Don't Believe A Word'; Elvis Presley 'The Girl Of My Best Friend'.

TOGETHERNESS SONGS: Difficult to pull off because they arouse envy in the listener.

The Carpenters 'We've Only Just Begun'; Paul McCartney 'Maybe I'm Amazed'; Bruce Springsteen 'If I Should Fall Behind'; The Turtles 'Happy Together'; Mama Cass 'Dream A Little Dream Of Me'; Dave Clark Five 'Glad All Over'; Four Tops 'I'm In a Different World'; The Casuals 'Never My Love'; The Beach Boys 'God Only Knows'; Herb Alpert 'This Guy's In Love With You'; The Beatles 'Something'.

EXISTENTIAL NEED SONGS: This is the 'I can't live without you' lyric. Deeply unfashionable since the 1990s at least.

The Four Tops 'I Can't Help Myself', 'Bernadette'; Harry Nilsson 'Without You'; Bob Dylan 'If Not For You'.

CONFLICT INSIDE A RELATIONSHIP:

Kate Bush 'Running Up That Hill'; U2 'With Or Without You', 'One'; Elvis Presley 'Always On My Mind', 'Suspicious Minds'; The Beatles 'Ticket To Ride', 'We Can Work It Out'; The Supremes 'You Keep Me Hanging On'; Stevie Nicks and Tom Petty 'Stop Draggin' My Heart Around'.

LOVE TRIANGLES:

Billy Paul 'Me And Mrs. Jones'; Mary MacGregor 'Torn Between Two Lovers'.

PARTING WHEN YOU DON'T REALLY WANT TO:

Moody Blues 'Go Now'; The Rolling Stones 'Angie'; Walker Brothers 'Make It Easy On Yourself'; Diana Ross 'Remember Me'; Blur 'Tender'; Roy Orbison 'It's Over'; Righteous Brothers 'You've Lost That Lovin' Feeling'; Carole King 'It's Too Late'; Fleetwood Mac 'Songbird'; Thelma Houston 'Don't Leave Me This Way'.

PARTING WHEN YOU WANT TO: Popular lyric subject in recent decades because it demonstrates emotional independence.

Carole King 'It's Too Late'; Bob Dylan 'It's All Over Now, Baby Blue'; 'Sooner Or Later One Of Us Must Know'; Dido 'Hunter'; Paul Simon '50 Ways To Leave Your Lover'; Soft Cell 'Say Hello, Wave Goodbye'; Fleetwood Mac 'Go Your Own Way'; Blondie 'Heart Of Glass'.

GETTING BACK TOGETHER AGAIN:

The Supremes 'Back In My Arms Again'; Jackson Five 'I Want You Back'; John Lennon '(Just Like) Starting Over'.

POST-SPLIT: Once likely to be an ode to unrestrained grief, the contemporary post-split song is more often a chance for celebrating self-determination.

Smokey Robinson 'Tracks Of My Tears'; Dionne Warwick 'Walk On By'; Gloria Gaynor 'I Will Survive'; Four Tops 'Ask The Lonely'; Dido 'White Flag'; Sinead O'Connor 'Nothing Compares 2 U'; The Zombies 'She's Not There'; Everly Brothers 'Cathy's Clown'; The Police 'Every Breath You Take'; R.E.M 'The One I Love'; The Supremes 'Reflections'; The Who 'A Legal Matter'.

REFUSING TO GIVE UP AFTER THE SPLIT:

Diana Ross 'I'm Still Waiting'; The Police 'I Can't Stand Losing You'; Elvis Presley 'A Fool Such As I'; Dusty Springfield 'I Just Don't Know What To Do With Myself'; The Supremes 'Someday We'll Be Together'; Phil Collins 'Take A Look At Me Now'.

JEALOUSY AND INFIDELITY:

Elvis Costello 'I Want You'; Pilot 'How Long'; Roxy Music 'Jealous Guy'; Dire Straits 'You And Your Friend'; Marvin Gaye 'I Heard It Through The Grapevine'; Stephen Stills 'Love The One You're With'; Velvet Underground 'Pale Blue Eyes'; Rod Stewart 'Reason To Believe'; Tremoloes 'Silence Is Golden'; Bryan Adams 'Run To You'.

Sex and desire

This theme is one of the most basic in popular music because of its connection with people going out and having a good time. The issue here is how explicit or subtle you want to be. In many lyrics what appears to be a love song is, consciously or unconsciously, really about sex. There are a huge number of songs about sexual encounters, covering all shades of innocence and explicitness.

Imagery, metaphor, and wordplay have a big role here in disguising the true subject, because that has often been the only way round the censor. Popular music has been courageous and daring at times in challenging oppressive social mores, at other times merely smutty or vulgar. How such a song is put across depends on your persona. Before attempting any explicit lyrics take a long, objective look at your performing style. The subject-matter and double entendres (or even single entendres) that Prince got away with in the 1990s might sound tawdry down at your local pub or club on a midweek evening in front of 50 people. You have to know what you can convincingly put across.

Genre also has an influence on how explicit lyrics can be. In some genres being explicit is a no-no. Blues, 1970s hard rock (see Led Zeppelin and Aerosmith), 1980s heavy metal, rap, and hip-hop are genres where rude and often misogynistic lyrics are endemic. This can be disguised to a certain extent by slang or innuendo, some of which can be amusing. For example, there's a difference between the innuendo of an AC/DC track like 'Dirty Deeds Done Dirt Cheap' and that of The Darkness's 'Holding My Own' because of the effect of the music. The Darkness track is brash but slightly mournful, which softens the *double entendre* of the title, making it half-funny, half-sad.

It is striking just how indecent some well-known songs are, especially considering they were released 30 or 40 years ago. Common metaphors for sexual activity include dancing, driving cars, activities in kitchens involving cooking and food. There are fine lines to tread between intelligibility and obscurity, and between ingenuity and the unintentionally comic. Heat, melting and fire are another group of images, with physiological origins.

Medicine and healing references can come across as unctuous and hypocritical – as though the singer is in some profound suffering when all they want to do is get laid. There's also quasi-Freudian stuff about riding horses and ponies, fish, cats, and snakes, and what might be termed human geography – all those references to "going down" or "going south".

Along with all this imagery goes a long-standing tradition of sexual boasting, both to the object of the seduction, and to the listener. One of the great sexual lyric clichés involves the phrase "all night long". Lovers in popular song seem never seem to get tired or have mornings feeling crushed by lack of sleep. Spare a thought for the character Lincoln Duncan in Paul Simon's song of that name, trapped in a motel room next to a couple who noisily make love all night.

A similar lack of realism is demonstrated by the fact that there are vastly fewer songs which deal with the *consequences* of sexual activity. This is why The Shirelles' 'Will You Still Love Me Tomorrow' was so powerful in voicing a common worry for young women, living in a society that exposed them to a sexual double standard. There aren't that many songs about abortions and miscarriages; Graham Parker's 'You Can't Be Too Strong' is a rare example of a lyric dealing with the former. The coded reference to menstruation as a "losing streak" in The Rolling Stones' 'Satisfaction' was amazingly daring for its time, and remains so (two other songs that refer to it are Alice Cooper's 'Only Women Bleed' and Tori Amos' 'Silent All These Years').

Sexual identity itself is an important lyric theme for teenagers who are exploring and defining their sexual roles. Relevant songs include The Who's 'I'm A Boy', Johnny Cash's 'A Boy Named Sue', The Kinks' 'Lola', Lou Reed's 'Walk On The Wild Side', Velvet Underground's 'Venus In Furs', Billy Bragg's 'Sexuality', Madness's 'House Of Fun', Undertones' 'Teenage Kicks', Blur's 'Girls and Boys', Garbage's 'Androgyny', and Aerosmith's 'Dude Looks Like A Lady'. An interesting story lies behind one of the most candid of sexual songs, The Who's 'Pictures Of Lily', about which Pete Townshend said, "The idea was inspired by a picture my girlfriend had on her wall of an old Vaudeville star – Lily Bayliss. It was an old 1920s postcard and someone had written on it 'Here's another picture of Lily – hope you haven't got this one.' It made me think that everyone has a pin-up period."[112]

Once upon a time writing lyrics about sex was genuinely rebellious. In a time as permissive as the present, where pornographic images are part of the mainstream, true rebellion may lie in doing something else.

The song-titles you may like to investigate are separated out into songs written or sung by men as opposed to women to get a sense of the difference. With some notable exceptions, the latter tend to be less explicit and crudely assertive, less apt to push emotion out of the picture.

SUNG BY MEN: Marvin Gaye 'Sexual Healing'; Led Zeppelin 'Whole Lotta Love'; Buzzcocks 'Orgasm Addict'; Bad Company 'Feel Like Makin' Love'; The Rolling Stones 'Let's Spend The Night Together'; Wings 'Hi Hi Hi'; Pulp 'This Is Hardcore'; Frankie Goes To Hollywood 'Relax'; Sam and Dave 'Hold On! I'm Comin''; The Kinks 'All Day And All Of The Night'; The Cure 'Let's Go To Bed'; George Michael 'I Want Your Sex'.

SUNG BY WOMEN: Tori Amos 'Professional Widow'; Aretha Franklin 'Natural Woman'; Madonna 'Erotica'; 'Justify My Love'; Siouxsie And The Banshees 'Slowdive'; Maria Muldaur 'Midnight At The Oasis'; Jane Birkin And Serge Gainsbourg 'Je t'aime (Moi Non Plus)'; The Shirelles 'Will You Still Love MeTomorrow?'; Dusty Springfield 'Some Of Your Lovin'; Rita Coolidge 'Help Me Make It Through The Night'; Peggy Lee 'Fever'; Kate Bush 'Feel It'.

Names

Since so many popular songs are about love, it's not surprising there are many whose titles include, or are, a woman's name (there are fewer songs with male names). Love is *the* great inspirer of songs. A song is conjured to fill (temporarily or permanently) the beloved's absence. There is a long tradition of singers attempting to win the affections of the person they desire by writing a song for this person. In which case, what better way to personalise the song than to name it after that person? And if you have *more* than one beloved, why not put them all in, as Lou Bega did with 'Mambo No. 5', whose lyric pays homage to Angela, Pamela, Monica, Erica, Rita, Tina, Sandra, Mary and Jessica. Likewise, Paul Simon used Gus, Lee, Roy, Stand and Jack and their respective rhymes in the chorus of '50 Ways To Leave Your Lover'.

A name in itself is not going to give you a story or a theme – no-one writes a lyric about a name – although some lyrics (like the B52s' '52 Girls') list them. But names can stir the imagination, and if you can find a rhyme for the name, that in itself might set off a lyric sketch. The origin of this is probably that when you're in love the name of your beloved is one of the most magical words in the language. Favourite names in lyrics are Carol, Caroline, Mary, Sue, and Jimmy.

As an example of a lyric named after a woman, take Leonard Cohen's 'Suzanne' (1967). 'Suzanne' is partly a portrait of a bohemian young woman who lives near a river, her exotic appeal captured in a wealth of colourful detail, like the tea she gives him, and oranges from China. She attempts to draw him into a relationship, though he is ambivalent about this. The second verse digresses into Christian myth, talking about Jesus as a sailor who walked on the water. Verse 3 implies there is something Christ-like about Suzanne – that she is a redemptive force. It is a song that evokes sensuality and a retreat far from the madding crowd.

A name doesn't have to stand alone as a title. You can attach a phrase to it, and this will often make it more interesting. The weakest tactic is to attach the word "song" (as in a title like 'Annie's Song'). It's great for the dedicatee but less engaging for everyone else (or at least, that section of the population which isn't going out with Annie or Bill or whichever name you've put). So as a title 'Mandy' is not as interesting as 'Mandy In The Morning' (which also has the virtue of alliteration) or 'Mandy's Dreaming', or 'Mandy, How Could You Do It?' – which intrigues us: how could she do what? Any addition to the name can hint at a theme. For example, 'Mandy and Christine Go Out To Play' suggests to anyone aware of 1960s British history that this lyric could be about Mandy Rice-Davis, Christine Keeler and the Profumo Affair.

A name title can originate in wordplay. David Bowie's character Jean Genie was derived from the French writer Jean Genet. Many albums have one song whose title is a name but, unusually, on The Cocteau Twins' *Treasure* (1984) every track was so titled.

Another way to use a name for a song title is to think of a famous person who embodies a particular quality, good or bad, and make that a title for a song whose lyric is about the quality but not specifically the person. Tori Amos did this with 'Jackie's Strength', where the Jackie is question is Jackie Kennedy and the "strength" is the fortitude she showed after the president's assassination in 1963.

Here is an A-Z of name-titles. I've excluded names of famous people (located in another part of **Section Nine**). This A-Z lets you see which names have been used and the variety of modifiers put with them. By checking the lyrics of names or titles of interest, you can see the ways songwriters have built lyrics round a name. Female names occur first, male names second.

A

Magnetic Fields 'Abigail, Bell Of Kilronan'; Elvis Costello 'Alison'; Boston 'Amanda'; Joni Mitchell 'Amelia'; The Rolling Stones 'Angie'; John Denver 'Annie's Song'; The Beatles 'Anna (Go To Him)'; Terrorvision 'Alice What's The Matter?'; Stackridge 'Amazing Agnes'; Long John Baldry 'Annabella'; Leonard Cohen 'Alexandra Leaving'.

Paul Simon 'You Can Call Me Al'; Jackson Browne 'Song For Adam'; The Killers 'Andy, You're A Star'; Christopher Cross 'Arthur's Theme'; Cilla Black 'Alfie'; Paul McCartney 'Uncle Albert'; Pink Floyd 'Arnold Layne'.

B

The Beach Boys 'Barbara Ann'; Michael Jackson 'Billie Jean'; Four Tops 'Bernadette'; Kiss 'Beth'; Ram Jam Band 'Black Betty'; Scott English 'Brandy'.

Janis Joplin 'Me And Bobby McGhee'; Bobbie Gentry 'Ode To Billie Joe'; The Marvellettes 'Don't Mess With Bill'; Pulp 'Seductive Barry'; The Jam 'Billy Hunt'; Kate Bush 'Bertie'; Elmore James 'Bobby's Rock'.

C

Elvis Costello 'Just Like Candy'; Joni Mitchell 'Carey'; Neil Sedaka 'Oh Carol'; Europe 'Carrie'; Neil Diamond 'Sweet Caroline'; Brian Wilson 'Caroline; No'; Hollies 'Carrie Ann'; Everly Brothers 'Cathy's Clown'; Simon and Garfunkel 'Cecilia'; Siouxsie and The Banshees 'Christine'; Jesus and Mary Chain 'Taste Of Cindy'; Gilbert O'Sullivan 'Clair'; Everly Brothers 'Claudette'; The Cure 'Charlotte Sometimes'; Bob Dylan 'Corinna, Corinna'; Little Richard 'Lawdy Miss Clawdy'.

Rickie Lee Jones 'Chuck E's In Love'; Vinegar Joe 'Charley's Horse'.

D

America 'Daisy Jane'; Tyrannosaurus Rex 'Deborah'; Tom Jones 'Delilah'; Paul Anka 'Diana'; Fleetwood Mac 'Oh Diane'; Frankie Vaughan 'Dolly'; Jimi Hendrix 'Dolly Dagger'; 10cc 'Oh Donna'; Ritchie Valens 'Donna'; Stackridge 'Dora The Female Explorer'; Louis XIV 'A Letter To Dominique'.

Blondie 'Denis'; Kinks 'David Watts'; Elton John 'Daniel'; The Levellers 'Dirty Davey'.

E-F

Joni Mitchell 'Edith And The Kingpin'; Dexy's Midnight Runners 'Come On Eileen'; Roy Wood 'Dear Elaine'; The Turtles 'Eleanor'; Franz Ferdinand 'Eleanor Put Your Boots On'; The Beatles 'Eleanor Rigby'; Stone Roses 'Elizabeth My Dear'; Barry Ryan 'Eloise'; Pink Floyd 'See Emily Play'; Laura Nyro 'Emmie'; Hot Chocolate 'Emma'

Tom Waits 'Poor Edward'; Small Faces 'Eddie's Dreaming'; Loudon Wainwright 'Edgar'; Roy Harper 'Francesca'; Abba 'Fernando'; Morrissey 'Our Frank'; Curtis Mayfield 'Freddie's Dead'; The Who 'Uncle Ernie'; Sandie Shaw 'Frederick'.

G-H-I

Clifford T. Ward 'Gaye'; Them 'Gloria'; Supergrass 'Grace'; Van Morrison 'Madame George'; Alex Harvey Band 'Isabel Goudie'; Ian Dury And The Blockheads 'Geraldine'; Huddie Ledbetter 'Goodnight Irene'; Jimi Hendrix 'Izabella'.

Violent Femmes 'Gordon's Message'; Rod Stewart 'The Killing Of Georgie'; Sham 69 'Hurry Up Harry'; ELO 'The Diary Of Horace Wimp'; Ian Dury And The Blockheads 'Mash It Up Harry'; Madonna 'Isaac'.

J-K

Tori Amos 'Jackie's Strength'; Franz Ferdinand 'Jacqueline'; R. Dean Taylor 'Gotta See Jane'; David Bowie 'Jean Genie'; Eddie Cochran 'Jeanie Jeanie Jeanie'; The Casuals 'Jesamine'; The Hollies 'Jennifer Eccles'; Mitch Ryder And The Detroit Wheels 'Jenny Take A Ride'; Hole 'Jennifer's Body'; Madonna 'Dear Jessie'; Bob Dylan 'Visions Of Johanna'; Dolly Parton 'Jolene'; John Lennon 'Julia'; Pink Floyd 'Julia Dream'; The Levellers 'Julie'; Shania Twain 'Juanita'; Van Halen 'Jamie's Crying'; John Fred And The Playboys 'Judy In Disguise'; Cockney Rebel 'Judy Teen'; Fats Domino 'My Girl Josephine'; The Band 'Jemima Surrender'.

The Beatles 'Hey Jude'; Undertones 'Jimmy Jimmy'; Manfred Mann 'My Name Is Jack'; Ray Charles 'Hit The Road; Jack'; The Rolling Stones 'Jumpin' Jack Flash'; David Bowie 'John, I'm Only Dancing'; Martha Reeves And The Vandellas 'Jimmy Mack'; Pearl Jam 'Jeremy'; Chuck Berry 'Johnny B. Goode'; The Who 'Happy Jack'; Bryan Ferry 'Tokyo Joe'; Jimmy Dean 'Big Bad John'.

Johnny Cash 'Katy Too'; Marillion 'Kayleigh'; Bruce Springsteen 'Kitty's Back'; The National 'Karen'; Josh Ritter 'Kathleen'; Simon and Garfunkel 'Kathy's Song'.

Manic Street Preachers 'Kevin Carter'; 'The Who 'Cousin Kevin'.

L

Cat Stevens 'Sad Lisa'; Derek And The Dominoes 'Layla'; The Who 'Pictures Of Lily'; Wings 'The Lovely Linda'; Scott Walker 'Big Louise'; Little Richard 'Lucille'; The Beatles 'Lucy In The Sky With Diamonds'; The Hunches

'Lisa Told Me'; The Jam 'Liza Radley'; Scissor Sisters 'Laura'; Al Stewart 'Lori Don't Go Right Now'; Smashing Pumpkins 'Lily (My One And Only)'. The Kingsmen 'Louie Louie'; Family 'Leroy'.

M

Rod Stewart 'Maggie May'; 10cc 'I'm Mandy Fly Me'; Tom Waits 'Martha'; Jacques Brel 'Mathilde'; The Association 'Along Comes Mary'; Donald Fagen 'Maxine'; Joe Cocker 'Marjorie'; The Monkees 'Mary Mary'; Rick Nelson 'Hello Mary Lou'; The Beatles 'Michelle', 'Martha My Dear'; Marianne Faithfull 'Lady Madeleine'; Procol Harum 'Magdalene (My Regal Zonophone)'; Jackson C. Frank 'Marlene'; Lloyd Cole 'Margo's Waltz'; Leonard Cohen 'So Long; Marianne'; Nick Drake 'The Thoughts Of Mary Jane'; Little Richard 'Good Golly Miss Molly'; Cosmic Rough Riders 'Melanie'; Al Stewart 'Waiting For Margaux'.

Franz Ferdinand 'Michael'; Toni Basil 'Mickey'; Cat Stevens 'Matthew and Son'; Bobby Darin 'Mack The Knife'.

N

Prefab Sprout ''Nancy (Let Your Hair Down For Me); Elton John 'Nikita'; Prince 'Darling Nikki'; Rufus 'Natasha'; The Killers 'Believe Me Natalie'.

XTC 'Making Plans For Nigel'; The Supremes 'Nathan Jones'.

P-Q

Wayne Fontana 'Pamela'; The Beatles 'Polythene Pam'; Paul and Paula 'Hey Paula'; No Doubt 'Paulina'; Bob Dylan 'Peggy Day'; Buddy Holly 'Peggy Sue'; Nirvana 'Polly'; The Beatles 'Dear Prudence'.

Monkees 'For Pete's Sake'; XTC 'The Ballad Of Peter Pumpkinhead'; Bob Dylan 'Quinn The Eskimo'.

R

Kevin Ayers 'The Lady Rachel'; Chuck Berry 'Ramona, Say Yes'; Small Faces 'Rene'; The Beach Boys 'Help Me Rhonda'; The Beatles 'Lovely Rita'; Bob Seger 'Rosalie'; Bruce Springsteen 'Rosalita'; Mungo Jerry 'Hey Rosalyn'; The Police 'Roxanne'; Tom Waits 'Ruby's Arms'; Four Tops 'Walk Away Renee'; Stackridge 'Ruth, Did You Read My Mind'; Dr Feelgood 'Roxette'; Grateful Dead 'Rosemary'; Neil Diamond 'Cracklin' Rosie'; Toto 'Rosanna'.

Steely Dan 'Rikki Don't Lose That Number'; Joni Mitchell 'The Last Time I Saw Richard'; Kenny Rogers And The First Edition 'Ruby, Don't Take Your Love To Town'; The Beatles 'Doctor Robert'; Simon and Garfunkel 'Richard Cory'; Lemonheads 'It's A Shame about Ray'.

S

The Beatles 'Sexy Sadie'; Bruce Springsteen 'Sandy'; Fleetwood Mac 'Sara'; The Knack 'My Sharona'; The Smiths 'Sheila, Take A Bow'; Frankie Valli and The Four Seasons 'Sherry'; Leonard Cohen 'Suzanne'; Ramones 'Suzie Is A Headbanger'; Everly Bothers 'Wake Up Little Suzie'; Dr Hook 'Sylvia's Mother'; Stone Roses 'Sally Cinnamon'; Pulp 'Sylvia'; Love 'Stephanie Knows Who'; Dion 'Runaround Sue'; Eels 'Susan's House'.

Eminem 'Stan'; Small Faces 'Happiness Stan'; Eddie Cochran 'Cut Across Shorty'; Cockney Rebel 'Sebastian'; Everything But The Girl 'Sean'; Al Stewart 'Samuel, Oh How You've Changed'; Randy Newman 'Simon Smith and His Amazing Dancing Bear'.

T-U-V-X-Y-Z
Debbie Reynolds 'Tammy'; The Cufflinks 'Tracy'; Barclay James Harvest 'Ursula'; Steve Winwood 'Valerie'; Pink Floyd 'Vera'; Elvis Costello 'Veronica'; Roxy Music 'Virginia Plain'; The Beach Boys 'Wendy'; The Association 'Windy'; Joni Mitchell 'Yvette in English'.

Hollies 'Lullaby To Tim'; The Smiths 'William; It Was Really Nothing'; Blondie 'Victor'.

Clothing

"There's a button at the top of my navy peacoat, and it's the hardest button to button. I thought that was a great metaphor for the odd man out in the family." (Jack White of The White Stripes on 'The Hardest Button To Button')[113]

An article of clothing can be the focus for a lyric. It could be something you have seen in a shop, or that a friend has, or that a celebrity is pictured or filmed wearing.

Build it into a title and write a lyric about the person who wears it, why they wear it, and what might happen when they wear it.

- Consider its colour, its texture, how common or rare, how cheap or expensive it is.
- What does it say about the individual who wears it?
- What do they want it to say about them? Is there a gap between the two?
- How does it make you feel?
- How do they look wearing it?
- What aspects of their personality might it express?
- What social situations does it suggest (you don't wear a coat indoors, you don't wear a ballgown on the street).

Song-lyrics about clothing often revolve around how attractive the character looks in that article of clothing. This is usually a woman who becomes lodged in a man's mind by her dress. As far as materials go, silk and velvet have always had a special cachet in the popular song, standing as they do for luxury, sensuality, and something out of the ordinary.

LADIES' FASHIONS: The Hollies 'Long Legged Woman In A Black Dress'; Mitch Ryder And The Detroit Wheels 'Devil With The Blue Dress'; Gene 'Long Sleeves For The Summer'; Kings Of Leon 'Taper Jean Girl'; Gene Vincent 'Bluejean Bop'; Pulp 'Pencil Skirt'; U2 'If You Wear That Velvet Dress'; Lori McKenna 'Pink Sweater'; Laurie Anderson 'Beautiful Red Dress'; Depeche Mode 'Blue Dress'; Neil Diamond 'Forever In Blue Jeans'; Eddie Cochran 'Pink Pegged Slacks'; Pulp 'Pink Glove'.

People express individuality and rebellion through clothing – hence the significance of songs about blue jeans in the 1950s-1960s when they were frowned on by many adults, and the persistently impressive effect of wearing coloured shoes. Even when a song is not organised around an image of clothing, lyrics will often make passing descriptive mention to evoke a character or a situation. In love songs that deal with how people meet, it can often be a style of dress that catches the eye of the protagonist. The phrase "blue collar" is associated with a certain economic class and the life that goes with it.

MEN'S WEAR: Ian Dury And The Blockheads 'New Boots and Panties'; ZZ Top 'Sharp Dressed Man'; Adam and The Ants 'Dirk Wears White Sox'; Bachman Turner Overdrive 'Blue Collar'; Tin Machine 'Black Tie White Noise'; The Tremeloes 'Blue Suede Tie'; Everclear 'White Men In Black Suits'; Johnny Cash 'The Man In Black'; Irving Berlin 'Top Hat White Tie And Tails'; Madness 'Baggy Trousers'; The Who 'Zoot Suit'; Paul Weller 'Peacock Suit'.

Black clothes denote power, mystery and sexuality. Sexuality is also expressed through clothes that reveal as much as they conceal, most notably underwear and swimwear.

BEDWEAR, UNDERWEAR, HOSIERY, AND SWIMWEAR: Paul Weller 'Moon On Your Pyjamas'; Bryan Adams 'Your Underwear'; Pulp 'Underwear'; ZZ Top 'A Fool For Your Stockings'; Babybird 'Man's Tight Vest'; Tori Amos 'The Power Of Orange Knickers'; Edie Brickell And The New Bohemians 'Oak Cliff Bra'; Brian Hyland 'Itsy-Bitsy Teeny-Weeny Yellow Polka Dot Bikini'; The Cramps 'Bikini Girls With Machine-Guns'.

FOOTWEAR: Shoes are also significant because of their association with dancing, dressing up and going out, attracting a partner, being on the move.

Boots tend to carry associations of dominance and a lack of elegance. Shoe colours tend to be conservative, so coloured shoes (especially for men) are quite radical.

Carl Perkins 'Blue Suede Shoes'; Elvis Costello 'Red Shoes'; Tommy Tucker 'High Heel Sneakers'; Jane Siberry 'Red High Heels'; Nancy Sinatra 'These Boots Are Made For Walking'; Velvet Underground 'Venus In Furs' (the most famous shiny boots of leather in rock); Jeff Beck 'Rock My Plimsoll'; Billy Joel 'Stiletto'; Traffic 'Hole In My Shoe'; Run DMC 'My Adidas'; The Beatles 'Old Brown Shoe'; Stereophonics 'Step On My Old Size Nines'; Jimmy Nail 'Crocodile Shoes'.

HATS: At one time hats were expressive of character, and characters in songs who travelled described hanging their hats somewhere temporarily. Hat-wearing might characterise a dandy in a society where that is not the norm. Berets have a special allure, the natural head-gear of the political radical (see Che Guevara) or the French sophisticate.

Bob Dylan 'Leopard-skin Pillbox Hat'; Prince 'Raspberry Beret'; Procol Harum 'Homburg'; Marvin Gaye 'Wherever I Lay My Hat'; Steeleye Span 'All Around My Hat'; Randy Newman 'You Can Leave Your Hat On'; The Go-Betweens 'Ghost And The Black Hat'; Kevin Ayers 'Hat Song'.

OUTDOOR WEAR: Since the weather is often rainy on Planet Pop, characters need a striking coat as they walk down rain-soaked boulevards of misery.

> **Leonard Cohen 'Famous Blue Raincoat'; Marty Robbins 'A White Sport Coat (And A Pink Carnation)'; Bob Dylan 'Man In The Long Black Coat'; Ice Cube 'Dirty Mac'; Bonzo Dog Doo Dah Band 'Button Up Your Overcoat'; XTC '1000 Umbrellas', Tori Amos 'Parasol'; Frank Zappa 'Little Umbrella'.**

JEWELLERY, ETC: A bit of jewellery or an accessory gets you noticed. It's also true that clothes need repair. Elton John wrote 'Tiny Dancer' about a young woman – the "blue jean baby" – who worked with his band to keep their clothes and stage gear in shape and repaired. The song reached a bigger audience on the soundtrack of the film *Almost Famous*.

> **Guy Mitchell 'She Wears Red Feathers'; Buzzcocks 'Lipstick'; The White Stripes 'The Hardest Button To Button'; R.E.M. 'Crush With Eye-Liner'; Patti Page 'Scarlet Ribbons'; Steely Dan 'Green Earrings'; Carl Perkins 'Lend Me Your Comb'; Glen Campbell 'Rhinestone Cowboy'; Shirley Bassey 'Diamonds Are Forever'; Marilyn Monroe 'Diamonds Are A Girl's Best Friend'; The Raspberries 'Rose-Coloured Glasses'; The Cramps 'Sunglasses After Dark'.**

SECONDHAND: If you can't afford new, sometimes you have to make do with 'pre-used' and the social stigma that goes with it.

> **Rod Stewart 'Handbags and Gladrags'; The Faces 'Three Button Hand Me Down'; Elvis Costello 'Big Sister's Clothes'.**

Put-down songs

We have already covered songs about being rejected in love. This is the section for satire, envy, and general put-downs. This is the type of lyric that appeals to your darker side. Imagine a person who seems to have it all, then write a lyric either describing how great it would be to be them, or your resentment that you are not in that position. For a rejection song say goodbye to someone in bitter tones. A subtler put-down song is where the "you" of the lyric is actually yourself, in a self-critical mocking piece.

The power of this type of lyric is governed by how technically sharp it is. Put-down songs are better witty than abusive, otherwise you raise suspicions against yourself. Multiple rhyme can be more effective here than in most lyrics. The invective in Blur's 'Beetlebum' is managed through repeated rhymes on the same sound: "gun", "done", "numb", "come", "young", "thumb", "bum". The repetitions of a refrain can be powerful, and other wordplay.

There is a sub-genre of songs about teenage envy, in which a young person sees another who is better advantaged or gifted, possibly a few years older, as in The Kinks' 'David Watts' and The Undertones' 'My Perfect Cousin'. This friction could be between siblings. There is also the self-loathing song, typified by Nirvana's 'I'm A Negative Creep', The Sex Pistols' 'Seventeen' and 'Pretty Vacant', and Radiohead's 'Creep'.

PUT-DOWN LYRICS: **Bob Dylan 'Like A Rolling Stone'; 'Positively Fourth St' (and many others!); Dido 'See You When You're Forty'; Carly Simon 'You're So Vain'; R.E.M. 'The One I Love'; Leonard Cohen 'Everybody Knows'; The Darkness 'Get Your Hands Off My Woman'; Radiohead 'Karma Police'; The O'Jays 'The Backstabbers'; Sex Pistols 'Liar'; Hole 'Celebrity Skin'.**

STEREOTYPES: In rock lyrics there is a tradition of mocking suburbia, and the people the hippies scorned as "straights" – people who go to work and do boring hum-drum jobs (thereby catering for hippies and punks when they get toothache or need a plumber). Married people, bureaucrats, politicians, and the clergy are also frequent targets. When this feeling runs rampant the satire is directed at the whole of humankind in a torrent of misanthropic invective (see songs by both Pink Floyd and Radiohead).

Manfred Mann 'Semi Detached Suburban Mr James'; Kinks 'Dedicated Follower Of Fashion'; The Jam 'Mr Clean'; Blur 'Charmless Man'; 'Mr Robinson's Quango'; Mungo Jerry 'Memoirs of a Stockbroker'; The Beatles 'The Continuing Story Of Bungalow Bill'; Jimi Hendrix 'If 6 Were 9'; Paul Kantner and Grace Slick 'White Boy'; Pink Floyd 'Another Brick In The Wall'; Elvis Costello 'This Year's Girl'.

MUSIC BUSINESS SATIRES: The music business is the target of songs from bands who have been mistreated by their managers and agents, critics, or other band members. Money and artistic freedom are the usual bones of contention.

Queen 'Death On Two Legs'; Stereophonics 'Mr Writer'; The Jam 'All Mod Cons'; Sex Pistols 'EMI'; Blur 'Beetlebum'; Siouxsie And The Banshees 'Drop Dead'; John Lennon 'How Do You Sleep?'; 'Serve Yourself'; Free 'Mr Big'; Graham Parker And The Rumour 'Mercury Poisoning'; Robert Plant 'Tin Pan Alley'; The Who 'They're All In Love'; The Beatles 'Only A Northern Song'.

Telephones

To paraphrase Chuck Berry, this lyric subject is about long distance information. Imagine a situation where you have to communicate – by phone, mobile, email, letter or even webcam. For the moment, let's confine it to the telephone:

- Who are you contacting?
- Why do you need to contact them?
- Why is this urgent?
- What happens if you don't make the call?
- Are you waiting for a call?
- Who are you waiting for?
- Why can't you call them first?
- How long have you been waiting?
- How long are you prepared to wait
- What happens if they don't make the call?

Answer these questions, create a scenario and write a lyric. In both cases pose the question: why can't you go and physically meet the person? Perhaps they are away in another town or country. Why is that? By asking the questions you generate the scenario; when you have the scenario you have something to write about.

The exchange of a phone number remains a significant moment in relationships, as is the universal anxiety that the person will accidentally lose it. Most communications in popular songs are made by lovers with a problem. Desire, fear, or rejection, make it necessary to make the call as soon as possible. These communications are urgent and therefore dramatic. Some older songs have come to quaintly record changes in social life because their lyrics depend on what is now antiquated technology. People no longer have to routinely talk to an operator on the phone system; the difficulty of placing long-distance calls or getting a number has diminished. There were songs where the distraught lover phones and pours out their story to the operator. It is also said that many people tried calling 'Beechwood 4-5789' after that record was a hit.

The mobile phone has changed things too. Calls used to be made on payphones in hotel lobbies or on the street in a call-box. That classic old film scene where someone has to wait in a call-box for a phone to ring has gone now. Modern communication is less picturesque. It was Marc Bolan who sang on T.Rex's 'Metal Guru' that God was all alone and without a telephone … maybe He now has a mobile too.

Undertones 'You've Got My Number (Why Don't You Use It'); Blondie 'Hanging On The Telephone'; ELO 'Telephone Line'; Four Tops 'Just Seven Numbers (Can Straighten Out My Life)'; Marvellettes 'Beechwood 4-5789'; Chuck Berry 'Memphis Tennessee'; Mercury Rev 'Pick Up If You're There'; R.E.M. 'At My Most Beautiful'; Phil Collins 'Don't Lose My Number'; Drifters 'You're More Than A Number In My Little Red Book'; Stevie Wonder I Just Called To Say I Love You'.

Letters

The letter form offers an easy way to lay out a story or a change of mood in a lyric. You begin, "Dear [name]," and take it from there. Gene Pitney's '24 Hours From Tulsa' remains a brilliant example of how the 'letter lyric' can tell a story in vivid detail. In it a man who travels for work reasons is returning home and is only a day away. He stops at a motel, meets a woman, falls in love, and decides he can't go home and resume his old life. For extra drama have your character write the letter in a life or death situation. To see how much can be done with this style of lyric look at *The Juliet Letters* by Elvis Costello And The Brodsky Quartet, where every track is a letter.

For a more dramatic form of communication, telegrams and telegraphs have been used by lyricists, as in Abba's 'S.O.S', and Edwin Starr's 'Stop Her On Sight (S.O.S)', which plays with the meaning of the acronym (which does not stand for "stop her on sight"). Cash on delivery (C.O.D.) is a postal abbreviation.

One interesting religious slant on this approach was the letter form used by Stevie B for the song 'Because I Love You (The Postman Song)', a US Number One in 1990. He turned a religious song into a pop song by pretending that the letter was written between lovers. This is an example of smuggling into a lyric what you want to say to avoid popular prejudice.

David Bowie 'Letter To Hermione'; Joe Cocker 'The Letter'; Roxy Music 'Strictly Confidential'; Stevie Wonder 'Signed Sealed Delivered'; Marvellettes 'Please Mr Postman'; Elvis Presley 'Return To Sender'; The Box-Tops

'The Letter'; The Beatles 'P.S.I Love You'; Bee Gees 'I've Gotta Get a Message To You'; Blondie 'Fan Mail'; Buddy Holly 'Mailman, Bring Me No More Blues'; Kristin Hersh 'The Letter'; Louis XIV 'A Letter To Dominique'.

Media songs: radio, newsprint, and television

"I was writing the song with the *Daily Mail* propped up in front of me on the piano, I had it open at their News In Brief, or Far or Near, whatever they call it. There was a paragraph about 4,000 holes in Blackburn, Lancashire, being discovered …' (John Lennon on 'A Day In The Life')[114]

An excellent way to get ideas for lyrics is to scan the newspaper and look for stories, images or phrases. In addition, the newspaper and the idea of a headline can in themselves become the start of a lyric. Imagine picking up a newspaper and a face or a story catches your eye. Maybe someone you once knew is unexpectedly in the paper. Why? Is the news good or bad? Is this how you find out about the new life they've made since they parted with you?

NEWSPAPERS, MAGAZINES, AND COMICS: Edwin Starr 'Headline News'; The Beatles 'A Day In The Life'; 'Paperback Writer'; The Jam 'News Of The World'; Joe Jackson 'Sunday Papers'; Billy Bragg 'Tatler'; Madonna 'Vogue'; J. Geils Band 'Centrefold'; Dire Straits 'Lady Writer'; Elvis Costello 'Everyday I Write The Book', Carter The Unstoppable Sex Machine 'Good Grief Charlie Brown'; The Royal Guardsmen 'Snoopy v. The Red Baron'; Tori Amos 'Not The Red Baron'; Spin Doctors 'Jimmy Olsen's Blues'; XTC 'That's Really Super, Supergirl'.

Songwriters have been concerned with the radio as the main channel by which their songs are heard. The effect of hearing someone else's song on the radio can be a powerful subject.

Songwriters have also attacked the radio for too-narrow playlists and conservatism. DJs can be figures of gratitude or dislike.

RADIO: R.E.M. 'Radio Free Europe'; Rush 'Spirit Of Radio'; The Smiths 'Panic'; Queen 'Radio Ga Ga'; Joni Mitchell 'You Turn Me On (I'm A Radio); Roxy Music 'Oh Yeah (On The Radio)'; Stereophonics 'I Wouldn't Believe Your Radio'; Elvis Costello 'Radio Radio'; Libertines 'Radio America'; Robbie Williams 'Radio'; Ramones 'Do You Remember Rock'n'Roll Radio'; Patti Smith 'Radio Baghdad'; The Wedding Present 'Don't Touch That Dial'.

Popular songs are almost invariably scathing about television, seeing it as a means of control of 'the masses' – which usually means everyone who's not in the band or on the tour bus. Individual singers and bands never consider themselves consumers, even as they try to persuade you to buy their CD. In future there may be more songs about the internet and chat rooms, like Blink 182's 'Online Songs'.

TELEVISION: 'TV Movie'; David Bowie 'TVC15'; Bruce Springsteen '57 Channels'; Vast 'My TV and You'; ZZ Top 'TV Dinners'; Billy Joel 'Sleeping With The Television On'; Terrorvision 'America TV'; John Fogerty 'I Saw It On TV'; Talking Heads 'Television Man'; Dead Kennedys 'MTV – Get Off The Air'; Blink 182 'TV'; AC/DC 'Blow Up Your Video'; Violent Femmes 'I Hate The TV'; Martha Wainwright 'TV Show'; Dire Straits 'Money For Nothing'.

Aside from the generic idea of television, specific shows have influence songwriters, as in the case of Portishead's 'Mysterons' (from puppet series *Captain Scarlet*), Radiohead's 'Paranoid Android' (a character in a BBC radio series *The Hitch-Hiker's Guide To The Galaxy*), Squeeze's 'Cool For Cats' (which namechecks British TV cop series *The Sweeney*), 10;000 Maniacs' 'Daktari', Oasis's 'Wonderwall' (a film with music by George Harrison), and The Police's 'Man In A Suitcase' (a British detective series).

Cinemas and drive-ins (see Eddie Cochran's 'Drive-In Show') were once significant in lyrics because they were places where teens could go to enjoy limited physical contact with the other sex. This significance has been partly eroded by home video and DVDs, not to mention the growth in television channels. Two famous songs about courting at the cinema are The Drifters' 'Saturday Night At The Movies' and 'Kissin' In The Back Row Of The Movies'. In terms of specific films, some songwriters are inspired by the imagery or mood of a film, or at the very least borrow the title because it will have connotations for the audience even before they have heard the song:

Dave Edmunds 'The Creature From The Black Lagoon'; Los Lobos 'Angels With Dirty Faces'; Bruce Springsteen 'Thunder Road' (named after a Robert Mitchum film); Siouxsie And The Banshees 'Bring Me The Head Of The Preacher Man' (*Bring Me The Head Of Alfredo Garcia*); Elton John 'Goodbye Yellow Brick Road' (alludes to *The Wizard Of Oz*); Kate Bush 'Hounds Of Love' (inspired by *Night Of The Demon*); Pulp 'Wickerman' (*The Wicker Man*).

Dances and parties

Popular music has always been bound up with dancing. What happened from the late 1950s on is that the distance between a lyric about a dance and the song being the dance narrowed. Popular songs of the 1920s and 1930s might be *about* a waltz but you couldn't necessarily waltz to them. But Chubby Checker's 'Twist' songs were meant for twisting. There are many songs which feature a dance reference in the title like bop, boogie, mambo, without being about those dances.

BOOGIE, BOP, JIVE, TWIST, MAMBO, TANGO: Bill Haley 'Rock A Beatin' Boogie'; Earth Wind & Fire 'Boogie Wonderland'; Heatwave 'Boogie Nights'; Ramones 'Blitzkreig Bop'; Gene Vincent 'Be-Bop-A-Lula'; Wizzard 'See My Baby Jive'; Bee Gees 'Jive Talkin''; Bill Haley 'Shake; Rattle and Roll'; Sam Cooke 'Twisting The Night Away'; Chubby Checker 'Let's Twist Again'; Elton John 'Your Sister Can't Twist (But She Can Rock'n'Roll)'; T.Rex 'Jitterbug Love'; Bill Haley 'Mambo Rock'; Lou Bega 'Mambo #5'.

Some dance lyrics give instructions on how to perform their dance. If you want your lyric to encourage people to dance set it in a venue where this might happen, like a club or a party.

BESPOKE DANCES: Bobby Pickett and The Crypt Kickers 'Monster Mash'; Little Eva 'Do The Locomotion'; Ashton Gardner and Dyke 'Resurrection Shuffle'; Roxy Music 'Do The Strand'; The Swinging Blue Jeans 'The Hippy Hippy Shake'; Duran Duran 'The Reflex'; Stackridge 'Do The Stanley'; The Table 'Do The Standing Still'; Smokey Robinson And The Miracles 'Mickey's Monkey'; Major Lance 'Come On Do The Jerk'; Rufus Thomas 'Do The Funky Chicken'.

Parties, clubs and dance-floors are places where people congregate to have fun, forget their troubles, enjoy the music, and find a partner, at the very least to dance with. One associated lyric theme is being where the 'in-crowd' are – however you define them. Dance-floors witness ego-driven competitions of display, immortalised in the image of a white-suited John Travolta strutting in Saturday Night Fever. Abba's 'Dancing Queen' and James Brown's 'Sex Machine' are other well-known lyrics in which one particular dancer becomes the centre of attention.

DISCO FEVER: Trammps 'Disco Inferno'; The Bee Gees 'Night Fever'; Pulp 'Disco 2000'; Michael Jackson 'Burn This Disco Out'; Arctic Monkeys 'I Bet You Look Good On The Dancefloor'; M/A/R/R/S 'Pump Up The Volume'; U2 'Discotheque'; KC And The Sunshine Band 'Queen Of Clubs'; Funkadelic 'One Nation Under A Groove'; Madonna 'Into The Groove'.

A variation on this is the lyric of brazen self-assertion as a seduction tactic. Thin Lizzy's 'The Rocker', Chuck Berry 'I'm A Rocker', The Black Crowes' 'Hard To Handle', Simple Minds' 'Don't You Forget About Me', The Spin Doctors' 'Two Princes', are examples of the self-assertion song – "look at me I'm brilliant, I'm larger than life". Dancing can also be a metaphor for sex, a parallel Elvis Costello exploited to good effect (and more wittily than most) in 'Mystery Dance'.

Sly And The Family Stone 'Dance To The Music'; Jackson Five 'Dancing Machine'; Martha Reeves And The Vandellas 'Dancing In The Street'; Edwin Starr 'Funky Music Sho' Nuff Turns Me On'; Smokey Robinson And The Miracles 'Going To A Go-Go'; Stevie Ray Vaughan 'The House Is Knockin''; Irene Cara 'Flashdance ... What A Feeling'; The Drifters 'Save The Last Dance For Me'; Robbie Williams 'Rock DJ'; Danny and The Juniors 'At The Hop'; Wanda Jackson 'Let's Have A Party'; Beastie Boys '(You Gotta) Fight For Your Right (To Party)'.

DANCES AND PARTIES: A more introverted party lyric evokes the emotional undercurrents of parties. This can express the shock of seeing someone you love with someone else, or going off with someone else; the thrill of seeing someone to whom you're attracted dressed up for the first time (think of the power of the reference to a "party dress' in Costello's 'Alison'), and, when it's over, the game of who is leaving with whom. This is captured in Costello's 'Party Girl' and Leslie Gore's 'It's My Party (And I'll Cry If I Want To)', and in the form of general alienation in Three Dog Night 'Mama Told Me Not To Come'.

Living in the city

Millions of people live and work in cities. Some would like to get away, dreaming of a better life somewhere else, but can't. This was the theme of Gerry Rafferty's 'Baker Street' and Stevie Wonder's 'Living In The City'. A dislike of city life is readily expressed through the cliché metaphor of the 'urban jungle'. On the other hand, some people like the city, as recorded in Hefner's 'We Love The City'. So write lyrics about the dramas of life in a modern city: the buzz, the speed of life, the unpredictability. Write about wanting to be there or wanting to get away. If you take as your starting point what daily city life is like for millions, you have a potential audience of millions.

For example, there is a specific city love song about the common experience of urban life – seeing a beautiful stranger in a crowd, or on the opposite side of the stair, and not being able to do anything about it, as in James Blunt's 'You're Beautiful'. Another possible theme arises from cities having shops. There are many general songs about shopping or that use it as a metaphor, like The Miracles' 'Shop Around', for finding a partner. Think about the variety of locations and buildings in a city, where people meet and relationships might start:

Hollies 'Bus Stop'; Babybird 'Corner Shop'; Rory Gallagher 'Laundromat'; Clash 'Lost In The Supermarket'; Animals 'House Of The Rising Sun'; Village People 'Y.M.C.A'; Sleepy John Estes 'Fire Department Blues'; Rose Royce 'Car Wash'; Muse 'Muscle Museum'; Dixie Cups 'Chapel Of Love'; Eels 'In The Yard; Behind the Church'; Laura Nyro 'Louise's Church'.

There are lyrics about landmarks, parks and other city features, including The Small Faces 'Itchycoo Park', James Gang 'Ashton Park', Richard Harris 'MacArthur Park', Prince 'Paisley Park', and Blur 'Park Life'. Some lyrics survey whole areas of a city, such as Petula Clark's 'Downtown', Dire Straits' 'Wild West End', The Pet Shop Boys' 'Suburbia', The Jam 'In The City', and Bruce Springsteen's 'Backstreets'.

Though a city is full of people, paradoxically this can make people feel lonely and isolated – hence the saying that you're never as alone as in a crowd. The complementary image for this is the individual isolated in a room or house. In lyrics, this can be a positive (the room or house as security) or a negative (the room or house as prison), depending on the individual's psychological state or state of romance. This theme is in songs like The Four Tops 'Seven Rooms Of Gloom', The Beach Boys' 'In My Room', Coldplay's 'In My Place', Dodgy's 'In A Room', Martha Reeves And The Vandellas' 'In My Lonely Room', and Depeche Mode's 'In Your Room'. The phrase "these four walls" is a related cliché.

Soft Cell 'Bedsitter'; Madness, CSN&Y 'Our House'; Jimi Hendrix 'Red House'; B52s 'Love Shack'; Jefferson Airplane 'The House At Pooneil Corner'; Asleep At The Wheel 'House Of Blue Lights'; Ryan Adams 'This House Is Not For Sale'; Badly Drawn Boy 'Rachel's Flat'; Mary J. Blige 'Mary's Joint'.

If you don't have a place of your own in the city, then you need somewhere to stay. Hotels are significant for characters in lyrics who are travelling or in-between different times in their lives. These lyrics are supplemented by those hubs of social activity, places where people eat:

Eagles 'Hotel California'; The White Stripes 'Hotel Yorba'; Elvis Presley 'Heartbreak Hotel'; Ryan Adams 'Hotel Chelsea Nights'; Pulp 'Bar Italia'; Carole King 'Hard Rock Café'; Suzanne Vega 'Tom's Diner'; Arlo Guthrie 'Alice's Restaurant'.

You can write songs about real streets and roads, or invented ones. Streets and roads are also spaces where people are seen by others. Often songs about real streets and places mythologise them so that it is as if they exist in a separate, unchanging world. This is certainly true of the relationship between the real place and the song in Springsteen's '4th Of July, Asbury Park', The Beatles' 'Penny Lane' and Scott Mackenzie's '(If You're Going To) San Francisco'.

Rod Stewart 'Gasoline Alley'; Nashville Teens 'Tobacco Road'; The Rolling Stones 'Exile On Main Street'; Bob Dylan 'Positively 4th St'; Bobby Darin 'On The Street Where You Live'; Van Morrison 'Cyprus Avenue'; Dire Straits 'Telegraph Rd'; Mamas and Papas 'Creeque Alley'; Paul Weller 'Stanley Road'.

The street can be a metaphor for a state of mind or a situation, as in the phrases "to go down a blind alley" and "that's right up my street". A dead end street is any situation that goes nowhere. Once there was a colloquial usage in American English that put the suffix "-ville" after a word denoting a mood or expression.

Asked what you thought of the party last night, the reply could be "dullsville". In the mid-1980s it was easy to interpret R.E.M.'s '(Don't Go Back To) Rockville' as an indie band's rejection of all things rockist, rather than a reference to an actual place. In this connection, think also of those current clichés: "don't even go there" and "let's not go down that road".

A one-way street is a metaphor for a situation where there's no going back. You cast a new light on metaphors when you combine them – so what about "one-way street over a burning bridge" which combines two similar ideas. Streets can be combined with dance and music references. In love songs the most magical street is the one where the beloved lives, as in 'On The Street Where You Live'. A love-affair could itself be regarded as a street, perhaps named after the beloved, or a park. A street could carry a moral quality, as in a title like 'Temperance Street'. Here are some examples of streets with modifiers:

The Kinks 'Dead End St'; Flying Burrito Brothers 'Dark End Of The Street'; Morrissey 'Late Night, Maudlin Street'; Prince 'Alphabet St'; Super Furry Animals 'Vulcan St'; Aerosmith 'One Way Street'; Bangles 'Walking Down Your Street'; Sisters Of Mercy 'Destination Boulevard'.

Some songwriters are excited by the lyric detail of having a numbered street or road:

The Wallflowers '6th Avenue Heartache'; Ryan Adams 'Shakedown On 9th Street'; Mick Ronson 'Slaughter On Tenth Avenue'; Rufus Wainwright '14th Street'; Gil Scott-Heron '17th Street'; Janis Ian Iron Maiden '22 Acacia Avenue'; '42nd St Psycho Blues'; Ramones '53 & 3rd'; Simon and Garfunkel 'The 59th Street Bridge Song (Feelin' Groovy)'; Bruce Springsteen 'Does This Bus Stop At 82nd?'

If a city has a waterfront it evokes the magic of being by the ocean whilst retaining the energy of the urban environment. Water juxtaposed with urban life can bring a sense of romance (as in the real life instances of Venice, Paris and Amsterdam).

Simple Minds 'Waterfront'; The Drifters 'Under The Boardwalk'; Blondie 'Love At The Pier'; Bruce Springsteen 'Seaside Bar Song'; Frankie Ford 'Sea Cruise'; All About Eve 'Martha's Harbour'; The Platters 'Harbour Lights'; Otis Redding 'Sittin' On The Dock Of The Bay'.

Money and work

"Everybody writes about love. I wanted to write about something different. But what? Then it popped into my head, the most obvious thing of all, the thing I needed most – money … Some will be shocked, some will think it's cute, some will think it's funny. I think I'll make money." (Berry Gordy, head of Motown, on writing 'Money (That's What I Want)'[115]

Naturally allied with the city is the work song. In this lyric, the speaker sings about whether they like or hate their job, whether it will lead anywhere, and if they want to escape it. A work lyric can describe the daily journey to and from work, friends and colleagues in the office, the morning coffee-stand, the lunch-hour, the commute home at the end of the day, and the contrast with the weekend.

The folk and blues song traditions have many songs about being exploited, working in terrible conditions, and about the privations and hazards of working in various trades, such as 'The Weaver And The Factory Maid', 'The Blacksmith', 'My Johnny Was A Shoemaker', 'Fisherman's Wife', and 'The Blackleg Miner'. Jimmy Webb's 'Wichita Lineman', about a man who repairs telegraph poles, has a potent tradition behind it. Alternatively, in Bacharach and David's 'Say A Little Prayer' the humdrum of the working day throws the speaker's romantic feelings into greater relief.

EMPLOYMENT: The Silhouettes 'Get A Job'; Miracles 'Got A Job'; Talking Heads 'Found A Job'; Elvis Costello 'Welcome To The Working Week'; Jane Wiedlin 'Rush Hour'; Cat Stevens 'Matthew And Son'; Aretha Franklin 'Say A Little Prayer'; Rose Royce 'Car Wash'; The Beach Boys 'I Get Around'; Paul McCartney 'Another Day'; R.E.M. 'Finest Worksong'; The Jam 'Man In The Cornershop'; Clash 'Career Opportunities'.

Work and money are universal concerns. Millions know how it feels to have no money or to work for peanuts, hence lyrics about wanting to make more money. The granddaddy of all songs about money is 'Buddy Can You Spare A Dime'.

Songs titled 'Money' have been recorded by Pink Floyd, Badfinger, Lovin' Spoonful, and most famously the Berry Gordy composition cited above, recorded in a no-nonsense manner by Barratt Strong in the early 1960s. Its lyric shocked people by challenging the proverbial wisdom that the best things in life are free, a view expressed successfully by The Beatles in 'Can't Buy Me Love'. The same cynicism apparent in Gordy's 'Money' is felt in 'Diamonds Are A Girl's Best Friend' and 'Diamonds Are Forever'. In the case of Pink Floyd's 'Money', the theme is handled from the other end of the bank account, where people have too much money.

The vocabulary of finance is a mine of similes and metaphors with which to colour a lyric – words like tender, account, and currency can have double meanings.

MONEY: Abba 'Money Money Money'; Chuck Berry 'No Money Down'; Simply Red 'Money's Too Tight To Mention'; Pet Shop Boys 'Opportunities (Let's Make Lots Of Money)'; Contours 'First I Look At The Purse'; Annie Lennox 'Money Can't Buy It'; Wham! 'Credit Card Baby'; Funkadelic 'Funky Dollar Bill'; Alice Cooper 'Billion Dollar Babies'; The Pretenders 'Brass In Pocket'; ZZ Top 'Just Got Paid'; Clash 'Working For The Yankee Dollar'; The Beatles 'Taxman'.

Country life

In song-lyrics the country exists as the polar opposite of the city. Where the latter is a technological, urban jungle – dangerous, exciting, modern – the country stands for a romantic pastoral vision of rootedness, belonging, beauty, tranquility, safety, healthy living, and getting back to nature. This symbolism was strengthened in the late 1960s by the growing environmental ethic, with its focus on self-sufficiency, communal living, the desire to escape capitalism. This contrasted with the aspiration of earlier generations employed in poorly paid jobs and often vulnerable to the unpredictable, destructive powers of nature. They could be glad to escape the country for the city, leaving behind small-town gossip and parochial attitudes. Now city-dwellers dream of escape to the country.

IN THE COUNTRY: Buddy Guy 'Country Man'; Elton John 'Country Comfort'; John Denver 'Take Me Home Country Roads'; Canned Heat 'Going Up The Country'; Rory Gallagher 'Country Mile'; Elton John 'Goodbye Yellow Brick Road'; Red Hot Chili Peppers 'Backwoods'; Neil Young 'Are You Ready For The Country'; James Taylor 'Country Road'.

In lyric writing, the country symbolically includes the small town (or village in the case of the UK) and the farm – so there are songs about working on farms. No-one should use a title with the word "farm" in it without being aware of Bob Dylan's 'Maggie's Farm'. In country music the countryside is seen as the place of traditional, conservative values, opposed to the decadent modernism of the city. For landscape features like rivers and woods, see topography metaphors in **Section Six**.

FARMS, COUNTRY HOUSES, CASTLES: The Faces 'Miss Judy's Farm'; Bob Dylan 'Maggie's Farm'; Mose Allison 'Parchman Farm'; Blur 'Country House'; Barenaked Ladies 'King Of Bedside Manor'; Wings 'Big Barn Red'; Eels 'Ant Farm'; Yoshikawa And The Blue Comets 'Blue Chateau'; Four Tops 'Keeper Of The Castle'; Jimi Hendrix 'Spanish Castle Magic'.

Amusement parks and the circus

We know from Shakespeare's plays that "all the world's a stage", and men and women are the players thereon, a notion re-stated in modern guise in the musical *Cabaret*. This sense of life as a play in which people have roles can be felt wherever people gather for entertainment. Hence lyrics about amusement parks and rides, carnivals, and circuses. These places and activities provide rich lyric material, whether literal or metaphorical. Everyone relates to the feeling of performing in social situations, sometimes enjoyably, sometimes not. For this reason, the line about being in the spotlight in R.E.M.'s 'Losing My Religion' struck a chord with many.

Young people haunt amusement parks; lovers wander through the crowds. At night they are noisy and colourful places, sometimes with fireworks. People gamble, win and lose. Each ride or attraction could individually be a metaphor, as in the case of Madness's 'House Of Fun', about a shy youth wanting to buy contraceptives in a chemist shop. The most often ride cited in lyrics is the tunnel of love, followed by the ghost train.

AMUSEMENT PARK AND RIDES: Madness 'House Of Fun', 'Ghost Train'; Dire Straits 'Tunnel Of Love'; Bruce Springsteen '4th Of July; Asbury Park (Sandy)'; The Beach Boys 'Amusement Parks USA'; 13th Floor Elevators 'Roller Coaster'; The Beatles 'Helter Skelter'; Richard Thompson 'Wall Of Death'; Hollies 'On A Carousel'.

The circus is a romantic symbol. Here are a bunch of people – often eccentric or playing eccentric roles – who live outside the usual world of work, and travel the country apparently with a freedom the majority do not have. In role, they are almost as a set of caricatures of what it is to be human, often with exaggerated powers or mis-shapen in some way. A circus also carries the derogatory meaning of an enterprise which is frivolous, unreal, and promises more than it delivers. The carnival is a closely-related possible setting.

CIRCUS: Bruce Springsteen 'Wild Billy's Circus Story'; The Beatles 'Being For The Benefit Of Mr Kite'; Procol Harum ''Twas Teatime At The Circus'; Junior's Eyes 'Circus Days'; Mountain 'The Animal Trainer And The Toad'; Butthole Surfers 'Human Cannonball'.

CARNIVAL: Tim Buckley 'Carnival Song'; The Seekers 'The Carnival Is Over'; The Coasters 'Little Egypt'; The Band ' The WS Walcott Medicine Show'; 'Life Is A Carnival'; Cher 'Gypsies; Tramps And Thieves'.

The central figure of the circus is the clown. The clown pretends to be funny and jovial but underneath is seen as solitary and alone. This image easily stands for the disappointed lover who wears a mask of pride to hide his or her hurt, the socially awkward, or the person made a fool of. The more literary version is the jester, an attractive figure to adolescents who feel clumsy and alienated. The clown is a tricky image to put in a lyric now because the happy outside/sad inside association has become a cliché.

CLOWNS: Smokey Robinson And The Miracles 'Tears Of A Clown'; Kinks 'Death Of A Clown'; Ron Sexsmith 'Clown In Broad Daylight'; Judy Collins 'Send In The Clowns'; Turin Brakes 'Last Clown'; Neil Sedaka 'King Of Clowns'.

Society itself can be seen as a set of people who are wearing masks, not showing their true feelings, and thus a "masquerade". Life becomes like a theatre performance.

The Band 'Stage Fright'; Graham Parker 'I'm Gonna Tear Your Playhouse Down'; Fish 'Black Masquerade' ; Leo Sayer 'I Won't Let The Show Go On'; 'The Dancer'; Marilyn McCoo and Billy Davis Jnr. 'You Don't Have To Be A Star (To Be In My Show)'; Badly Drawn Boy 'Exit Stage Right'; Van Morrison 'Ballerina'.

Geography: places in the USA

Geography easily evokes pictures and suggests a story which can make a lyric. A geographical title is more interesting if a verb or adjective is attached to the place-name, rather than it stand on its own. The additional word can lend drama and imply what the song is about. This technique is more important the better known the place. Let's face it, if you decide to call a song 'New York' you're up against some stiff competition.

Consider Leonard Cohen's 'First We Take Manhattan'. The title refers to a place but it conveys something else. The hyperbole is intriguing – what does he mean by "take'? Literally? Is this a war song? And then he has the word "first' which begs the question, what happens second? (They take Berlin.) Some place names are intrinsically more evocative than others. A place-name like Phoenix, for example, has poetic possibilities because of the association with the legendary bird that renews its immortality by burning in a pyre and rising from the ashes. With Jimmy Webb's 'By The Time I Get To Phoenix' the title immediately makes us wonder, "by the time he gets to Phoenix ... what?' Similarly, 'Do You Know The Way To San Jose?' has us thinking, why is the speaker asking? Why does she want to get there?

The geography of America, and the idealism associated with its origins, lends itself to a projection of imagined values and dreams which would not be prevalent in a smaller country. A lyric like The Beach Boys' 'Surfin' USA' is exhilarating as it criss-crosses the continent naming places. There are many songs about the U.S.A., including

Chuck Berry 'Back In The USA', Ramones 'I'm So Bored With The USA', Steve Miller Band 'Living In The USA', MC5 'Back In The USA', Bruce Springsteen 'Born In The USA', Ray Charles 'America The Beautiful', Simon and Garfunkel 'America', Elvis Presley 'An American Trilogy'.

Travel often expresses a desire to find a better life. This has been the case from the time of the old blues songs, when African Americans freed from slavery in the South journeyed by whatever means they could towards the cities. This impulse to make a better life somewhere else is re-expressed in the songs of Bruce Springsteen, which initially focused on travel as escape but matured to ask what happens when you arrive at your so-called dream place. Another group of people liable to write songs about different places are musicians themselves, since they spend so much time touring.

Singer-songwriter Sufjan Stevens has recorded two albums recently dedicated to individual states: *Michigan* (2003) and *(Come On Feel The) Illinoise* (2005). He has an ambition to do an album for all 50 states. There are thousands of songs whose titles refer to places in America, with California one of the most popular of the states, with Brian Wilson 'California Girls, Led Zeppelin 'Going To California', Mamas and Papas 'California Dreaming', Red Hot Chili Peppers 'Californication', Dead Kennedys 'California Uber Alles', R.E.M. 'I Remember California', Joni Mitchell 'California', and The Move 'California Man' among them. Here are some other state-based songs:

SONGS OF THE STATES: The Doors 'Alabama Song'; Bee Gees 'Road To Alaska'; Los Lobos 'Arizona Skies'; James Taylor 'Carolina In My Mind'; Lyle Lovett 'North Dakota; Perry Como 'Delaware'; Bob Seger 'Get Out Of Denver'; Ray Charles 'Georgia On My Mind'; R. Dean Taylor 'Indiana Wants Me'; Elvis Presley 'Kentucky Rain'; Bee Gees 'Massachusetts'; Jerry Lee Lewis 'What Made Milwaukee Famous'; Mountain 'Mississippi Queen'; Neil Young 'Ohio'; Al Stewart 'Katherine Of Oregon'; Elton John 'Philadelphia Freedom'; Capt Beefheart 'Moonlight On Vermont'; America 'Old Virginia'.

The prime subjects of place-name song-lyrics in the U.S. are New York, Los Angeles, and Hollywood. Cities closely associated with music, such as Memphis, Nashville and Detroit also feature. In the 1960s San Francisco had songs written about it when it was the capital of the hippy counter-culture.

Barney Hoskyns' *Waiting For The Sun: The Sound Of Los Angeles* (1996) has an appendix listing songs about Los Angeles.

SONGS OF NEW YORK: Frank Sinatra 'New York, New York'; Bruce Springsteen 'New York City Serenade'; Sting 'Englishman In New York'; Don Henley 'New York Minute'; Arrow 'New York Groove'; Barbara Streisand 'New York State Of Mind'; The Pogues And Kirsty MacColl 'Fairytale Of New York'; Ryan Adams 'My Blue Manhattan'; Van Morrison 'Coney Island'; Beastie Boys 'No Sleep Til Brooklyn'; Drifters 'On Broadway'; Simon and Garfunkel 'Bleecker Street'; Nat King Cole 'On The Streets Of New York'.

SONGS OF HOLLYWOOD AND SAN FRANCISCO: Fleetwood Mac 'Hollywood'; Corrs 'Queen Of Hollywood'; Eagles 'King Of Hollywood'; Thin Lizzy 'Hollywood (Down On Your Luck)'; System Of A Down 'Lost In Hollywood'; Eagles 'Hollywood Waltz'; Scott McKenzie 'San Francisco'; Flowerpot Men 'Let's Go To San Francisco'; Tony Bennett 'I Left My Heart In San Francisco'; Eric Burdon And The Animals 'San Franciscan Nights'.

OTHER LOCATIONS IN THE US: Neil Young 'Albuquerque'; Bruce Springsteen 'Atlantic City'; Tim Hardin 'The Lady Came From Baltimore'; Paul Butterfield Blues Band 'Born In Chicago'; David Bowie 'Panic In Detroit'; Martha And The Muffins 'Echo Beach'; Glen Campbell 'Galveston'; Albert King 'Kansas City'; Mott The Hoople 'All The Way From Memphis'; Bob Dylan 'Nashville Skyline'; Tim Buckley 'Monterey'; Loudon Wainwright III 'Ode To Pittsburgh'; R.E.M. 'All The Way To Reno'; Nanci Griffith 'San Diego Serenade'; Everclear 'Santa Monica'; The Byrds 'Tulsa County Blue'; Blondie 'Union City Blue'; Glen Campbell 'Wichita Lineman'.

Places in the UK

Songs about places in the UK are rarer than those about the USA. Since the UK is geographically smaller, it is harder to feel that your dreams and the answer to your problems lie at the end of a long motorway drive. It is also a fact that British musicians are less inclined to overt patriotism. Songs about England, for example, usually start from a sense that the theme is problematic, assuming they aren't outright attacks. Blur's album *Modern Life Is Rubbish* was an attempt to write songs about definite characters who would illustrate the romantic and sinister aspects of English life. Popular songs about England, post-1960s, tend to be sceptical, verging on cynical. This is felt strongly in punk bands like The Sex Pistols.

ENGLAND: Oysterband 'Another Quiet Night In England'; Roy Harper 'One Of Those Days In England'; The Clash 'Something About England'; Kate Bush 'Oh England (My Lionheart)'; Kirsty MacColl 'England'; Waterboys 'Old England'; The Clash 'This Is England'; Billy Bragg 'I'm Not Looking For New England'; Sex Pistols 'Anarchy In The UK'.

British songwriters have only recently started to overcome the sense that to write songs about journeys or places in the UK is bathetic. It is still unexpected to examine a CD and find a title like 'Clouds Over Carlisle' or 'Meet Me In Lincoln'. In the British context, Carter The Unstoppable Sex Machine's '24 Minutes From Tulse Hill' is a funny allusion to Gene Pitney's '24 Hours From Tulsa', and Billy Bragg's 'A13 Trunk Road To The Sea' is the unromantic British version of 'Route 66'.

As is the case with most countries, there are plenty of songs about the capital city, London and its districts, though probably more in the pre-rock'n'roll era than after (standards like 'Maybe It's Because I'm A Londoner', 'Doing The Lambeth Walk', 'Underneath The Arches', etc.). In the mid-1960s it was briefly hip to write songs about London when it was centre of the pop world (until the axis shifted to San Francisco). When England was 'swinging' the New Vaudeville Band could write a hit lyric like 'Winchester Cathedral'.

LONDON AND ENVIRONS: The Clash 'London Calling'; Catatonia 'Londinium'; Gene 'London, Can You Wait?'; Ralph McTell 'Streets Of London'; Blur 'London Loves'; ELO 'Last Train To London'; Pet Shop Boys 'West End Girls'; Elvis Costello 'I Don't Want To Go To Chelsea'; The Clash 'White Man In The Hammersmith Palais'; Gerry Rafferty 'Baker Street'; Donovan 'Hampstead Incident'; Kirsty MacColl 'Soho Square'; The New Vaudeville Band 'Finchley Central'; The Kinks 'Waterloo Sunset'; Cat Stevens 'Portobello Road'; Ian Dury 'Billericay Dickie'.

Counties are not as glamorous as American states, as they're smaller, and geographical contrasts in the UK are not as pronounced as in the US. An exception is traditional folk song, which dates from a time when people mostly travelled on foot, and often didn't meet anyone who lived further away than the nearest village (see Simon And Garfunkel's recording of 'Scarborough Fair'). In reality, the counties of England do have their own character and history; it just takes more imagination to see it. But they do not represent modernity in the way that America always has, and popular songs are bound up with modernity. Consequently, the counties are almost invisible in popular song lyrics (a title like Bill Nelson's 'Adventures In A Yorkshire Landscape' is very rare), whereas towns and cities do figure.

CITIES: ELO 'Birmingham Blues'; Bangles 'Going Down To Liverpool'; Gerry And The Pacemakers 'Ferry Cross The Mersey' (Liverpool); Stone Roses 'Mersey Paradise'; Simple Minds 'Belfast Child'; Manic Street Preachers 'Cardiff Afterlife'; Happy Mondays 'Manchester Rave On'; Fat Boy Slim 'You're Not From Brighton'; Lindisfarne 'Fog On The Tyne' (Newcastle); Alan Price 'Jarrow Song'.

TOWNS AND OTHER GEOGRAPHICAL REFERENCES: Oysterband 'The Oxford Girl'; Peter Gabriel 'Solsbury Hill'; Waterboys 'The Glastonbury Song'; Siouxsie And The Banshees 'Land's End'; Manic Street Preachers 'Blackpool Pier'; Pink Floyd 'Grantchester Meadow'; Traffic 'Berkshire Poppies'; Blur 'Clover Over Dover'; Badly Drawn Boy 'Stockport'; Robyn Hitchcock 'No, I Don't Remember Guildford'; Doves 'Shadows Of Salford'; Roy Harper 'Watford Gap'; The Fall 'Bournemouth Runner'; Arctic Monkeys 'Rotherham'.

Places in the rest of the world

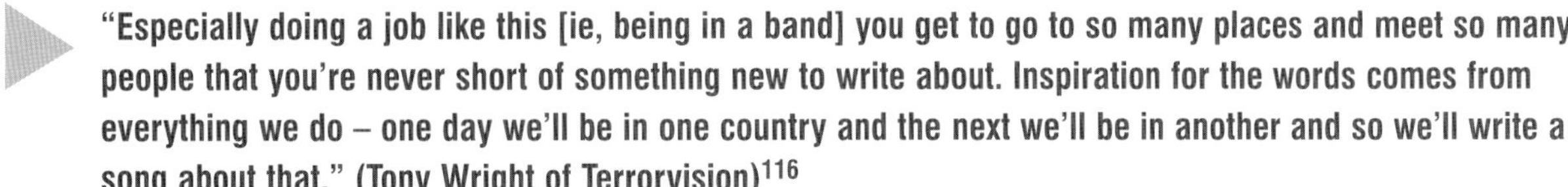

"Especially doing a job like this [ie, being in a band] you get to go to so many places and meet so many people that you're never short of something new to write about. Inspiration for the words comes from everything we do – one day we'll be in one country and the next we'll be in another and so we'll write a song about that." (Tony Wright of Terrorvision)[116]

Songs about countries other than the one you live in might be inspired by a holiday, by current events, history, politics, the desire to go there, or because that country represents to you a theme or an emotion. All countries have a geographical reality and a cultural reality in the mind (including the country you live in). All landscapes are also imagined; all geography is also the cultural topography of symbols and values.

These lyrics are not confined to being about the country concerned; that may just be the backdrop to something else.

When it comes to arranging and recording a song, a country's own music might suggest native instruments. The West Indies are associated with calypso, Jamaica with reggae, Cuba with the music of the Buena Vista Social Club, India with its scales, sitars and tablas, and evoking the Far East might make you put a pentatonic scale to other uses than are found in John Lee Hooker.

This list of titles does not include songs in indigenous languages. For example, Edith Piaf, Jacques Brel, Francoise Hardy, Maurice Chevalier, and Serge Gainsbourg could supply hundreds of songs about France ... in French. This book restricts itself to the Anglo-American tradition.

CANADA: Songs about Canada will often focus on the great outdoors and the symbolism of north.

> **Echobelly 'Canada'; Billy Bragg 'Ontario Quebec and Me'; The Byrds 'Blue Canadian Rockies'; Eliza Carthy 'Quebecois'; Violent Femmes 'Vancouver'; Jeff Buckley 'Vancouver'; Andy Williams 'Canadian Sunset'.**

CENTRAL AMERICA: Here it is the heat, laid-back life, corruption, and political revolution which provide themes.

> **Long John Baldry 'Mexico'; Marty Robbins 'El Paso'; Stan Getz & Joao Gilberto 'The Girl From Ipanema'; Jackson Browne 'Jamaica Say You Will'; Bruce Cockburn 'Nicaragua'; Zutons 'Havana Gang Brawl'; R.E.M. 'The Flowers Of Guatemala'; Arcade Fire 'Haiti'; Bobby Bloom 'Montego Bay'; Billy Ocean 'Caribbean Queen'; Athlete 'El Salvador'; Minutemen 'Untitled Song For Latin America'.**

SOUTH AMERICA: This continent evokes lyrics about tropical weather, tyranny, escape, and ecology.

> **Julie Covington 'Don't Cry For Me Argentina'; Kirsty MacColl 'Columbia'; Stackridge 'The Road To Venezuela'; Pink Flag 'Brazil'; Duran Duran 'Rio'; Crass 'Sheep-Farming In The Falklands'; Martin Stephenson And The Dainties 'Boat To Bolivia'; Bob Martin 'Silver Rails to Rio'; Neil Young 'Like An Inca'; Toad The Wet Sprocket 'Chile'.**

WESTERN EUROPE: These countries offer much in the way of sense of place and history, and sophistication, though they have not figured much in Anglo-American lyrics.

> **Nelson Riddle 'In Old Lisbon' ; John Cale 'Andalucia'; Three Dog Night 'Never Been To Spain'; Mink Deville 'Spanish Stroll'; Joni Mitchell 'Free Man In Paris'; Supergrass 'Road To Rouen'; Verve 'Monte Carlo'; Red Hot Chilli Peppers 'Venice Queen'; Rufus Wainwright 'Greek Song'; The Rakes 'Strasbourg'; Pavement 'Zurich Is Stained'; Elvis Costello 'Luxembourg', 'New Amsterdam'; Beautiful South 'Rotterdam (Or Anywhere); Scott Walker 'Copenhagen'; Al Stewart 'Night Train To Munich'; The Associates 'White Car In Germany'; Lou Reed 'Berlin'; Billy Joel 'Vienna'.**

SCANDINAVIA AND EASTERN EUROPE: Head to the Scandinavian countries and you really are in virgin territory for lyrics. Some ideas you might like to think about include deep fjords, snow, pine forests, wilderness, northern lights. Head east and, despite the changing political scene in those countries, your lyrics are likely to be entering Cold War and spy country.

> **Eliza Carthy 'Sweden'; David Bowie 'Warszawa'; Joy Division 'Warsaw'; Jethro Tull 'Budapest'; Matt Monroe 'From Russia With Love'; The Beatles 'Back In The USSR'; Sting 'Russians'; The Levellers 'Belaruse'; Al Stewart 'Roads To Moscow'; Blondie 'Contact In Red Square'.**

MIDDLE EAST: The popular song lyric has never been interested in the geo-political realities of the Middle East, preferring instead to conjure with visions of an older Arabia of camels, deserts, and the ancient monuments of Egypt.

> **The Police 'Tea In The Sahara'; Siouxsie And The Banshees 'Israel'; The Coral 'Arabian Sand'; Kate Bush 'Egypt'; Cure 'Fire In Cairo'; Bangles 'Walk Like An Egyptian'; The Teardrop Explodes 'Thief Of Baghdad'; Human League 'The Lebanon'; The Clash 'Rock The Casbah'.**

AFRICA: The humanitarian needs of the continent have meant that in lyrics (especially for charity songs) Africa is often the place of starvation, conflict and disease. It is also likely to bring political themes into focus, as was the case with apartheid in South Africa.

> **Toto 'Africa'; Bob Marley 'Africa Unite'; Gretchen Petersen 'Over Africa'; Roy Harper 'South Africa'; Bob Dylan 'Mozambique'; Billy Joel 'Zanzibar'; The Housemartins 'Johannesburg'; Kanye West 'Diamonds From Sierra Leone'; Peter Gabriel 'Biko'; Paul Simon 'Under African Skies'.**

FAR EAST: Lyrics about the Far East stress its apparent exoticism, with India and Tibet being the focus for imagined secret spiritual wisdom from the mid-1960s onwards.

> **Big Star 'The India Song'; Lawrence Welk 'Calcutta'; Led Zeppelin 'Kashmir'; Cat Stevens 'Katmandu'; David Bowie 'Seven Years In Tibet'; Tom Waits 'Singapore'; Babybird 'Hong Kong Blues'; Tom Waits 'Burma Shave'; Dead Kennedys 'Holiday In Cambodia'; Freddy Cannon 'One Night In Bangkok'; Deep Purple 'Woman From Tokyo'; Elvis Costello 'Tokyo Storm Warning'; Japan 'Visions Of China'; David Bowie 'China Girl'.**

PACIFIC: There seem to be very few lyrics about countries in the southern Pacific, perhaps reflecting their geographical isolation and remoteness from the experience of most pop musicians and their relative youth as countries compared to those that colonised them. With global warming we may yet hear a few more songs about the Antarctic.

> **Smashing Pumpkins 'Galapagos'; Moby Grape 'Omaha'; Men At Work 'Down Under'; Manic St Preachers 'Australia'; John Cale 'Antarctica Starts Here'; Al Stewart 'Antarctica'; Icehouse 'Great Southern Land'.**

Journeys

"Travelling is a big inspiration. Just being in motion, a train, a plane. As soon as I'm mobile I start to write things down, usually from the first line onwards ... If my opener doesn't work for the first verse, I usually move it to the end of the second verse." (Paul Heaton of The Beautiful South)117

Describe a journey and you can sketch a lyric by stating

- Where it started.
- Why it started.
- Where it's going.
- By what means you are travelling
- Where you are now.
- What this journey means to you.
- How long it might take.
- What needs to happen to get there.
- If you think you will make it.

That's plenty of stimulus for a lyric. In popular songs people have walked, cruised the freeways on bikes or in cars, hitch-hiked, jumped on trains, and taken jet-planes. (They have even been through deserts on horses that had no name!)

The road is a rich source of metaphor – you can turn the wrong way down a one-way street, or live life in the "fast lane". Life itself can be interpreted as a journey, with right turnings and wrong turnings, as in the Isley Brothers' 'The Highways Of My Life'.

ROAD SONGS: America 'Ventura Highway'; Deep Purple 'Highway Star'; Joni Mitchell 'Refuge Of The Roads'; Robert Johnson 'Crossroads'; Eagles 'Life In The Fast Lane'; Edwin Starr '25 Miles'; Tom Robinson Band '2-4-6-8 Motorway'; Pretenders '2000 Miles;' Lovin' Spoonful 'On The Road Again'; Robert Plant 'Big Log'; Talking Heads 'Road To Nowhere'; Tom Waits 'Wrong Side Of The Road'; Van Morrison 'Bright Side Of The Road'; Sheryl Crow 'Everyday Is A Winding Road', Jimi Hendrix 'Burning Of The Midnight Lamp'.

All that's required is to connect a term like "border" or "road" with an abstract noun like "love", "hope", "fear", "doubt", etc, as in a couplet like "I can't live this way any longer / In the borderland of doubt." These metaphors broaden out into geographical references such as borders and compass points in songs like Thin Lizzy's 'Borderline', Dire Straits' 'Southbound Again', Elton John's 'Border Song', Richard and Linda Thompson's 'When I Get To The Border', Little Feat's 'Down Below The Borderline', and ELO's 'Across The Border'.

There are many lyrics about life on the road, a topic close to the heart of touring musicians who spend much of their lives on the move from concert to concert – as Madonna sang in *Evita*, a matter of 'Another Suitcase In Another Hall'. The figure of the ever-travelling man (it usually is a man) is part of the folklore of song-lyrics.

TRAVELLERS: Jimi Hendrix 'Highway Chile'; Junior Walker And The All Stars '(I'm A) Road Runner'; Free 'Travelling Man'; Mountain 'Crossroader'; Dion 'The Wanderer'; The Who 'Going Mobile'; Bob Seger 'Travellin' Man'; Bonnie Raitt 'The Road's My Middle Name'; Roger Miller 'King Of The Road'; Boston 'Hitch A Ride'; Creedence Clearwater Revival 'Travellin' Band'.

TRAVELLING HOMEWARD

Lyrically, home is a 'hot-button' word – a concept that is emotive for most people. We become adults as we leave home, and there's no going back. A vast number of people at any given time are thinking about home, wanting to get back home, or making a home. The journey home and inward is the balance to all the journeys in popular song that go away and outward. Home might be a place, or be defined as something else, like a person; home can be in the country or the city. Sometimes these songs take on a certain death-longing about them, as the return home can be associated with a sense of spiritual exile from heaven. You can check for this when a lyric associates rest, stasis, nightfall, autumn, etc, with home.

Carole King 'Goin' Back'; The Beatles 'There's A Place'; 'The Long And Winding Road'; Simon and Garfunkel 'Homeward Bound'; Bruce Springsteen 'My Hometown'; Meredith Brooks 'My Little Town'; Rory Gallagher 'Going To My Home Town'; Ten Years After 'Going Home'; Slade 'Take Me Back 'Ome'; Andy Williams 'Home Lovin' Man'; Slim Whitman 'Home On The Range'.

Transport

"I buy the local papers every day, and they're full of car wrecks and ... I guess it all depends on what it is in the paper that attracts you. I'm always drawn to these terrible stories." (Tom Waits)[118]

Writing about people travelling can give your lyric drama and movement. When people go on journeys things can happen; they meet other people, they see new things, they have new thoughts and new feelings and so on. Springsteen once pointed out that he was less interested in cars than the people in the cars. So the question becomes which mode of transport.

CARS

Rock'n'roll and cars have been linked since Chuck Berry tunes like 'No Particular Place To Go' and 'Maybellene' celebrated the joys of being young and mobile. The birth of rock'n'roll in the 1950s coincided with a classic period of American car manufacture, when cars got bigger and more elaborately contoured, with chrome, fins and extravagant tail-lights. Chevrolets and pink Cadillacs are as much rock icons as blue-suede shoes or a guitar-shaped swimming pool. Specific brand names became significant:

Bruce Springsteen 'Cadillac Ranch'; The Clash 'Brand New Cadillac'; Hot Chocolate 'Heaven Is In The Back Seat Of My Cadillac'; Gene Vincent 'Pink Thunderbird'; Chuck Berry 'Jaguar And The Thunderbird'; Janis Joplin 'Mercedes Benz'; Commander Cody and His Lost Planet Airmen 'Hot Rod Lincoln'; Prince 'Little Red Corvette'; Wilson Pickett

'Mustang Sally'; Nanci Griffith 'Ford Econoline'; The Beach Boys 'Little Deuce Coupe'; 'Little Honda'; 1910 Fruitgum Company 'Firebird'; Bob Dylan 'From A Buick 6'.

If you didn't want to be specific, it didn't matter. The idea of the car was powerful enough:

The Rolling Stones 'Black Limousine'; Big Star 'Big Black Car'; Dan Seals 'My Old Yellow Car'; Kristina Olsen 'The Man With The Bright Red Car'; Bachman Turner Overdrive 'Four Wheel Drive'; Big Star 'Back Of A Car'; U2 'Fast Cars'; Beck 'Magic Stationwagon'; Gary Numan 'Cars'.

Most modern cars lack the same romance as their older forebears, and modern brands don't have the same glamour. Can you imagine writing a lyric about a gas-guzzling 4x4? In the age of global warming, driving a car is no longer be a gesture of rebellion.

In the USA in the affluent 1950s, a car was a teenager's easiest means to circumvent adult rules about who you saw and how much you saw of them. The car was a status symbol; learning to drive was an important rite of passage. As you earned more money you could buy a bigger car. A bigger car was a way of attracting girls. Racing cars was a way of proving your manhood, as in The Beach Boys' 'Don't Worry Baby'. The car was a place where you could live fast and die young. In reality, car wrecks claimed popular figures like Eddie Cochran, actress Jayne Mansfield, and actor James Dean.

Picking up the driving imagery, The Beatles wrote 'Drive My Car' and 'Day Tripper'. Rock stars are driven around in limos, a fact symbolised by Marc Bolan's reference to a Rolls-Royce in T.Rex's 'Children Of The Revolution'.

For a lyric, a car automatically evokes people, movement and new experiences, which amounts to the chance of something dramatic happening.

MOVING CARS: Gene 'A Car That Sped'; Joni Mitchell 'Car On A Hill'; Bruce Springsteen 'Stolen Car', 'Drive All Night'; Chuck Berry 'No Particular Place To Go'; Jimi Hendrix 'Crosstown Traffic'; Lucinda Williams 'Car Wheels On A Gravel Road'; Iggy Pop 'The Passenger'; Tracy Chapman 'Fast Car'.

Cars and driving provide a considerable source for smutty sexual metaphors. 'Drive My Car' and 'Mustang Sally' are relatively innocent examples, but Prince's 'Little Red Corvette' and Led Zeppelin's 'Trampled Underfoot' are bolder. The vocabulary of cars and driving lends itself to punning metaphors, as do many related words and concepts, as the following titles indicate.

ASSOCIATED IMAGES AND PHRASES: Meatloaf 'Paradise By The Dashboard Light'; Alice Cooper 'Under My Wheels'; Pearl Jam 'Rear View Mirror'; Go-Gos 'Skidmarks On My Heart'; Elvis Costello 'Five Gears In Reverse'; Jackson Browne 'Runnin' On Empty'; Mitchell 'Yellow Taxi'; Queen 'I'm In Love With My Car'; Dictators '(I Live For) Cars and Girls'; Prefab Sprout 'Cars and Girls'; Paul Simon 'Cars Are Cars'; Shania Twain 'In My Car (I'll Be The Driver)'.

Part of the drama of driving is the fact that things can go seriously wrong, and the appeal of the car and the open road can turn sour, as the following songs demonstrate.

Paul Anka 'Tell Laura I Love Her'; Jan and Dean 'Dead Man's Curve'; Shangri-Las 'The Leader Of The Pack', The Beatles 'A Day In The Life' (ought to have noticed that the lights had changed); Bruce Springsteen 'Racing In The Streets' (speeding in a residential area); David Bowie 'Always Crashing In The Same Car' (especially careless driving); Mungo Jerry 'In The Summertime' (doing 125mph!); Dave Edmunds 'Crawling From The Wreckage'; Soundgarden 'Limo Wreck'; Catatonia 'Road Rage'.

MOTORCYCLES AND BUSES

Motorcycles retain their rebel image, hence a recent band choosing the name Black Rebel Motorcycle Club and George Michael choosing to be photographed in a BSA jacket. Rockers in 1950s England and 1960s Hell's Angels are forever associated with rock music. The Vespa scooter, favourite vehicle for the Mods, has proved more appealing visually than in song. Truckers are also romanticised in popular song as outsiders.

Steppenwolf 'Born To Be Wild'; Bruce Springsteen 'Born To Run'; Chris Spedding 'Motor Bikin''; Iggy Pop 'Motorcycle'; Manic Street Preachers 'Motorcycle Emptiness'; Shangri-Las 'Leader Of The Pack'; Sinead O'Connor 'Black Boys On Mopeds'; Richard Thompson '1952 Vincent Black Lightning'; The Who 'Magic Bus'; The Beatles 'One After 909'; Count Five 'Double Decker Bus'; CW McCall 'Convoy'.

TRAINS

In lyrics, trains have different associations to cars. For a start, you don't own a train. You could even jump aboard without paying in the old days. Trains travel long distances so they are associated with the size of the continent of the USA. A train journey takes you far away from where you are or it separates you from someone you love. The most famous train in popular lyric is Elvis's 'Mystery Train' (sixteen coaches long), closely followed by Glen Miller's 'Chatanooga Choo-Choo'. There are thousands of train songs in blues and skiffle, like Bukka White's 'Panama Limited' and 'Special Streamline', or Lightnin' Slim's 'Mean Old Lonesome Train'. There seem to be far fewer lyrics about train stations. Simon And Garfunkel's 'Homeward Bound' is set at a railway station, and Wings 'Hi Hi Hi' starts at one.

Monkees 'Last Train To Clarksville'; Los Lobos 'The Train Don't Stop Here'; No Doubt 'Big City Train'; James Brown 'Night Train'; The Cure 'Jumping Someone Else's Train'; Jimi Hendrix 'Hear My Train A-Comin''; Clash 'Train In Vain'; Tiny Bradshaw 'The Train Kept A-Rollin'; Doobie Bros 'Long Train Runnin''; Elvis Presley 'Mystery Train'; Paul Simon 'Train In The Distance'; The The 'Slow Train To Dawn'; O'Jays 'Love Train'; Gladys Knight and The Pips 'Midnight Train To Georgia'; Ocean Colour Scene 'The Day We Caught The Train'.

BOATS AND PLANES

Travel by ship is far too luxurious and slow to fit in with the lyrics of the rock era.

If a lyric uses the image of a ship it is usually a metaphor and often unconsciously archaic (as in 'Sailing', with its boat on thoroughly allegorical "stormy waters". Ship travel for pleasure, as in a cruise, is linked to the first three decades of the 20th century. There are more lyrics referring to modern sea travel in songs of the 1920s-1940s.

Billy J. Kramer 'Trains And Boats And Planes'; Bebop Deluxe 'Ships In The Night'; Neil Young 'Cripple Creek Ferry'; The Beatles 'Yellow Submarine'; The Beach Boys 'Sloop John B.'; Rod Stewart 'Sailing'; Gordon Lightfoot 'The Wreck of the Edmund Fitzgerald'; Procol Harum 'Salty Dog'; Creedence 'Proud Mary'; The Doors 'The Crystal Ship'; CSN&Y 'Wooden Ships'.

In the late 20th century air travel took over as a means of getting across vast distances – but this does not seem to have inspired many songwriters.

Joni Mitchell 'This Flight Tonight'; The Byrds 'Eight Miles High'; John Denver 'Leaving On A Jet Plane'; Elton John 'Take Me To The Pilot'; John Sebastian 'Red Eye Express'; Roy Harper 'Twelve Hours Of Sunsets'; Nanci Griffith 'Outbound Plane'; Joni Mitchell 'Amelia'; The Rose Garden 'Next Plane To London'; The Motors 'Airport'; Frank Sinatra 'Come Fly With Me'.

Crime and punishment

Popular music has always loved the outsider (it is itself an 'outsider' from the world of high art). The past 50 years of music are rooted in rock'n'roll, a teenager's music, and teenagers are self-defined as outsiders, belonging neither to the adult world nor that of children. So the criminal as an outsider becomes something of a heroic figure. Guns, murders, love triangles, fires, riots all provide vivid dramatic material for song-lyrics. They also provide dramatic images and metaphors for other types of song. Few metaphors are as 'arresting' as that of a gun or gangster, as with the Steve Miller Band's metaphorical 'Gangster Of Love'.

The general rules for committing homicide in a lyric appear to be: first, if your woman is unfaithful shoot first and ask questions later; second, make sure you have someone to tell it to; and three, be close enough to the border to make a getaway to Mexico. If you do get caught, deliver an eve-of-execution confession detailing how much you loved her, or how she done you wrong, or how you just couldn't take it (anymore). Needless to say, rap and hip-hop have built a whole genre on antisocial lyrics about crime, guns, homicides, car-theft and domestic violence.

Homicide and firearms in lyrics mean the drama and tension of life and death situations :

Jimi Hendrix 'Hey Joe'; Queen 'Bohemian Rhapsody'; Dave Dee Dozy Beaky Mick and Tich 'Last Night In Soho'; Tom Jones 'Green Green Grass Of Home'; Eric Clapton 'I Shot The Sheriff' (but the defendant pleads not guilty to shooting the deputy); Elvis Costello 'Shot With His Own Gun'; Boomtown Rats 'I Don't Like Mondays'; Body Count 'Cop Killer'; Ice T 'Six In The Morning'; Clash 'Guns On The Roof'; Black Rebel Motorcycle Club 'Six Barrel Shot Gun'; ZZ Top 'Six Shooter'.

Grievous bodily harm, rape, and affray are generally treated from the view of the victim, unless the victim has turned into the representative of a despised social order:

The Jam 'Down In The Tube Station At Midnight'; The Prodigy 'Smack My Bitch Up'; Tori Amos 'Me And A Gun'; Nirvana 'Rape Me'; Eurythmics 'Sex Crime 1984'; The Smiths 'I Started Something That I Just Couldn't Finish'; The Clash 'White Riot'; Bobby Fuller Four 'I Fought The Law'; The Rolling Stones 'Street Fighting Man'; Kaiser Chiefs 'I Predict A Riot'.

A small number of lyrics deal with child abuse and bullying. Great skill and sensitivity is required of the lyric writer in handling such topics:

Siouxsie and The Banshees 'Candyman'; Suzanne Vega 'Luka'; The Mission 'Amelia'; Pearl Jam 'Jeremy'; The Who 'Fiddle About'; 'I'm A Boy'; Tasmin Archer 'In Your Care'; Loudon Wainwright 'Hitting You'.

Arson and explosives in lyrics also mean high drama. Fire will often feature in a social/political context of unrest:

Jimi Hendrix 'House Burning Down'; Elton John 'Burn Down The Mission'; The Jam 'Funeral Pyre'; The Prodigy 'Firestarter'; The Ruts 'Babylon Is Burning'; Siouxsie And The Banshees 'Burn The House Down'; Public Enemy 'Burn Hollywood Burn'; Green Day 'Letterbomb'; Mothers Of Invention 'Trouble Every Day (The Watts Riot Song)'; Stiff Little Fingers 'Suspect Device'.

Robbery and petty damage in lyrics are sometimes connected with teenage frustration and minor brushes with the law:

Kate Bush 'There Goes A Tenner'; Clash 'Bank Robber'; Georgie Fame 'Ballad Of Bonnie And Clyde'; The Smiths 'Shoplifters Of The World Unite'; The Slits 'Shoplifters'; U2 'I Threw A Brick Through A Window'; Nick Lowe 'I Love The Sound Of Breaking Glass'; Arctic Monkeys 'Riot Van'.

Illegal substances feature in many lyrics as a potent symbol of counter-culture values, of living by different rules to the norm. The drug featured will vary from youth cult to youth cult, from one age to another. There are also cautionary tales about the damage caused by drug use:

Supergrass 'Caught By The Fuzz'; Thin Lizzy 'Opium Trail'; Eels 'Novacaine For The Soul'; The Beatles 'What's The New, Mary Jane?'; Velvet Underground 'Heroin'; J.J. Cale 'Cocaine'; Queens Of The Stone Age 'Feel Good Hit Of The Summer'; The Rolling Stones 'Sister Morphine'; Black Sabbath 'Sweet Leaf'; Ramones 'Now I Wanna Sniff Some Glue'; Neil Young 'The Needle And The Damage Done'; Grandmaster Melle Mel 'White Lines (Don't Do It)'.

Courts, judges and jail are taken as the embodiment of a social order which the rebel may be challenging. Less frequently they will be seen as bulwarks against chaos. The jail break-out offers dramatic story-telling possibilities.

Shorty Long 'Here Comes The Judge'; 10cc 'Good Morning Judge'; Travis 'Re-Offender'; Thin Lizzy 'Jailbreak'; 10cc

'Rubber Bullets'; Elvis Presley 'Jailhouse Rock'; Sham 69 'Borstal Break-out'; Coolio 'Gangsta's Paradise'; The Offspring 'When You're In Prison'; Blind Lemon Jefferson 'Prison Cell Blues'; Johnny Cash '25 Minutes To Go'; The Adverts 'Gary Gilmore's Eyes'; Dr Feelgood 'Riot In Cell Black #9'; Motorhead 'Jailbait'.

Lyrics have also been spun round the related figures of the sheriff, the policeman, and the private detective. The sheriff (may not be available outside the US) is often a positive figure, the policeman is usually reviled, and the detective has a seedy glamour.

Clash 'Police and Thieves'; Charley Patton 'High Sheriff Blues'; Cypress Hill 'Looking Through The Eye Of A Pig'; Asian Dub Foundation 'Officer XX'; Everything But The Girl 'Good Cop Bad Cop'; The Strokes 'New York City Cops'; Bruce Springsteen 'Highway Patrolman', 'American Skin (41 Shots)'; Dire Straits 'Private Investigations'; Elvis Costello 'Watching The Detectives'.

Time past and memory

When it comes to arousing emotions in the listener, there are few more potent words than "yesterday". Memory, reflections on how things used to be, old selves, past lovers – everything to do with time past is a rich subject area for lyrics. Such themes speak of universal concerns with being young, being old, maturing; with looking forward and back. This normal facet of human life is stimulated and exacerbated by the pace of modern life, the way familiar objects, activities, fashions, ways of doing things, the very buildings of our towns and cities, change seemingly before our eyes.

These emotions are so strong that they can stop people hearing the real intent of a lyric. The Beatles 'In My Life' is often heard simply as a lament for the past, when actually the song's emotional calculations come out in favour of the present.

The challenge for a lyric writer is to avoid easy nostalgia (as the joke goes, even nostalgia isn't what it used to be). A more interesting lyric about the past will balance its attractions with genuinely good things about today. If you want a bittersweet combination of golden past with happy present listen to a song like Love Affair's 'Bring On Back The Good Times', where past joys thought lost are experienced more sharply as they are recovered in the present.

Stevie Wonder 'Yester-me, Yester-you, Yesterday'; The Beatles 'Yesterday'; Gene Pitney 'That Girl Belongs To Yesterday'; Four Tops 'Yesterday's Dreams'; Simply Red 'Holding Back The Years'; Led Zeppelin 'Ten Years Gone'; Diana Ross 'Remember Me'; Mary Hopkin 'Those Were The Days'; Jethro Tull 'Living In The Past'; Sting 'Fields Of Gold'; The Faces 'Love Lived Here'; Dean Martin 'Memories Are Made Of This'; Barbara Streisand 'The Way We Were'; The Byrds 'My Back Pages'; Love Affair 'Bring On Back The Good Times'.

Historical dates

You might also consider writing a lyric about a recent historical event. These could form the subject of a song, or provide the backdrop for a personal experience (there is more about historical themes further on). Here are some titles that relate to a date, place and/or event, imagined or real, in the past 50 years.

The Police 'Born In The 50s'; Morrissey 'Munich Air Disaster 1958'; Four Seasons 'December 1963 (Oh What A Night)'; Family 'Summer 67'; The Stooges, The Vines '1969'; Bryan Adams 'Summer of '69'; The Stooges '1970'; The Connells '74-75'; Wayne County And The Backstreet Boys 'Max's Kansas City 1976'; The Clash '1977'; Smashing Pumpkins '1979'; Simple Minds 'New Gold Dream (81-82-83-84)'; Van Halen '1984'; Manic Street Preachers '1985'; Travis 'Tied To The 90s'; Blur '1992'; Pulp 'Disco 2000'.

Alternatively, focus on a historical event that interests you and is felt to be significant. Again, the challenge is to describe it in a compressed way. The chorus of such a song is where to state what it is that matters about the event. Leave the verses for narrating the story. The bridge can also be used as a place where deductions can be made about the event's significance. A lyric can only be a snapshot of a big event, but snapshots can be memorable. Consider the imaginative power of a song like The Band's 'The Night They Drove Ol' Dixie Down'.

DATED EVENTS: Randy Newman 'Dayton, Ohio 1903'; Al Stewart 'Somewhere In England, 1915', 'Laughing Into 1939'; David Bowie '1917'; John Cale 'Paris 1919'; The Who '1921'; Randy Newman 'Louisiana 1927'; Aimee Mann 'Fifty Years After The Fair' (alludes to New York World's Fair of 1939); Bee Gees 'New York Mining Disaster 1941'.

Childhood, youth and school

Popular music is associated with youth, so it contains a huge number of songs about being young, growing up, clashing with authority figures, feeling confused, struggling with identity, and negotiating the rites of adolescence. The innocence of childhood (children's voices on records almost always signify innocence) is itself an important theme:

Brian Wilson 'Child Is Father of the Man'; Billy J. Kramer 'Little Children'; Tyrannosaurus Rex 'Child Star'; Page and Plant 'When I Was A Child'; Madonna 'Dear Jessie'; 'This Used To Be My Playground'; CSN&Y 'Teach Your Children'; R.E.M. 'The Wrong Child'; Neil Young 'I Am A Child'; Siouxsie And The Banshees 'Playground Twist'.

Where there are children there must be parents, and such relationships can be written about from both ends:

Bruce Springsteen 'Independence Day'; Cat Stevens 'Father and Son'; Queen 'Father To Son'; The Beatles 'She's Leaving Home'; Paul Simon 'Mother And Child Reunion'; Gilbert O'Sullivan 'We Will'; Manfred Mann 'My Name Is Jack'; Tori Amos 'Winter'; Kate Bush 'Mother Stands For Comfort'; David Bowie 'The Bewlay Brothers'; Madonna 'Papa Don't Preach'; John Lennon 'Mother'.

There is the subject of the sexual awakening of teen years, sometimes celebrated by those who would like to take advantage of it:

Yardbirds 'Good Morning Little Schoolgirl'; The Knack 'My Sharona'; Neil Sedaka 'Happy Birthday Sweet Sixteen'; Johnny Burnette 'You're Sixteen'; Undertones 'Teenage Kicks'; MC5 'Teenage Lust'; Ramones 'Teenage Lobotomy'; Flamin' Groovies 'Teenage Head'; Wheatus 'Teenage Dirtbag'; Tori Amos 'These Precious Things'.

Conflict with parents, authority figures, and alienation from society (or what the adolescent imagines as 'society') is often expressed in an anthem for the current teenage generation:

> **The Sweet 'Teenage Rampage'; The Who 'The Kids Are Alright'; 'My Generation'; Nirvana 'Smells Like Teen Spirit'; Mott The Hoople 'All The Young Dudes'; Alice Cooper 'Generation Landslide'; T.Rex 'Children of the Revolution'; Lovin' Spoonful 'Younger Generation'; Eddie Cochran 'Summertime Blues'; Richard Hell And The Voidoids 'I Belong To The Blank Generation'; Bob Dylan 'The Times They Are A-Changing'; Dion And The Belmonts 'Lonely Teenager'; Frankie Lymon And The Teenagers 'I'm Not A Juvenile Delinquent'.**

If you've left school, write a lyric about schooldays. If you're still at school write about some of your experiences there, good and bad. Write about what it feels like to be away from school in the holiday. Write about what it will be like to leave forever.

There are a fund of songs about school and its timetables and the joy (expressed with joyful recklessness in David Bowie's 'Kooks') of chucking away homework and going out instead. There seem to be far fewer university songs.

> **Supertramp 'School'; Alice Cooper 'School's Out'; Chuck Berry 'School Day (Ring Ring Goes The Bell!)'; Jerry Lee Lewis 'High School Confidential'; Madness 'Baggy Trousers'; Pink Floyd 'Another Brick In The Wall'; The Darkness 'Friday Night'; Janis Ian 'At Seventeen'; Bruce Springsteen 'Growing Up'; X-Ray Spex 'Germ-Free Adolescents'; The Beach Boys 'Be True To Your School'; The Jam 'When You're Young'; Boomtown Rats 'Mary Of The Fourth Form'; Adverts 'Bored Teenagers'; Marty Wilde 'Why Must I Be A Teenager In Love?'**

Think of a childhood experience, good or bad, and write about it. How typical do you think it might be of many people's experiences?

Time present

> **"He [Berry Gordy, head of Motown] told me to 'never write a song like it's past, always write a song like it's happening right now so people can associate with it.' So when I decided to write 'You've made me so very happy', I said 'he's making me happy now' even though I was very sad because I had a bad love affair, a boyfriend that walked out on me. So I said 'I'm gonna write a song like this is the happiest day of my life'." (Brenda Holloway)[119]**

Since popular music likes to be fashionable and of the moment, there are plenty of songs with the word "modern" in the title. These include The Jam's 'This Is The Modern World', David Bowie's 'Modern Love', Bloc Party's 'This Modern Love', Black Mountain's 'Modern Music', The Strokes' 'The Modern Age', and Sheena Easton's 'Modern Girl'. Other songs which celebrate the moment are Madonna 'Holiday', Bruce Springsteen 'Better Days', The Beach Boys' 'Here Today', Smashing Pumpkins' and Jefferson Airplane's 'Today', Bryan Adams' 'On A Day Like Today', Aimee Mann's 'Today's The Day', Kate Bush's 'Moments Of Pleasure', Roy Harper's 'Frozen Moment', Lovin' Spoonful's 'Daydream', and Fat Boy Slim's 'Right Here, Right Now'.

Time present can also be summed up in expanded form as a lyric about whatever is happening today:

> **Kinks 'Days'; Lou Reed 'Perfect Day'; Badfinger 'Day After Day'; Haircut 100 'Fantastic Day'; Bill Withers 'Lovely Day'; Talking Heads 'Happy Day'; The Cure 'In Between Days'; Mariah Carey 'One Sweet Day'; U2 'Beautiful Day'; Altered Images 'Happy Birthday'; The Beatles 'Birthday'; 'Stevie Wonder 'Happy Birthday'.**

Divisions of the day

Many lyrics describe something happening at a particular time of day, or what that time of day suggests by way of a mood. Each portion of the day is associated in song lyrics with a variety of activities. The Moody Blues' concept album *Days Of Future Passed* actually went all the way through a single day in songs and instrumentals. Kate Bush's *Aerial* has a nine-song suite that extends over a day. Roger Waters' *The Pros and Cons of Hitch-Hiking* has a number of parts, each of which are titled a couple of minutes apart between four and five in the morning. Chuck Berry's 'Reelin' and Rockin' relates events as the hours go by, and Bill Haley used the clock as a structuring device in 'Rock Around The Clock'.

> **DAWN AND EARLY MORNING: Rolf Harris 'Sun Arise'; Cream 'Sunshine Of Your Love'; Eagles 'Tequila Sunrise'; The Supremes 'Here Comes The Sunrise'; Bette Midler 'Delta Dawn'; Boo Radleys 'Wake Up Boo'; Wham! 'Wake Me Up Before You Go Go'; The Blue Nile '7am'; Peter Paul And Mary 'Early In The Morning'; The Four Seasons 'Early In The Morning; Peter, Paul and Mary 'Early Morning Rain'.**

> **MORNING: The Rascals 'Beautiful Morning'; Joni Mitchell 'Chelsea Morning'; The Beatles 'Good Day Sunshine'; Nick Drake 'From The Morning'; Monkees 'Sometime In The Morning'; Verve 'Velvet Morning'; Free 'Come Together In The Morning'; Bob Dylan 'Meet Me In The Morning'; Diana Ross 'Touch Me In The Morning'; Dusty Springfield 'Breakfast In Bed'.**

> **AFTERNOON: Kinks 'Sunny Afternoon'; Starland Vocal Band 'Afternoon Delight'; Small Faces 'Lazy Sunday Afternoon'; Supergrass 'Late In The Day'.**

> **TWILIGHT AND SUNSET: Roy Harper 'Twelve Hours Of Sunsets'; Elton John 'Don't Let The Sun Go Down On Me'; Kinks 'Waterloo Sunset'; Sting 'Lithium Sunset'; Nick Drake 'Day Is Done'; Thin Lizzy 'The Sun Goes Down'; Fleetwood Mac 'When The Sun Goes Down'; Chemical Brothers 'Setting Sun'; Gordon Lightfoot 'Sundown'.**

Night-time is the most frequently cited time because of its associations with adventure, going out, mystery, excitement, socializing, dancing, seducing, and making love.

> **EVENING AND DARKNESS: Patti Smith 'Because The Night'; Bruce Springsteen 'Spirit In The Night'; Moody Blues 'Nights In White Satin'; Lionel Ritchie 'All Night Long'; The Police 'Bring On The Night'; Paul Simon 'Late In The Evening'; Them 'Here Comes The Night'; The Doors 'End Of The Night'; R.E.M. 'Nightswimming'; Phil Collins 'In The Air Tonight'; Bobby Vee 'The Night Has A Thousand Eyes'; Frank Sinatra 'Strangers In The Night'.**

MIDNIGHT: The Rolling Stones 'Moonlight Mile'; Wilson Pickett 'In The Midnight Hour'; Eric Clapton 'After Midnight'; The Stargazers 'I See The Moon'; Jimi Hendrix 'Burning Of The Midnight Lamp'; Monkees 'Midnight Train'; Ocean Colour Scene '40 Past Midnight'; Blondie '11:59'; David Gray 'A New Day At Midnight'; Howlin' Wolf 'Moanin' At Midnight'.

EARLY HOURS: Busted '3am'; Gene 'Sleep Well Tonight'; My Bloody Valentine 'When You Sleep'; Pretenders 'I Go To Sleep'; KLF '3 am Eternal'; Frank Sinatra 'In The Wee Small Hours Of The Morning'; Boo Radleys '4am Conversation'; The Strokes '12:51'; Gary U.S. Bonds 'Quarter To Three'; Skip James '4'O Clock Blues'; Johnny Winter 'Five After Four A.M.'; Judy Tzuke 'Stay With Me Till Dawn'.

Days of the week

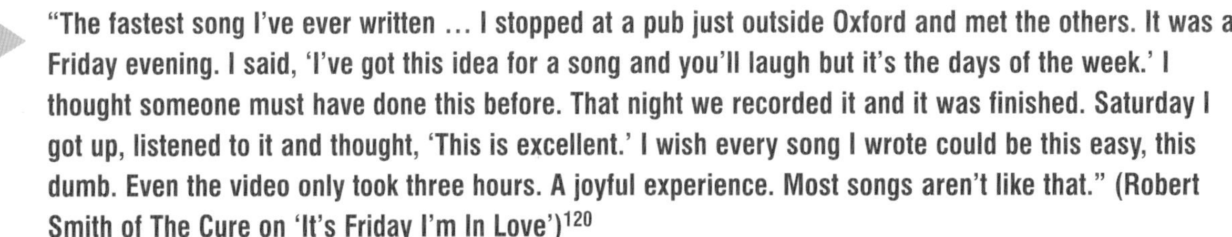

"The fastest song I've ever written … I stopped at a pub just outside Oxford and met the others. It was a Friday evening. I said, 'I've got this idea for a song and you'll laugh but it's the days of the week.' I thought someone must have done this before. That night we recorded it and it was finished. Saturday I got up, listened to it and thought, 'This is excellent.' I wish every song I wrote could be this easy, this dumb. Even the video only took three hours. A joyful experience. Most songs aren't like that." (Robert Smith of The Cure on 'It's Friday I'm In Love')[120]

"It leans very heavily on fairy tales, especially the macabre ones that seem very innocent when you're little, but as you get older, the real meanings come out. It's got the Red Riding Hood figure in there, and these three characters that are basically part of the same person – the Monday, the Tuesday and the Sunday person. And they go through a bit of a mess in the song … They can only really function when they're all part of the same thing and, at the end of the song, they all come together. When they're not in sync, the person isn't functioning or happening at all." (Julianne Regan of All About Eve on 'Tuesday's Child')[121]

Choose a day of the week. What associations does it have for you? Are these based on something that happened to you on that day? Do you associate a certain day with a memory, a happy or sad occasion, a mood, an activity? Develop a lyric from this idea. In most lyrics the days around the weekend have strong associations relating to work, leisure time, and socialising. To write a song about a day in the week some writers have drawn on the proverb about children born on the various days:

Monday's child is fair of face
Tuesday's child is full of grace
Wednesday's child is full of woe
Thursday's child has far to go
Friday's child is loving and giving
Saturday's child works hard for its living
And the child that's born on the Sabbath day
Is fair and wise and good and gay

(Note that "gay" here means "happy and joyful".) There is a less well-known rhyme about which day of the week to hold a wedding:

Monday for wealth, Tuesday for health,
Wednesday the best day of all;
Thursday for crosses, Friday for losses
Saturday no luck at all.

A lyric can be structured around the seven days, as was done by The Cure in 'Friday I'm In Love', U2's 'Some Days Are Better Than Others', Sting's 'Seven Days', Craig David's '7 Days', and Etta James 'Seven Day Fool'.

MONDAY is often dreary and no fun because it's the return-to-work day; "blue Monday' is something of a cliché.

Bangles 'Manic Monday'; Mamas and Papas 'Monday Monday'; Boomtown Rats 'I Don't Like Mondays'; Carpenters 'Rainy Days And Mondays'; Fleetwood Mac 'Monday Morning'; T-Bone Walker 'Stormy Monday'; Bobby Bland 'Stormy Monday Blues'; Fats Domino 'Blue Monday'; Nick Heyward 'Atlantic Monday'; Marillion 'Chelsea Monday'; Janis Ian 'Might As Well Be Monday'.

TUESDAY has moderate appeal as the day after Monday if there has been an adjustment back into the working week.

All About Eve 'Tuesday's Child'; Moody Blues 'Tuesday Afternoon'; Chairmen of the Board 'Everything's Tuesday'; Melanie 'Ruby Tuesday'; David Bowie 'Love You Till Tuesday'; Kristin Hersh 'Tuesday Night'; Stone Temple Pilots 'Church Of Tuesday'; Cat Stevens 'Tuesday's Dead'; Eliza Carthy 'Tuesday Morning'; Cowboy Junkies 'Sun Comes Up; It's Tuesday Morning'.

WEDNESDAY AND THURSDAY have hardly registered in lyrics.

Simon and Garfunkel 'Wednesday Morning 3 a.m.'; Tori Amos 'Wednesday'; Undertones 'Wednesday Week'; Self 'Wednesday Again'; Lisa Loeb and Nine Stories 'Waiting For Wednesday'; John Lee Hooker 'Wednesday Evening'; Hey Mercedes 'Our Weekend Starts On Wednesday'.

David Bowie 'Thursday's Child'; Cat Stevens 'Sweet Thursday'; Jim Croce 'Thursday'; Townes Van Zandt 'Like A Summer Thursday'; The Hollies '10:15 Thursday Morning'; Morphine 'Thursday'; The Millennium 'To Claudia On Thursday'.

FRIDAY is happy because it's the end of the week, it's a going-out night, and probably no homework if you're at school.

The Cure 'It's Friday, I'm In Love'; The Darkness 'Friday Night'; The Easybeats 'Friday On My Mind'; The Specials 'Friday Night Saturday Morning'; Will Young 'Friday's Child'; Love and Kisses 'Thank God It's Friday'; Paul Weller 'Friday Street'; David Ackles 'Another Friday Night'; Van Morrison 'Friday's Child'; Steely Dan 'Black Friday'; Joe Jackson 'Friday'.

SATURDAY is shopping, socializing, and Saturday night can mean a raucous party, a dancing late-nighter, or a punch-up.

> **Elton John 'Saturday Night's All Right For Fighting'; The Drifters 'Saturday Night At The Movies'; David Bowie 'Drive-in Saturday'; Nick Drake 'Saturday Sun'; Monkees 'Saturday's Child'; Graham Parker 'Saturday Nite Is Dead'; Chicago 'Saturday In The Park'; Sam Cooke 'Another Saturday Night'; Nils Lofgren 'One More Saturday Night'; Suede 'Saturday Night'; The Eels 'Saturday Morning'; Eddie Cochran 'Weekend'.**

SUNDAY morning is lying in, possibly church-going (though not often in popular lyrics); Sunday evening is calm and reflective.

> **Small Faces 'Lazy Sunday'; Monkees 'Pleasant Valley Sunday'; Morrissey 'Every Day Is Like Sunday'; Velvet Underground 'Sunday Morning'; Lionel Ritchie 'Easy Like Sunday Morning'; Elvis Costello 'Sunday's Best'; Blondie 'Sunday Girl'; The Shirelles 'I Met Him On A Sunday'; The Doobie Brothers 'Another Park, Another Sunday'; The Harptones 'A Sunday Kind Of Love'; Rain Tree Crow 'A Reassuringly Dull Sunday'.**

Seasons and months

Think about the months of the year, which in turn represent the seasons with their rich symbolic overtones of birth, growth, maturity, decay and death. Traditionally in the northern hemisphere spring is March-April-May, summer is June-July-August, autumn (Fall) is September, October, November, winter is December-January-February (allowing for where you live and the impact of global warming). Crowded House offered the metaphor of 'Four Seasons In One Day'. Needless to say, the most popular season for lyrics is summer, because as The Beach Boys put it, 'Summer Means New Love'. Here are some seasonal songs:

> **SPRING: Pentangle 'Springtime Promises'; Mel Brooks 'Springtime For Hitler'; Black Crowes 'The Colour of Spring'; Judy Collins 'So Early, Early In The Spring'; The Go-Betweens 'Spring Rain'.**

> **SUMMER: Mungo Jerry 'In The Summertime'; The Temptations 'It's Summer'; Style Council 'Long Hot Summer'; Lovin' Spoonful 'Summer In The City'; All About Eve 'Our Summer'; Jimi Hendrix 'Long Hot Summer Night'; Eddie Cochran 'Summertime Blues'; Cliff Richard 'Summer Holiday'; Marshall Crenshaw 'Starless Summer Sky'; The Beach Boys 'All Summer Long'; Don Henley 'The Boys Of Summer'.**

> **AUTUMN: Siouxsie And The Banshees 'Halloween'; Justin Hayward 'Forever Autumn'; Roger Williams 'Autumn Leaves'; The Vines 'Autumn Shade'; Peter Paul And Mary 'Autumn To May'; Procol Harum 'In The Autumn Of My Madness'; Francoise Hardy 'Autumn Rendez-vous'.**

> **WINTER: Simon and Garfunkel 'Hazy Shade of Winter'; Tori Amos 'Winter'; Tyrannosaurus Rex 'The Throat Of Winter'; The Doors 'Winter Love'; Darlene Love 'Winter Wonderland'; Leonard Cohen 'Winter Lady'; Aztec Camera 'Walk Out To Winter'; Queen 'A Winter's Tale'.**

Some of the characteristics attributed to seasons can be also associated with the appropriate months. For ideas, think also of special days that fall in certain months – Valentine's Day (February), April Fool's Day, Easter (April), Independence Day (July), Halloween (October), Guy Fawkes Night and Thanksgiving (November), Christmas (December), all of which could figure in a lyric. I have deliberately excluded Christmas songs (there are too many) but if you want to investigate them start with the Phil Spector-produced album *A Christmas Gift To You*.

Here are songs using a month in the title – with the exception of March as no-one seems to set lyrics in March.

JANUARY AND FEBRUARY: Pilot 'January'; U2 'New Year's Day'; Lindisfarne 'January Song'; Abba 'Happy New Year'; Tori Amos 'Black Dove (January)'; David Gray 'January Rain'; Jeff Buckley 'New Year's Prayer'; The Breeders 'New Year'; Frank Sinatra 'June In January'; Cole Porter 'My Lovely Valentine'; ABC 'Valentine's Day'; Paul McCartney 'Valentine Day'; Lou Reed 'Christmas In February'; Foo Fighters 'February Stars'; Billy Bragg 'Valentine's Day Is Over'; 'The Fourteenth Of February; Oleander 'February Son'.

APRIL: Simon and Garfunkel 'April Come She Will'; Pat Boone 'April Love'; Oysterband '20th Of April'; Jesus and Mary Chain 'April Skies'; Al Jolson 'April Showers'; Prince 'Sometimes It Snows In April'; The Associates 'Tell Me Easter's On Friday'; Black Crowes 'Good Friday'; Ron Sexsmith 'April After All'; Loudon Wainwright III 'Fool's Day Morn'.

MAY AND JUNE: The Bee Gees 'First Of May'; Blue Oyster Cult 'Then Came The Last Days Of May'; Tremoloes 'May Morning'; B52s 'June Bug'; Kinks 'Rainy Day In June'; Jamiroquai 'Seven Days In Sunny June'; Heather Nova 'One Day In June'; The Wannadies 'Love In June'; The Minutemen 'June 16th'.

JULY AND AUGUST: Bruce Springsteen '4th Of July Asbury Park'; Stevie Wonder 'Hotter Than July'; Aimee Mann '4th Of July'; Ocean Colour Scene 'July'; Uriah Heep 'July Morning'; Neil Diamond 'Hot August Night'; Clapton 'August'; Love 'August'; Funkadelic 'Friday Night, August 14th'; Counting Crows 'August And Everything After'.

SEPTEMBER AND OCTOBER: Carole King 'It Might As Well Rain Until September'; Earth, Wind and Fire 'September'; Big Star 'September Gurls'; Green Day 'Wake Me Up When September Ends'; Neil Diamond 'September Morn'; Kurt Weill and Maxwell Anderson 'September Song'; XTC 'Harvest Festival'; Incredible String Band 'October Song'; Amy Winehouse 'October Song'; U2 'October'; Pet Shop Boys 'My October Symphony'.

NOVEMBER AND DECEMBER: Guns and Roses 'November Rain'; Sandy Denny 'Late November'; Gorillaz 'November Has Come'; The National 'Mr November'; Morrissey 'November Spawned A Monster'; David Gray 'December'; Wendy and Lisa 'I Think It Was December'; Edie Brickell 'Air Of December'; Counting Crows 'A Long December'; Everything But The Girl '25th December'; Roberta Flack 'The 25th Of Last December'; The Who 'Christmas'; John Lennon 'Happy Xmas (War Is Over)'.

Time future: dystopias, space, aliens

"Dreams are all the promises of the future that never seem to get here." (Jim White)[122]

Another potentially interesting subject area is the future. This extends from short-term to long-term, and from personal to collective. Future songs at their simplest mean the lyric idea "I'm so looking forward to seeing Marsha (or Bill) on Friday night" (which happens to be tomorrow), or a sense of romantic foreboding, as in Marvin Gaye's 'I Heard It Through The Grapevine'. People in love songs swear they will love each other until mountains crumble into the sea (see Ben E. King), rivers dry up and stars fall out of the sky. The end of the world thus becomes an image for romantic loss. This long-vision leads to titles like 'Forever And A Day' and paradoxes like The Moody Blues *Days Of Future Passed*.

TOMORROW TITLES: Monkees 'Look Out Here Comes Tomorrow'; The Beatles 'Tomorrow Never Knows'; Sheryl Crow 'Tomorrow Never Dies'; Badfinger 'Maybe Tomorrow'; Shirelles 'Will You Still Love Me Tomorrow'; Carpenters 'Our Day Will Come'; The Chiffons 'One Fine Day'; Aqualung 'Good Times Gonna Come'.

At the furthest reach, there are lyrics about humanity and life in the distant future, including King Crimson's '21st Century Schizoid Man', Zager and Evans' 'In The Year 2525', Barry MacGuire's 'Eve Of Destruction' and The Fifth Dimension's 'Aquarius'. Future lyrics can be personal - projecting an optimistic vision for lovers into the immediate future - or about society – a utopia. If the vision is of a world gone wrong, the lyric is a dystopia. A lyric about a dystopia is usually by default a protest song. David Bowie has written more visions of the future than most, including 'The Man Who Sold The World', 'Five Years', 'Drive-in Saturday', 'Diamond Dogs', 'Aladdin Sane', and others. If you write a song about a specific year in the future you might live to see it pass by, which in turn will affect the meaning of the lyric. The notorious 1984 didn't turn out quite so bad after all. Such songs include Jimi Hendrix's '1983', David Bowie's '1984', Wings' 'Nineteen Hundred and Eighty-Five', Jamiroquai's 'Revolution 1993', and Prince's '1999'.

The development of rockets and space exploration in the 1950s and 1960s, coupled with the popularity of outer space science fiction, T.V. series and cinema films, and the phenomenon of UFO sightings, resulted in a number of songs about aliens and spaceships.

SPACE AND ALIENS: David Bowie 'Space Oddity'; 'Life On Mars'; T.Rex 'The Visit'; 'Planet Queen'; Graham Parker 'Waiting For The UFOs'; Goldfinger 'Girl From Mars'; Neil Young 'After The Goldrush'; Blue Oyster Cult 'E.T.I. (Extra Terrestrial Intelligence)'; Stackridge 'Purple Spaceships Over Yatton'; Jimi Hendrix 'House Burning Down'; 'Third Stone From The Sun'; The Byrds 'Mr Spaceman'; Peter and Gordon 'Everyone's Gone To The Moon', Elton John 'Rocket Man', Queen '39'.

Smart answers: parody, response

"... I get fed up with the alternative/indie world ... They're so sombre. They have no time for humour. They can't get above themselves – they're so clearly trapped in themselves that nothing is funny.

They're in pain, and that's their universe, and that's what they want the world to pay for." (Liz Phair)[123]

" … I was criticised terribly for writing novelty songs; people were very snobbish. Although there was a tradition of humour in folk, it was exorcised in the '60s. 'Ugh, go away funny man,' they said." (Loudon Wainwright)[124]

"For me one of the greatest lyricists of all time is George Formby. His more obscure songs are so hilarious, the language was so flat and Lancastrian and always focused on domestic things. Not academically funny, not witty, just morosely humorous, and that really appealed to me." (Morrissey 1984)[125]

"I don't really like a lot of bands who write lyrics about themselves all the time, wallowing in self-pity. You've gotta laugh at yourself as well. If you don't do it all comes across too melodramatic and over the top. People don't believe it." (Kelly Jones of The Stereophonics)[126]

One way to start a lyric is to write a 'smart answer' to another. Shaping a response to the original gets you going on one of your own.

The response can take various forms. This could be a witty adjustment to a title, or an extended engagement with the source material. The former might not carry through into the song's meaning and theme; it could just be an eye-catching title.

If I write a song called 'I Want To Hold Your Head' people would relate it to The Beatles' 'I Want To Hold Your Hand', but the lyric might not take the allusion any further. What you need is an eye for a pun or a similarity of wording, for how a word changes if one letter is altered, or if a phrase is inverted, as with Joni Mitchell's 'The Pirate Of Penance' (*The Pirates Of Penzance*) or Public Enemy's 'Rebel Without A Pause' (*Rebel Without A Cause*).

Freak Power 'Turn On; Tune In; Cop Out' (1960s slogan 'turn on; tune in; drop out'); Carter The Unstoppable Sex Machine '101 Damnations' (*101 Dalmatians*); The Hives 'Abra Cadaver' (abracadabra); Badly Drawn Boy 'Everybody's Stalking' ('Everybody's Talking'); Soul Asylum 'Somebody To Shove' ('Somebody To Love'); Dustball 'Send In The Clones' ('Send In The Clowns'); The Beautiful South 'Old Red Eyes Is Back' (a reference to Frank Sinatra, whose nickname was 'Ol' blue eyes'); Al Stewart 'League Of Notions' (League of Nations); XTC 'Knights In Shining Karma' (instead of 'armour'); Sufjan Stevens *(Come On Feel The) Illinoise* album title is a play on Slade's 'Come On Feel The Noize'.

A clever way of generating such titles is to find a well-known phrase and transpose initial letters of key words, or move words around from something familiar:

Kula Shaker 'Grateful When You're Dead' (The band); Kirsty MacColl 'Electric Landlady' (plays on *Electric Ladyland*); Butthole Surfers 'Hairway To Steven' ('Stairway To Heaven'); Half Man Half Biscuit 'Trouble Over Bridgewater' ('Bridge Over Troubled Water'); The Tremoloes 'Breakheart Motel' ('Heartbreak Hotel').

Here are some other titles which involve an element of wordplay, but done with more than just the change of a letter or two:

> **Squeeze 'Stranger Than The Stranger On The Shore' ('Stranger On The Shore'); Ryan Adams 'English Girls Approximately' (Dylanesque); Radiohead 'Subterranean Homesick Alien' ('Subterranean Homesick Blues'); Teenage Fanclub 'Neil Jung' (Carl Jung meets Neil Young); X 'Your Phone's Off The Hook But You're Not'.**

At a deeper level, choose a famous song and write a lyric taking the opposite view of the theme and/or the imagery. This need not be a parody or comic – though such an approach is a good method for generating a funny song. The Arrows' 'I Love Rock'n'Roll' (later a hit for Joan Jett) was written as an answer to The Stones' 'It's Only Rock'n'Roll (But I Like It)' because the writers took exception to the implication of the word "only". On the larger scale this could create something like Liz Phair's *Exile In Guyville* album, a response to the Stones' *Exile On Main Street*.

The 'straight' (non-parody) approach is to choose a famous song you like and write a lyric on a similar theme. How would you translate its world into a lyric you would feel comfortable singing? What are the nearest equivalent perceptions and experiences in your own daily life? Or take a famous song and write a continuation to the situation or the emotion that it represents. If the original song was about two people dreaming of escaping to another place and building a better life, your lyric could describe what happened to them when they did it.

Consider a title like The Supremes' 'Love Is Here (And Now You're Gone)'. Imagine the fun to be had with people's expectations if we write a love song called 'Love Is Here (And Now I'm Gone)'. The Jam memorably turned Nevil Shute's novel *Town Called Alice* into 'Town Called Malice'. From this we could derive a song called 'Malice In Wonderland', or Smokie's pop 'Living Next Door To Alice' could be wittily grunged into 'Living Next Door To Malice'.

Having written 'Peggy Sue' Buddy Holly wrote 'Peggy Sue Got Married' to continue the story. The Miracles' 'Got A Job' answered The Silhouettes' 'Get A Job'. Many songwriters have echoed Chuck Berry's 'Johnny B. Goode', including T.Rex with 'Jason B. Sad' and Mungo Jerry with 'Johnny B. Badde'.

> **ANSWERING BACK: Kaiser Chiefs 'Caroline, Yes' ('Caroline, No'); David Ackles 'Surf's Down' ('Surf's Up'); Squeeze *East Side Story* (musical *West Side Story*); Starsailor 'Silence Is Easy' (proverb 'silence is golden'); Tears For Fears 'Brian Wilson Said' ('Jackie Wilson Said'); Half Man Half Biscuit 'Back In The DHSS' ('Back In The USSR'); Billy Bragg 'I Dreamed I Saw Phil Ochs Last Night' (Bob Dylan 'I Dreamt I Saw St Augustine'); The Detergents 'Leader Of The Laundromat' (parody of 'Leader Of The Pack').**

Comedy songs

Writing comedy songs is an art in itself. Some comedians have made a name singing comedy songs not necessarily written by them. George Formby, Flanders and Swann, Tom Lehrer and Randy Newman are well-known for comic songs. Eric Idle and Neil Innes extended their spoof on The Beatles, The *Rutles*, across a double album, and Spinal Tap's parody of heavy rock is the most famous film to satirise rock.

There are also groups like Half Man Half Biscuit and The Bonzo Dog Doo-Dah Band. The Monty Python team wrote comic songs, including a Eurovision send-up and the notorious 'Always Look On The Bright Side Of Life' from *Life Of Brian*.

The type of comedy song where you write a new lyric for the original's music, requires copyright clearance and permission; it also means you only get royalties for the words.

Billy Connolly parodied Tammy Wynette's 'D.I.V.O.R.C.E' by re-writing the lyric but retaining the music.

Ray Stevens 'Bridget The Midget'; Bernard Cribbins 'Right Said Fred', 'My Brother'; Charlie Drake 'Please Mr Custer'; The Wurzels 'Combine Harvester' (a re-write of Melanie's 'Brand New Key'); The Goons 'The Ying Tong Song'; The Bonzo Dog Doo Dah Band 'I'm The Urban Spaceman'; Tom Lehrer 'Poisoning Pigeons In The Park'; The Firm 'Star Trekkin''; Allan Sherman 'Hello Mudduh, Hello Fadduh'.

Inspired by the arts

"Read a book – any book – but to make it interesting, begin to read one that you've not read before. With a pencil underline every situation or statement in the first chapter that suggests a song idea, entering them all in your notebook." (Jimmy Webb)[127]

"I had a rhythm idea with a synth line I took home to work on one night. While I was playing it this repeated Yes came to me and made me think of Molly Bloom's speech right at the end of *Ulysses* … I went downstairs and read it again, this unending sentence punctuated with 'yeses', fantastic stuff, and it was uncanny, it fitted the rhythm of my song … [the James Joyce estate refused her permission to use the actual text] I tried to write it like Joyce. The rhythm at least I wanted to keep. Obviously I couldn't do his style. It became a song about Molly Bloom, the character, stepping out of the page … ' (Kate Bush on 'The Sensual World')[128]

"The album's doing well [*International Velvet*], although we named that after a film as well – perhaps people think it's a soundtrack album. I think from now on we should stick to naming our songs after things on telly or films – adverts, even." (Owen Powell of Catatonia who had a hit with 'Mulder and Scully')[129]

One way to avoid the dreaded writer's block is to draw ideas for lyrics from the arts.

This means not only singers and musicians of earlier periods, but literature, painting, sculpture, theatre and films. Such inspiration could come simply as a title or a one-line allusion; it could be a character or a concept or a feeling. At its most ambitious, such a song might try to approximate the overall experience of the source work.

Paintings lend themselves well to treatment in a lyric because they are a single image. They can be taken in much faster than a novel, for example (at least on a superficial level), and if they have any narrative element it may be implied rather than developed, which gives the songwriter an opportunity to tell that story in a lyric (or make one up that fits the picture). The lives of artists have also formed song subjects.

PAINTERS AND PAINTINGS: David Bowie 'Andy Warhol'; Paul Simon 'Rene and Georgette Magritte With Their Dog after The War'; Don McLean 'Vincent' (Van Gogh); Brian and Michael 'Matchstick Men and Matchstick Cats And Dogs (L.S. Lowry); Queen 'The Fairy Feller's Master-Stroke' (Richard Dadd); Wings 'Picasso's Last Words'; David Bowie 'Pablo Picasso'; Ocean Colour Scene 'Mona Lisa Eyes'; Marianne Faithful 'Witches Song' (inspired by Goya drawings).

Poetry is an art-form with a complex relationship to songs, since it is the art-form closest to the song-lyric – so much so that the two forms are often confused. Some songs have been inspired by poems, and of course there is always the option of setting a poem to music, although you may will need copyright clearance to do this in public.

PLAYS AND POETRY: Billy Bragg 'Walt Whitman's Niece'; Clifford T. Ward 'Not Waving – Drowning' (named after a Stevie Smith poem); The Jam 'Tonight At Noon' (named after a poem by Liverpool poet Roger McGough); Oasis 'Don't Look Back In Anger' (play *Look Back In Anger* by John Osborne); Iron Maiden 'Rime Of The Ancient Mariner' (Coleridge); Rush 'Xanadu' (poem 'Kubla Khan' by Coleridge); Joni Mitchell 'Slouching Towards Bethlehem' (W. B. Yeats 'The Second Coming'); The Waterboys 'The Stolen Child' (W.B. Yeats')'; Dire Straits 'Romeo and Juliet'; Lou Reed 'Romeo Had Juliette'; Adam Cohen 'Cry Ophelia'.

May songwriters find prose fiction stimulates ideas for songs. Travelling musicians have plenty of time to read when they are on the road.

Kate Bush's hit 'Wuthering Heights' evokes the romantic intensity of Emily Bronte's novel, but as she admitted, "It was a real challenge to *précis* the whole mood of a book into such a short piece of prose." Without being specific to one book, Elvis Costello's 'Watching The Detectives' conjured up the *milieu* of pulp fiction.

In 1987, in connection with *Nebraska*, Bruce Springsteen revealed that he had been reading William Price Fox, author of the novel *Dixiana Moon* and numerous short stories. The song 'Open All Night' was inspired by Fox's writing. Springsteen revealed in 1996 that he got into short story writers like James M. Cain, Jim Thompson, and Flannery O'Connor. *The Ghost Of Tom Joad* draws on John Steinbeck's classic novel, The Grapes Of Wrath (1939).

In 1986 Morrissey revealed, "I've never made any secret of the fact that at least 50 per cent of my writing can be blamed on Shelagh Delaney, who wrote *A Taste Of Honey*.'[130]

WRITERS AND FICTION: 10;000 Maniacs 'Hey Jack Kerouac'; Metallica 'For Whom The Bell Tolls' (story by Ernest Hemingway); America 'Watership Down' (novel by Richard Adams); Ash 'Day Of The Triffids' (novel by John Wyndham); Graham Parker 'Just Like Herman Hesse'; Genesis 'Unquiet Slumbers for the Sleepers'; '...In That Quiet Earth' (Emily Bronte); Billy Bragg 'The Man In The Iron Mask' (Alexandre Dumas); Belle and Sebastian 'The Loneliness Of The Middle Distance Runner' (alludes to Alan Sillitoe's novel *The Loneliness Of The Long Distance Runner*); John Cale's 'Paris 1919' (alludes to *A Child's Christmas In Wales* by Dylan Thomas); Prince 'The Ballad Of Dorothy Parker'.

Famous people and historical events

Many songwriters have periods where they either don't want to write about themselves or get bored with doing so. One way out of this is to write about famous and infamous characters from history, and historical events. Here's how to approach it:

- Choose a character who made an impression on the world who interests you. Better still, be sufficiently open-minded and curious about the world and one will find you.
- Try to get to the root of why they interest you. That will be the personal core of the song which helps take it beyond a mere exercise.
- Research this person. Read a book or article about them, watch a film about them. Biographical entries in any good encyclopaedia make a useful starting point. Don't overdo the note-taking – you're gathering material for a lyric, not a novel.
- Make a list of short phrases that encapsulate the person, what they did, their life, how others saw them. Out of these phrases may come the title and the beginning of a lyric.
- Look for the essence of this person's life, or what they represent. Can you distil it in an image or a phrase? This could be the chorus or refrain.
- Look for a story. Is there a sequence of events which typify this character? You can't tell the whole story in detail of a person's life in a song lyric. But a narrative element will give the lyric drama. The more events you want to include, the more you have to master the art of using an image or a short phrase to represent that life. This requires compression.

HISTORY: The Smiths 'Some Girls Are Bigger Than Others' (Antony and Cleopatra); Supergrass 'Richard III'; Orchestral Manoeuvres In The Dark 'Joan Of Arc'; 'Enola Gay'; Nico 'Genghis Khan'; Boney M 'Rasputin'; Joni Mitchell 'Amelia' (pilot Amelia Earhart); Simon And Garfunkel 'So Long Frank Lloyd Wright'; Magnetic Fields 'Death Of Ferdinand De Saussure'; Morrissey 'Jack The Ripper'; Belle And Sebastian 'Marx and Engels'; Neil Young 'Cortez The Killer'; Bill Hayes 'The Ballad of Davy Crockett'; Beastie Boys 'Paul Revere'.

One such historical figure might be the escapologist Harry Houdini (1874-1926). He was the subject of Kate Bush's song 'Houdini', not only because of his escape stunts but because his life touched on the question of life after death, as Bush explained:

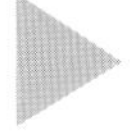

"He and his wife made a decision that if one of them should die and try to make contact, that the other would know it was truly them through a code that only the two of them knew ... It is such a beautiful and strange story that I thought I had very little to do, other than to tell it like it was. But in fact it proved to be the most difficult lyric of all the songs and the most demanding."[131]

This lyric also suggested the photography for the album sleeve (*The Dreaming*) on which it was released. If a person or event is really well-known their name only has to appear in the title/hook for the meaning to be clear, as is the case with Elvis Costello's 'Two Little Hitlers' and Abba's 'Waterloo'. You may need to consider whether listeners in different parts of the world will understand the historical references. Elvis Costello knew an American audience wouldn't get a reference to 1930s British fascist Oswald Mosley in 'Less Than Zero'. He re-wrote a verse so that Oswald became Lee Harvey Oswald, alleged assassin of JFK.

Rather than writing a whole lyric about a famous person, writers sometimes use them as simply a colourful comparison. Ben Folds Five released a song called 'Julianne' in which the first line compares a girl to Axl Rose, and Bananarama's 'Robert De Niro' is another example. A famous person as an image carries a certain ambience. When sketching a lyric this ambience can act as a magnetic field, attracting other ideas into the imagined space, and stepping over any initial feeling you may have of not knowing precisely what you want to say. Film stars and recent politicians often serve this purpose well.

FILM STARS: Sheryl Crow 'Steve McQueen'; Elton John 'Candle In The Wind' (Marilyn Monroe); Madonna 'Vogue'; Kim Carnes 'Bette Davis Eyes'; Blue Oyster Cult 'Joan Crawford'; Underworld 'Bruce Lee'; Bauhaus 'Bela Lugosi's Dead'; Madness 'Michael Caine'; Carly Simon 'You're So Vain' (Warren Beatty); Billy Bragg 'Ingrid Bergman'.

RECENT POLITICS AND POLITICIANS: R.E.M. 'Exhuming McCarthy'; Manic Street Preachers 'The Love Of Richard Nixon'; U2 'MLK'; 'Pride (In The Name Of Love)'; Chicago 'Harry Truman'; Mercury Rev 'Lincoln's Eyes'. John F. Kennedy's assassination influenced The Byrds 'He Was A Friend Of Mine'; Phil Ochs 'Crucifixion'; The Beach Boys 'The Warmth Of The Sun'; Peter Gabriel 'Family Snapshot'; Marvin Gaye 'Abraham, Martin and John'; Tori Amos 'Jacqueline's Strength'.

Musicians

"I liked [Buddy] Holly because he spoke to me. He was a symbol of something deeper than the music he made." (Don McLean, who wrote about Holly's death in 'American Pie')[132]

It's hardly surprising that songwriters might want to honour singers, bands and musicians they admire. Normally, there is a certain length of time before such songs are written, partly to establish that the subject really is of an importance to deserve a song, and to wait until they belong to a different generation. Otherwise there is the danger that the singer or band providing the homage might look as though they were too close to the subject, which would call into question their originality. There is an assumption that to write a song about another musician means you secretly want to be them, even if this isn't the case.

Elvis Presley's status as "king of rock'n'roll" and his relatively early death have made him popular as a subject. In many lyrics he symbolises loneliness in the midst of worldly success, and the cost of fame (see also David Bowie's 'Fame' on this subject).

SONGS INSPIRED BY ELVIS PRESLEY: Dire Straits 'Calling Elvis'; Kate Bush 'King of the Mountain'; Gillian Welch 'Elvis Presley Blues'; Thin Lizzy 'The King Is Dead'; Jimmy Webb 'Elvis and Me'; Belle And Sebastian 'A Century Of Elvis'; Manic Street Preachers 'Elvis Impersonator: Blackpool Pier'; Kirsty MacColl 'There's A Guy Works Down The Chip Shop Swears He's Elvis'.

At the other end of the popularity scale, writing a song about a musician is a means to draw attention to someone whose music has, in your view, been neglected, either because their career went into decline, or (as with many professional songwriters) they were never known to the public in the first place.

Such songs can excite curiosity in a generation too young to have known the music first time round. Don McLean's 'American Pie' begins as an account of his sadness at the death of Buddy Holly in February 1959 and then turns into an allegory on the 1960s. There is an increasing frequency of these songs as popular music since the 1950s develops a sense of its history and tradition and the key players in it. This would apply to songs like The Boo Radleys' 'Jimmy Webb Is God', Barenaked Ladies' 'Brian Wilson', and The Replacements' 'Alex Chilton' (of Big Star).

Even if you don't want to build a whole lyric about a musician, they can sometimes make for an effective allusion or detail. T.Rex's 'Ballrooms Of Mars' name-checks Bob Dylan, John Lennon and the disc jockey Alan Freed, and the album *The Slider* (1972), to which it belongs, has other songs that mention film-maker Pasolini and New York street musician Moondog.

Billy Bragg 'Levi Stubbs' Tears' (lead singer of The Four Tops); ABC 'When Smokey Sings' (Smokey Robinson); Big Audio Dynamite 'James Brown'; Dexys Midnight Runners 'Jackie Wilson Said'; Dexys Midnight Runners 'Oh Geno' (Geno Washington); Ian Dury 'Sweet Gene Vincent'; Buddy Holly 'Bo Diddley'; Happy Mondays 'Donovan'; Neil Young 'From Hank To Hendrix'; Oasis 'Cast No Shadow' (written about Richard Ashcroft of The Verve); John Martyn 'Solid Air' (for Nick Drake); Free 'My Brother Jake' (about guitarist Paul Kossoff); George Harrison 'When We Was Fab'; David Bowie 'Song For Bob Dylan'.

Going slightly further afield, songwriters occasionally mention performers and composers in fields of music such as jazz and classical music. Writing lyrics about jazz musicians is, of course, terribly hip. The stand-out hit of this kind is Stevie Wonder's 'Sir Duke', a tribute to Duke Ellington, which also mentions Ella Fitzgerald, Glen Miller, Count Basie, and Louis Armstrong. Lyrics about classical figures often vent popular music's resentment towards high culture, as in Chuck Berry's 'Roll Over Beethoven' and Roy Wood's 'Bend Over Beethoven'. A few exceptions include Kate Bush's 'Delius (Song Of Summer)', Siouxsie And The Banshees' 'The Last Beat Of My Heart' (Shostakovich), Eurythmics' 'Beethoven (I Love To Listen To)', and Falco's 'Rock Me Amadeus' (inspired by the film *Amadeus*, about Mozart).

Songs about songs

When songwriters get stuck for a subject they sometimes fall back on describing what they do – and so we get lyrics about songs and wanting to write a song. Many of these lyrics are suffocatingly self-conscious. For a start, admitting out loud that you're not feeling inspired doesn't make for an inspiring lyric. Such a lyric can make you look smugly self-engrossed, with an inflated sense of your musical talent. Some of these lyrics are so portentously self-absorbed that they invite not sympathy for the songwriter's predicament but the response: so you can strum three chords and write a song? Ever looked at a score by Stravinsky? See a difference? There is also a sense that a song about a song is a form of postponement, just as a story about telling stories puts us one remove from a story. Beware of seeming like a waiter who thinks reading the menu is a substitute for bringing the food.

More meaningful is when music itself becomes a metaphor for other types of harmony, such as that felt between lovers. This lyric motif can also be used in spiritual songs, where music is an expression of cosmic harmony, part of the order of things. This goes back at least as far as Greek philosophy and the belief in the 'music of the spheres'. Both these musical metaphors themes can be found in The Who's output, the first in 'Getting In Tune', and the second in 'Pure And Easy'. The tenacity of Pete Townshend's pursuit of this notion of the universal power of music, during the years 1968-73, is probably unparalleled by anyone in rock music.

In addition to songs glorifying the singer-songwriter and his/her art, there are truckloads of songs celebrating music-making, there are songs about instruments, and, last but not least, songs about specific genres such as rock'n'roll.

THE GUITAR MAN AND THE BAND

In the mid-1950s, when the electric guitar became the symbol and voice of rock'n'roll rebellion, the guitarist became a folk hero who could make huge amounts of money and wield a magic spell over increasingly large audiences. The quintessential lyric on this topic is Chuck Berry's 'Johnny B Goode', a narrative about a country boy who learns rhythm by imitating trains and whose rise to fame is prophesised by his mother. The extended sense of the *electric* guitarist as a 'shaman' is encapsulated in Jimi Hendrix's 'Voodoo Chile'. Here are songs about singers, players, bands, and their rise and fall.

Chuck Berry 'Johnny B Goode'; Dire Straits 'Sultans Of Swing'; 'Walk Of Life' (about a busker); Bread 'Guitar Man'; The Carpenters 'Superstar'; David Bowie 'Ziggy Stardust'; Elton John 'Bennie and The Jets'; Oasis 'Rock'n'Roll Star'; Hole 'Rock Star'; The Byrds 'So You Want To Be A Rock'n'Roll Star'; Nickelback 'Rockstar'; Moody Blues 'I'm Just A Singer (In A Rock And Roll Band)'; Bruce Springsteen 'Where The Bands Are'; Grand Funk Railroad 'We're An American Band'.

THE GUITAR

It isn't surprising that the guitar should be venerated, as an object of beauty, of longing (if you're young and can't afford a Fender or a Gibson), of power, of sex appeal, and as a route to riches. The guitar is also sometimes anthropomorphised, as in The Beatles' 'While My Guitar Gently Weeps' and Bon Jovi's 'My Guitar Lies Bleeding In My Arms', so that it becomes the embodiment of the singer's emotions.

Townes Van Zandt, Moody Blues, Susan Werner 'Blue Guitar'; Loudon Wainwright III, U2 'Red Guitar'; XTC 'My Brown Guitar'; Pete Townshend 'Sheraton Gibson'; Squeeze 'F-Hole'; Bebop Deluxe 'Sunburst Finish'; David Sylvian 'Dobro'; Neil Young 'This Old Guitar'; Magnetic Fields 'Acoustic Guitar'; Joe Brown 'Talking Guitar'; Billy Bragg 'This Guitar Says Sorry'.

OTHER INSTRUMENTS AND ACCESSORIES

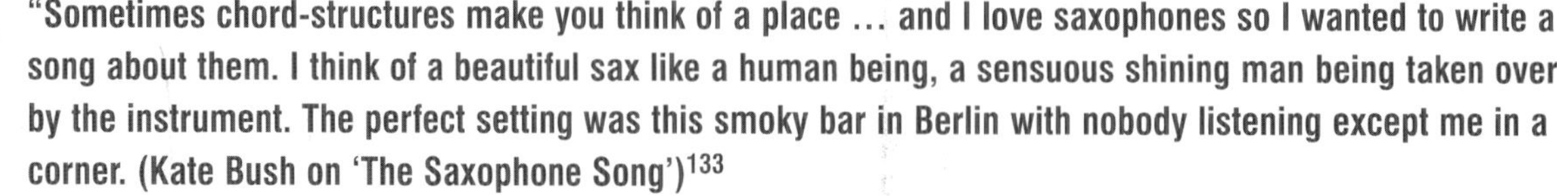
"Sometimes chord-structures make you think of a place … and I love saxophones so I wanted to write a song about them. I think of a beautiful sax like a human being, a sensuous shining man being taken over by the instrument. The perfect setting was this smoky bar in Berlin with nobody listening except me in a corner. (Kate Bush on 'The Saxophone Song')[133]

Even if you don't want to write a whole lyric about an instrument, it could suggest a central metaphor for a situation. The black and white keys of a piano were taken as an image of racial harmony in the McCartney and Wonder song 'Ebony And Ivory'. It is also worth considering the use of proverbial phrases linked with instruments, such as a phrase like "second fiddle". The lyrics of Sly And The Family Stone's 'Dance To The Music' introduce the musicians/instruments one by one. For comic purposes so does The Bonzo Dog Doo-Dah Band's 'The Intro & The Outro', name-checking Adolf Hitler on vibes. Such lyrics obviously invite the inclusion of the instrument in the arrangement, or the effects device in the case of R.E.M.'s 'E-Bow The Letter'.

Kate Bush 'Violin', 'The Saxophone Song'; Nick Drake 'Cello Song'; David Gray 'Wurlitzer'; The Who 'Squeeze Box'; Squeeze 'Farfisa Beat'; Freddie And The Dreamers 'Susan's Tuba'; Mantronix 'Bassline'; Stone Roses 'She Bangs The Drums'; Bob Dylan 'Mr Tambourine Man'; Gomez 'Love Is Better Than A Warm Trombone'; Bjork 'Headphones'; Genesis 'Guide Vocal'; The Who 'Success Story' (the trials of recording).

STAGE SONGS AND CROWD-PLEASERS

One particular self-referential lyric celebrates live performance and holds a mirror to the audience. It is the sort of lyric in which the word "tonight" looms large and rock bands ask their audiences if they're ready to rock. This is a crowd-pleasing move, a "we're all in this together" gesture, even if the song can sound contrived and self-conscious. The showbiz recognition of the performer as entertainer can clash with rebel counter-establishment pretensions, as expressed in The Who's 'Join Together'. This list also includes several songs about festivals.

The Who 'Long Live Rock'; Bryan Adams 'Kids Wanna Rock'; Wings 'Rock Show'; Led Zeppelin 'The Ocean'; Status Quo 'Rockin' all Over The World'; Alice Cooper 'Hello Hurray'; Chuck Berry 'House Lights'; Queen 'We Will Rock You'; Robbie Williams 'Let Me Entertain You'; AC/DC 'For Those About To Rock'; Mountain 'For Yasgur's Farm' (about Woodstock); Joni Mitchell 'Woodstock'; Echo And The Bunnymen 'Altamont'; David Bowie 'Memory Of A Free Festival'.

GENERAL PAEANS TO ROCK

Here is a short list of songs with "rock" or "rock'n'roll" in the title. The phrase can among other things be shorthand for having a good time, having sex, or playing 12-bars at high volume.

Chuck Berry 'Rock And Roll Music', 'Sweet Little Rock and Roller'; Ian Dury 'Sex And Drugs And Rock'n'Roll'; Joan Jett And The Blackhearts 'I Love Rock'n'Roll'; Led Zeppelin 'Rock And Roll'; Billy Joel 'It's Still Rock'n'Roll To Me'; The Rolling Stones 'It's Only Rock'n'Roll (But I Like It)'; Mott The Hoople 'Golden Age Of Rock'n'Roll'; Johnny Winter 'Golden Days Of Rock and Roll'; Argent 'God Gave Rock And Roll To You'; Black Rebel Motorcycle Club 'Whatever Happened To My Rock And Roll'; Danny And The Juniors 'Rock And Roll Is Here To Stay'.

ABOUT SONGS

The song can be a metaphor for an old relationship. There are songs about couples who have adopted a song because they heard it when they met. This becomes 'their' song and said song becomes devastating after they break up. Cue subject for a lyric. Motown writers Holland-Dozier-Holland were audacious enough to draw attention to repeating their own musical formulae with The Four Tops when they wrote 'It's The Same Old Song' as a love song.

Elton John 'Sad Songs (Say So Much)'; Jim Croce 'I'll Just Have To Say I Love You In A Song'; Roberta Flack 'Killing Me Softly With His Song'; B.J. Thomas '(Hey Won't You Play) Another Somebody Done Somebody Some Wrong Song'; Travis 'Sing'; M 'Pop Muzik'; Genesis 'Abacab'; Wings 'Silly Love Songs'; Elton John 'Your Song'; The Who 'Guitar and Pen'; John Miles 'Music'; The Beatles 'Only A Northern Song'; Smokey Robinson 'Melody Man'.

CLASSICAL REFERENCES

To add a touch of pretension and grandeur to your lyric, borrow a structural term from the vocabulary of classical music. Suitable terms include melody, overture, opera, serenade, rhapsody, suite, symphony, and references to keys. The Moody Blues named an album after the mnemonic for the the musical stave: *Every Good Boy Deserves Favours*. With the exception of the word "melody", there is no connection between song-form and any of these large-scale musical structures.

ELO '10538 Overture'; 'Concerto For A Rainy Day'; Righteous Brothers 'Unchained Melody'; Verve 'Bitter Sweet Symphony'; The Supremes 'I Hear A Symphony'; The Beach Boys 'Winter Symphony'; Keith West 'Excerpt From A Teenage Opera'; David Gates 'Suite: Clouds, Rain'; Lindisfarne 'Train In G Major'; Billy Bragg 'Way Over Yonder in the Minor Key'; Red Hot Chili Peppers 'Mellowslip Slinky In B Major'.

Politics and protest

"You've got to be aware that whatever you say to someone, it's only your opinion. You get political bands like Rage Against The Machine – and I'm not slagging them off because they've got good songs – but it's a bit too much. Music's entertainment and politics isn't. Ramming your opinion down someone's throat is not entertaining." (Tony Wright of Terrorvision)[134]

"When I see contemporary songs quoted by contemporary music critics, they say, "This is a great lyric," and they'll isolate a line, and I'll think, What's great about that? There's no nourishment in that line. There's not even alliteration or linguistic colour, you know? "Everybody's gay". You know – it's a statement, but there's not art. ... Is it all distilled down to its simplest essence and therefore it's valid? Or do people just not know how to express themselves very well?' (Joni Mitchell)[135]

The state of the world offers an endless source of potential lyric themes, and eventually most songwriters are tempted to have their say about something that bugs them. Writing a protest song makes you feel you have said something significant in the larger scheme of things. The challenge is not to allow this satisfaction to eclipse the more relevant one of artistic judgement. No matter how right you think you are about the issue, your first concern must be artistic: is this a good song/lyric? Good intent does not guarantee artistic success, nor is it a measure of it.

The counter-culture's opposition to the Vietnam war brought about a rock version of the protest song. As far as topics go, the songwriter can count on an audience thinking that war and violence are bad things, so, as protest lyrics go, these are safer subjects than most. Some of the best examples include:

WAR AND VIOLENCE: Edwin Starr 'War'; Marvin Gaye 'What's Going On'; Bob Dylan 'Masters Of War'; Happy Mondays 'Altogether Now'; John Lennon 'Give Peace A Chance'; 'Happy Xmas (War Is Over)'; Peter Gabriel 'Games Without Frontiers'; Bruce Springsteen 'Born In The USA'; Country Joe and The Fish 'I Feel Like I'm Fixin' To Die Rag'; Paul Hardcastle '19'; Frankie Goes To Hollywood 'Two Tribes'; Jimi Hendrix 'Machine Gun'; U2 'Bullet The Blue Sky'; 'Sunday Bloody Sunday'; Black Sabbath 'War Pigs'.

Unemployment and poverty touch a chord of identification and sympathy in the majority of people. Not everyone has fought in a war, or been gunned or bombed, but almost everyone knows what it is to (at the least) fear poverty.

POVERTY AND UNEMPLOYMENT: Marvin Gaye 'Inner City Blues'; Isley Bros 'Harvest For The World'; George Harrison 'Bangla Desh'; Band Aid 'Do They Know It's Christmas'; The Police 'Driven To Tears'; The Specials 'Ghost Town'; Grandmaster Flash And The Furious Five 'The Message'; Tracy Chapman 'Talkin' 'Bout A Revolution'; UB40 'One In Ten'; Elvis Presley 'In The Ghetto'.

Few traps are so powerfully sprung for the unwary songwriter as writing a song with a 'message'. 'Message' songs are bywords for slogans and platitudes over which a sticky goo of generalised sentiment has been poured. The notion of writing a song with a message is itself flawed because it implies a simplistic relation of form and content. It implies once you get the 'message' you might as well throw away the song as if it were no more than a sweet wrapper. This should be borne in mind by songwriters who want to tackle current ecological issues. The earliest ecological protest songs date from the 1960s and chiefly concern pollution rather than the then unknown global warming:

ENVIRONMENTAL AND GREEN: Joni Mitchell 'Big Yellow Taxi'; Marvin Gaye 'Mercy Mercy Me (The Ecology)'; Four Tops 'That's The Way Nature Planned It; 'Moody Blues 'A Question Of Balance'; Pete Seeger 'Where Have All The Flowers Gone?'; Spirit 'Nature's Way'; Cliff Richard 'Silvery Rain'.

In the early 1960s, the hey-day of protest, both Bob Dylan and Phil Ochs wrote protest songs about Medgar Evans, but Dylan is alleged to have said to Ochs, "You're not a songwriter, you're a journalist.'[136] Songs about politics and protest were more visible in the 1960s than at any time since, because popular music was undergoing a revolution. Initially such songs were associated with 'folk' music (itself allied to a variety of left-wing causes) and singers such as Woody Guthrie. It reached a bigger audience than the folk clubs because of the involvement of singers like Pete Seeger, Bob Dylan, and Joan Baez. Only five years after The Beatles had gone to Number One all over the world with 'She Loves You', they were recording 'Revolution'. Since then political songs have emerged from punk, new wave, rock and heavy rock.

POLITICS AND POWER: Pete Seeger 'We Shall Overcome'; Elvis Costello 'Night Rally'; The Who 'Relay'; Buffalo Springfield 'Ohio'; The Rolling Stones 'Street Fighting Man'; The Police 'Invisible Sun'; Peter Gabriel 'Biko'; The Specials 'Nelson Mandela'; The Beatles 'Revolution'; Thunderclap Newman 'Something In The Air'; U2 'Mothers Of The Disappeared'; Billy Bragg 'There Is Power In A Union'; The Chi-Lites '(For God's Sake) Give More Power To The People'; Plastic Ono Band 'Power To The People'; Temptations 'Ball Of Confusion'.

Alert to the turn rock was taking, soul music of the late 1960s increasingly reflected the trials and aspirations of frustrated African-Americans, the civil rights movement, and black power.

RACIAL: Stevie Wonder 'Heaven Help Us All'; James Brown 'Say It Aloud (I'm Black And I'm Proud'); Public Enemy '911 Is A Joke'; Billie Holiday 'Strange Fruit'; Tracy Chapman 'Across The Lines'; Bob Dylan 'The Ballad Of Medgar Evans'; Eminem 'White America'; Curtis Mayfield 'Miss Black America'; Artists United Against Apartheid 'Sun City'; Sam Cooke 'A Change Is Gonna Come'; Manic Street Preachers 'IfWhiteAmericaToldTheTruthForOneDayItsWorld-WouldFallApart'.

Writers perceived as deviating into protest can get into commercial difficulties. In the 1970s Jackson Browne established himself as a singer-songwriter writing about love and loss, but in the 1980s he released many songs that dealt with broader themes.

When his 1993 album *I'm Alive* was released, Elektra issued an ad subtitled "Jackson Browne Resurfaces" (the sleeve was his head emerging from water). Apparently, to return from protest songs was to come up for air.

The ad reassured the prospective buyer that these were love songs reflecting recent events in Browne's personal life. The sub-text was, "Hey, it's okay, it's safe to buy *this* one, he's not doing political/protest stuff now."

Keep a sense of perspective with the protest song. Why should the ability to strum chords mean you have answers to great political and social questions?

Aware of the absurdity lurking in this scenario, songwriter Barry Mann released a single in 1968 called 'Young Electric Psychedelic Hippy Flippy Folk and Funky Philosophic Turned On Groovy 12-String Band', that satirised the desire of performers to comment on anything and everything and the eagerness of the media to listen to them.

A GUIDE TO WRITING PROTEST LYRICS

- to make big issues seem real, a lyric must be grounded in human particulars, because they flesh out the abstraction.
- be clear where you stand, and humanise your doubts or make a virtue of them.
  look for the details from which the theme emerges. This makes it easier for people to relate to.
- be wary of assuming a stance of personal moral superiority.
- if you want to write a chant that crowds can take up, keep things simple, as in 'Power To The People' or 'Give Peace A Chance'.
- having your heart in the right place will not save a crude or incompetent lyric.

Fantasy and myth

"See like how they got the Greek gods and all that mythology. Well, you can have your own mythology scene. Or write, you know, fiction. Complete fiction though, you know … the way I write things, I just write them with a clash between reality and fantasy mostly. You have to use the fantasy in order to show different sides of reality." (Jimi Hendrix)[137]

"[Genesis] were writing songs that were surreal, escapist, not your average lyric. And that's all well and good until you've got to sing them. We were listening to some of our old live tapes, and 'bread bin' was in one of the lyrics. You try and sing 'bread bin' – it's a difficult word to put anything to." (Phil Collins on taking over vocals in Genesis)[138]

"I grew up in the suburbs and it was all very prosaic and dull … as a writer, fantasy is really an excellent vehicle for expressing ideas in their purest sense, without any preconceptions. There's nothing better than having your own made-to-order extra-terrestrial world." (Neil Peart of Rush)[139]

If you want to have a break from the real world, write a lyric which is fantasy or based on myth. Inspiration could come from fantasy stories, science-fiction, as well as children's stories. A lyric does not have to be crudely realistic and every day to be truthful about life, the human condition, or to express feelings. Fantasy songs can express emotions obliquely. Like dreams, they relate to our inner lives and unconscious. Children's songs often have a fantastical element.

The fantasy lyric received a strong impetus in the 1960s. This was partly due to the influence of psychedelia and books the hippies were reading, notably Tolkien's epic *Lord Of The Rings*. Between 1968-1970 Marc Bolan wrote five albums' worth of songs based on a Tolkienesque world of elves and wizards. Tolkien also influenced Led Zeppelin's 'Ramble On' and 'Battle Of Evermore', and provided the title of 'Misty Mountain Hop'. Other key fantasy texts included C.S. Lewis' *Narnia* chronicles, Lewis Carroll's *Alice In Wonderland*, and books by Ray Bradbury. The Beatles 'I Am The Walrus', Jefferson Airplane's 'White Rabbit', and Elton John's 'Mona Lisas And Mad Hatters', allude to Carroll. Nursery rhymes can also be re-set and given an adult meaning, or lend an image to a title.

NURSERY RHYMES AND CHILDREN'S STORIES: Adam and The Ants 'Prince Charming'; Robert Plant; Joss Stone And The Firm 'All The King's Horses'; Sam The Sham And The Pharaohs 'Li'l Red Riding Hood'; Squeeze 'Pinocchio'; Stevie Ray Vaughan 'Mary Had A Little Lamb'; Death In Vegas 'Aladdin's Story'; Kate Bush 'In Search Of Peter Pan'.

Glam rockers like David Bowie, Roxy Music, progressive bands like Genesis (*The Lamb Lies Down On Broadway*), Hawkwind, Pink Floyd, Yes, and Rush (see 2112) often invented fantasy stories. Tubeway Army's 'Are Friends Electric' was based on Philip K. Dick's novel *Do Androids Dream Of Electric Sheep*? More sinister fantasy informed the lyrics of heavy rock groups. Metallica and other HM bands draw on the stories of H. P. Lovecraft for songs like 'The Call Of Kthulu'. Alice Cooper made up horror stories for *Welcome To My Nightmare*.

Inexperienced young songwriters, especially in rock bands who lean towards sword and sorcery, often unconsciously default to fantasy lyrics of courtly love imagery derived third-hand from an idealised Middle Ages. This stuff is comprised of castles, lakes, magic woods, swords, maidens, ladies, queens, kings, fools, jesters, wizards and witches, soldiers, crystals, etc. Unless you are in a certain kind of prog-rock band, I would avoid this except for sending it up. Gordon Lightfoot's 'If You Could Read My Mind' is interesting in this connection because it has some of this imagery, derived from paperback romance, but undercuts it. The details are ascribed to a film or book that the speaker and the woman he's addressing have seen or read. It's a clever lyric that includes within itself the act of interpretation.

Fantasy itself as a psychological habit can be the subject of a lyric. The Jam's 'Billy Hunt', Pink Floyd's 'Arnold Layne' and 'See Emily Play', are about people lost in fantasy. The Temptations 'Just My Imagination (Running Away With Me)' is a good example of the way that lovers are fantasists; the entire lyric leads the listener up the garden path.

FANTASY: 'In Search Of Space'; Pink Floyd 'Astronomy Domine'; Queen 'Seven Seas Of Rhye'; The Beatles 'Lucy In The Sky With Diamonds'; King Crimson 'The Court of the Crimson King'; Bob Dylan 'Mighty Quinn'; David McWilliams 'Days Of Pearly Spencer'; The Beatles 'Magical Mystery Tour'; Rory Gallagher; King Crimson 'Moonchild'; Iron Maiden 'Seventh Son Of A Seventh Son'; Genesis 'Eleventh Earl Of Mar'; Rush 'The Temples Of Syrinx'.

If you don't feel you could invent a fantasy world there are always Greek and Roman myths, the root of Western art and literature for centuries. They have been recycled and interpreted by writers, painters, sculptors, composers, etc. A myth can provide a parallel for the situation you're writing about. Greek and Roman myths have been considered too highbrow for chart lyrics, so there have been few hits with such references. Prog-rock bands, who want their music to be viewed as art, not ephemeral pop, have less reservations about working such myths into songs. For them it could signal that they were serious musicians. Nevertheless, chart-wise Sting alluded to the two rocks Scylla and Charybdis in 'Wrapped About Your Finger', a reference to the Sirens who tempted Odysseus occurs in Radiohead's 'There There', and there is an allusion to the Trojan horse in Manfred Mann's '5-4-3-2-1'.

GREEK AND ROMAN MYTH: Led Zeppelin 'Achilles Last Stand'; The Herd 'From The Underground' (Orpheus and Eurydice); Nick Cave and The Bad Seeds 'The Lyre Of Orpheus'; Cream 'Tales Of Brave Ulysses'; The Hollies 'King Midas In Reverse'; Incredible String Band 'The Minotaur's Song'; Wishbone Ash 'Persephone'; The Waterboys 'The Pan Within'; Mercury Rev 'Hercules'; Tin Machine 'Pallas Athena'; Wings 'Venus and Mars'; Ash 'Aphrodite'; Procol Harum 'Pandora's Box'; Iron Maiden 'The Flight Of Icarus'; Al Stewart 'Helen And Cassandra'; XTC 'Jason And The Argonauts'; Elvis Costello 'Poor Fractured Atlas'.

If the song can stand it, classical references add grandeur. Otherwise, juxtapose a classical reference with the everyday, as Dylan sometimes did in the mid-1960s, and as did Prefab Sprout ('Venus Of The Soup Kitchen') and Mercury Rev ('Goddess On A Highway'). In both instances a soup kitchen and a highway are the last places you would expect to find an immortal being. The most popular figure from classical myth (unsurprisingly) is Venus, the goddess of love. Outside of classical stories, Randy Newman wrote an album of songs about the Faust myth and Dylan titled a song 'Isis' after an Egyptian deity. No self-respecting heavy rock band is without its tableau of riffing Viking pillage, following Led Zeppelin's 'Immigrant Song', an idea taken to a final, ridiculous extreme by the Finnish winners of the 2006 Eurovision song contest.

The supernatural

"Well, we all have demons inside. I've witnessed a lot of self-destruction in the world I'm in, and writing about it is my way of dealing with it." (Lucinda Williams)[140]

"I'd pick up the guitar, come up with a riff, and go 'That sounds a bit evil.' The words had to fit that mood." (Toni Iommi of Black Sabbath)[141]

Most ghosts, and demons in song-lyrics are strictly metaphorical. Such imagery is an easy-to-apply shorthand for the trauma of lost love, or to describe self-destructive impulses, as the Lucinda Williams quote makes clear. These days everyone is "haunted", everyone has their "personal demons". In this connection see Gene's 'Haunted By You', Kristin Hersh's 'Your Ghost', and Here Come The Tears' 'The Ghost Of You'. Songs such as 'Haunted' and 'Bring Me To Life' by Evanescence are typical of a type of overwrought lyric saturated with Gothic imagery of dying, being undead, bleeding, screaming, being pulled down, of salvation and deliverance.

Astrology has provided some colourful titles and vivid imagery for songs. R.E.M. recorded a song called 'Saturn Return' which refers to a 29-year astrological cycle alleged to reflect our struggles to mature, Deep Purple did 'Maybe I'm A Leo', and astrology is implied in song titles like 'Cancer Moon', 'Scorpio Girl', etc, and Albert King's 'Born Under A Bad Sign' (but let's not talk about The Floaters).

E.S.P, parapsychology, prophecy, synchronicity, and out-of- the-body experiences have all been fruitful lyric subjects.

Al Stewart 'Nostradamus'; Kate Bush 'Strange Phenomena'; Paul Kantner And Grace Slick 'Your Mind Has Left Your Body'; The Police 'Synchronicity'; Ash 'Astral Conversations With Toulouse-Lautrec'; Buzzcocks 'ESP'; Stevie Wonder 'Superstition'.

Sometimes songwriters want to spook their listeners, make them curious, or revel in occult power by proxy. The blues and R'n'B have a long tradition of stories of doing deals with dark forces to get what you want, a legend attached to Robert Johnson ('Hellhound On My Trail'). If you like this sort of thing check out Dr John's album *Gris-Gris*. It was okay for Jimi Hendrix to claim he was a "voodoo chile" but harder if you were born in the deep south of Sussex. Other voodoo songs include The Prodigy's 'Voodoo People', Boney M's 'Voodoonight', Aerosmith's 'Voodoo Medicine', and Siouxsie And The Banshees' 'Voodoo Dolly'.

Fleetwood Mac 'Black Magic Woman'; The Rattles 'The Witch'; Donovan 'Season of the Witch'; Jethro Tull 'The Witch's Promise'; Redbone 'Witch Queen Of New Orleans'; Fleetwood Mac 'Rhiannon'; Eagles 'Witchy Woman'; John Mayall 'I'm Your Witchdoctor'; John Kongos 'Tokoloshe Man'; The Darkness 'Black Shuck'.

It is no surprise, given rock music's long history as the voice of rebels, that it should contain many songs about the archetypal rebel, Satan, and hell. The use of occult imagery in lyrics by early heavy rock bands like Black Sabbath and Black Widow at the start of the 1970s had by the 1990s created a whole genre of the stuff.

Atomic Rooster 'Devil's Answer'; Van Halen 'Runnin' With The Devil'; The Rolling Stones 'Dancing With Mr D'; Crazy World Of Arthur Brown 'Fire'; Meatloaf 'Bat Out Of Hell'; Chris Rea 'Road To Hell'; 'AC/DC 'Highway To Hell'; Saxon 'Beyond The Grave'; Iron Maiden 'The Number Of The Beast'; Blue Oyster Cult 'Don't Fear The Reaper', Ozzy Osbourne 'Mr. Crowley'; Black Widow 'Come To The Sabbath'.

Spirituality

"I was told that if I insisted [on the title 'Deal With God'] the radio stations in at least 10 countries would refuse to play it because it had 'God' in the title – Spain, Italy, America, lots of them. I thought it was ridiculous. Still, especially after *The Dreaming*, I decided I couldn't be bloody-minded. You have to weigh up the priorities ..." (Kate Bush on 'Running Up That Hill')[142]

"I think I felt good about incorporating sex-and-death imagery, especially if I found it in the Old Testament. That felt good to me. That felt kind of cool. That felt kind of rock'n'roll." (Charles Thompson of The Pixies)[143]

The main use of positive religious imagery in song-lyrics has been as a metaphor for romance, as in Belinda Carlisle's 'Heaven Is A Place On Earth', The Elgins' 'Heaven Must Have Sent You', Tavares' 'Heaven Must Be Missing An Angel' and Madonna's 'Like A Prayer'. Falling in love is the most common experience of expanded consciousness, however flawed or transient. As Amen Corner posed it, 'If Paradise Is Half As Nice'. The Monkees 'I'm A Believer' was romance as conversion.

Ultra-romantic lyrics appropriate the imagery of religion and drain it of any metaphysical meaning. It is possible to write a lyric that can be interpreted as a love song or as religious (devotional). During their first four albums U2 were very good at this. Images for this kind of ambiguity include terms like "soul", "salvation" and "angel". Fleetwood Mac, Madonna, Jimi Hendrix and Bruce Springsteen, all wrote songs called 'Angel', and there have been plenty along the lines of B.B. King's 'Sweet Little Angel', or Roxy Music's 'Angel Eyes'. The biggest song of Robbie Williams' career so far is 'Angels', a New Age scenario in which God never puts in an unwelcome appearance. This sort of vague belief, which asks nothing of the ego, is acceptable to a mass audience in a way that traditional or more defined belief generally is not.

Back in 1971, George Harrison fused East and West, combining "hallelujah" with "hare Krishna", on 'My Sweet Lord', a Number One in the UK and the U.S., without his credibility suffering. But that was because you can't argue with an ex-Beatle with near-guru status, a great slide solo, and a Phil Spector production that's almost a religious experience in itself. The power of music is sometimes sufficient to overcome a tepid reaction to religious lyrics. The Strawbs' hymn 'Lay Down' was helped by the Les Paul power-chords which punctuated the verses. Back in the mid-1960s, The Byrds took several verses from Old

Testament text *Ecclesiastes* into the chart with Pete Seeger's 'Turn Turn Turn'. For many years U2 closed their set with '40', the words of which come from Psalm 40, and Boney M had a hit with 'The Rivers Of Babylon', another Old Testament text.

By contrast, consider the critical disdain that affects Cliff Richard's mainstream religious material, and that nearly eclipsed even Bob Dylan during his evangelical phase. No such critique has ever touched the Rastafarian songs of Bob Marley ('Exodus', 'Redemption Song') which are treated as beyond criticism. Gospel is, of course, always liable to generate a hit by virtue of its emotive and declamatory style (as with the Edwin Hawkins Singers' 'Oh Happy Day') and is viewed as 'authentic' because of its connection with the blues. A different standard is applied to, say, Cat Stevens doing 'Morning Has Broken' than is applied to Marvin Gaye singing about saving the children. To many, Lennon's humanist anthem 'Imagine' is more palatable, and it remains one of the most popular 'belief' songs ever written.

A song can use spiritual imagery without being about religion. There are a few artists whose prior critical reputation has enabled them to use more Christian imagery than would normally be considered hip. Springsteen, who came from a Catholic household, put Biblical allusions in songs like 'Adam Raised A Cain', 'Pink Cadillac' (Adam and Eve), 'Lion's Den' (Daniel), 'The Promised Land', 'The Price You Pay' (Moses and the chosen land), and 'Ice Man' (the flaming sword that guards the garden of Eden mentioned in *Genesis*). The story of Cain and Abel occurs in many songs (see Elvis Costello's 'Blame It On Cain'). The Doors' song 'Break On Through' has the phrase "The gate is strait, deep and wide' which is Biblical. The second verse of Leonard Cohen's 'Suzanne' alludes to Jesus's miracle of walking on the water. Elvis' 'Hard Headed Woman' refers to Samson and Delilah, and Adam and Eve.

BIBLICAL REFERENCES: Billy Bragg 'King James Version'; Mott The Hoople 'Roll Away The Stone'; Gretchen Peters 'Like Water Into Wine'; Boo Radleys 'Lazarus'; Elton John 'Where To Now St Peter?'; Bob Dylan 'Gates Of Eden'; Badly Drawn Boy '40 Days, 40 Nights'; Depeche Mode 'Judas'; Stones Roses 'I Am The Resurrection'; Virgin Fugs 'The 10 Commandments'; Aphrodite's Child 'The Four Horsemen'; 10;000 Maniacs 'Noah's Dove'; Joni Mitchell 'The Sire Of Sorrow (Job's Sad Song)'.

The 1960s counter-culture bequeathed Eastern terms like zen, nirvana, and karma to pop's language, and Van Morrison's songs include other esoteric terms like "astral" and "dweller on the threshold". T.Rex's 'Cosmic Dancer' and CSNY's 'We Have All Been Here Before' are both about reincarnation. The Police's 'Secret Journey', Kate Bush's 'Sat In Your Lap', and The Waterboys' 'The Glastonbury Song', are all about pilgrimage. More general songs about belief or lack of it include:

John Lennon 'God'; David Bowie 'Word On A Wing'; Norman Greenbaum 'Spirit In The Sky'; Led Zeppelin 'In My Time Of Dying'; The Wallflowers 'God Says Nothing Back'; Joan Osborne 'One Of Us'; The Byrds 'Jesus Is Just Alright With Me'; Wishbone Ash 'The King Will Come'; The Who 'Bargain'; 'Pure And Easy'; Johnny Cash 'Personal Jesus'; George Harrison 'Awaiting On You All'; The Police 'Spirits In The Material World'; Blind Faith 'Presence Of The Lord'.

Jerry Leiber

Interviewed by Sean Egan

Lyricist Jerry Leiber is a giant in the world of songwriting. With composer Mike Stoller he formed one of the most successful writing teams of all time. They ruled the pop charts in the late 1950s and early 1960s, penning hits for Elvis Presley, The Drifters, The Coasters and many others. 'Jailhouse Rock'. 'Houndog' and 'Spanish Harlem' are just a few of the duo's classic songs.

When did you first become interested in songwriting?

The whole family were songwriters and I was exposed to this general influence that seemed to me a lot of fun. I was getting more and more interested in the lyrical end of songs. My family didn't know what I was doing. I could have been hijacking trucks. They didn't really know what I was about. Later on, when I started to have a modicum of success, I'd tell my mother and she'd be pleased at the success, or I'd show her a royalty check, but her attitude was always, "That's very nice Jerry but I really think you should get a job." Nobody was making any judgment about anything. Nobody was that interested either.

When did songwriting start to become something you might make a living from?

After school, I would work at Norty's Record Shop, which was two blocks down the street from the school. Lester [Sill, of Modern Records] came into Norty's Record Shop to more or less test out the viability of the new records that he had coming out. I was a clerk there at the time and Lester came in and struck up a conversation with me. At some point, he said, "So what do you want to do when you grow up?" And I said, "I want to be a songwriter." He said, "Really? Have you written any songs?" I said, "Yes but I don't have any proper music put to them yet." "Well could you sing me a song or two?" I said, "In here? Norty'll fire me." He was in the back doing inventory. Lester said, "Don't worry about Norty. He's a friend of mine. Sing me a song." So I sang him part of a song. He said, "You're going to be a good songwriter. Now you get yourself a partner who can write these lyrics and music down on a lead sheet." He explained to me what a lead sheet was. And then it all started to come together because I think I had Stoller's number in my pocket then and I knew there was an urgency in calling him because I needed someone to write the music down.

I said, "Are you Mike Stoller?" He said, "Yes." I said, "Do you play piano?" He said, "Yes." I said, "Do you read music?" He said, "Yes." I said, "Can you write notes on paper?" He said, "Yes." And I said, "Well, I was told that you might be interested in writing songs, and that's why I'm calling you. Would you like to write songs with me?" He said, "No." I was shocked! I had to bug him for another 45 minutes on the phone to convince him to let me come over and talk to him.

After that, though, you clicked fairly quickly as writing partners?

We had a sort of instant rapport, especially writing. We just fell in together. In the early days, it was always spontaneous. Those lyrics that I had in my notebook, they were written and I would present them to Mike and he would go to the piano and he'd fiddle around with some riffs, some licks and some rhythm patterns and chords till we found something that we both liked. Not all these songs that are twelve- or eight-bar blues have what you would call conventional melodies.

Was it always the case that you wrote the words, and Mike wrote the music? Did you ever swap roles?

Once in a while I may come up with a note or two and once in a while he may come up with a word. But certainly I'm not a composer and Mike is not a lyric writer.

Did songwriting come easily to you? Has your level of productivity always been the same?

Our stream of productivity is kind of strange and kind of unpredictable. We started off writing like machines. We were writing five songs a day for the first seven or eight or nine years. And then we slowed down somewhere, somehow, for whatever reason. It's been very spotty in a way.

What inspired those early songs?

Nothing's based on a true story. All these things are more or less influenced by the '30s, '40s, and '50s radio plays. 'Riot In Cell Block No. 9' was based on a show called *Gangbusters*. In fact, it opened with a machine gun just like the one I used on the record. It's not one thing, it's a conglomerate of influences.

All these things are about a bigger-than-life kind of story that was often heard on radio. It's a combination of soap operettas, pulp fiction, suspense stories, and cartoons.

Is it harder to write ballads?

I think it was maybe for me back then. I had a tendency to avoid sentimentality and romantic material. I always felt more at home with humor and with irony and with some kind of action, a cliffhanger of some kind, and love ballads tend to be a lot more passive and not as rife with action.

How did you come to write 'Hound Dog'?

We saw Big Mama Thornton and she was singing some soulful blues. I turned to Mike and I said, "Let's get out of here and write our song – she's the one." On the way to his house – which was only about twelve, fifteen minutes away – I was beating out this kind of rhythm on the roof of the car and I was singing some catch phrases to try and get the feeling for the song.

I was looking for something insinuating and funky and kind of sexy. And out came "You ain't nothin' but a hound dog." And Mike said, "Hey man, that's not bad." I said, "Oh that's so lame compared to 'Dirty Mother Furrier' [by Furry Lewis]. It just doesn't say anything." He said, "I think it says enough. 'Dirty Mother Furrier' I don't think ever got played on the radio." I argued with him for most of the ride to his house. When we finally got there he went right to the piano and he started playing this rhythm that I was beating out on the roof of his car. He had it down. He could do that. He could latch onto a nuance of an idea and bring it on home.

What did you think when you heard, several three years later, that Elvis was going to record it?

I didn't find out he was gonna do it. I found out that he had done it and it was already a hit. Harry Goodman called me and said, "Hey man – you've got a big, big hit." "Big Mama Thornton all over again?" He said, "No, Elvis Presley."

Colonel Parker and Jean Aberbach called us up – the manager and the publisher – and asked us if we would consider writing some new material for Elvis. We said we'd love to.

We always felt that he was a great white Southern singer who had certain kinds of slight coloration that were tinted black but we didn't feel that he was a black singer at all. I thought he was a mixture of country & western and somewhat gospel (but not necessarily black gospel – he sounded white Baptist to me). To me, rock'n'roll was not black, rock'n'roll was white. Black is rhythm & blues and rock'n'roll is a hybrid. We have been attributed with inventing it and maybe we have done things that might indicate that, but we have never really experienced ourselves as rock and roll songwriters.

For instance, we wrote a song for Big Mama Thornton and it became a big hit. And now comes the big transition: a white singer from Memphis who's a hell of a singer – he does have some black attitudes – takes the song over, does it and sells five or eight million copies compared to her half a million and saturates the world with his presence. But here's the thing: we didn't make it. His version is like a combination of country and skiffle. It's not black. He sounds like Hank Snow. In most cases where we are attributed with rock and roll, it's misleading, because what we did is usually the original record – which is R&B – and some other producer (and a lot of them are great) covered our original record.

Did you give any thought to your prospective audience as you wrote?

I never self-consciously constructed an idea in a song to appeal to any specific audience. The material came straight out of a very spontaneous impulse. It had nothing to do with "Who will this appeal to?" or "Who will this not appeal to?" That's something that we've never done. I would think that most good writers really don't design things that consciously. I don't think they think about the market.

I don't think I've ever sat down and said "I'm not gonna write this for a white audience." I don't think I ever specifically said, "I'm gonna write this for a black audience." The thing was, we worked in that milieu [blues] to begin with almost exclusively and as things began to change, we just kept writing. I don't think we ever, ever said. "We're gonna write this because this is what's happening in the market." I wrote to amuse myself.

Did you write with a specific singer in mind? The songs you wrote for The Coasters, for instance, seem very different to the ones you wrote for Elvis.

They were more elaborate and more intricate and more complex because they had characters speaking words of dialogue and singing words of dialogue that were scored. That took a lot more fashioning in terms of lyric writing. The lyrics had to be absolutely precise because if something was off a syllable or whatever, it wouldn't work. And the same thing with the music.

I was designing the lyrics and the voices. I used to do the voices for them. I used to do line readings to demonstrate the way they were to be performed.

How did you come to write 'Stand By Me' with Ben E. King?

The title was from an old gospel song. Ben E. King brought me a fragment of the song. It sounded like a church song. I said, "I like the sound of that." "I like it too," he said, "but I can't get past the first four or five bars." I said, "Do you want me to write it with you? I can write it with you, we can get it finished today and we'll record it." And he got very excited because he liked the song very much but he figured that he's not going to be able to write it. Then later Mike walked in and came up with the crowning stroke: he wrote the bass pattern.

'On Broadway' [a 1960 hit for The Drifters] is interesting in that it is credited to you and Mike Stoller, and also to the Brill Building songwriting duo Barry Mann and Cynthia Weil.

[Don Kirshner, music publisher] said, "Leiber, I've got an almost great song. I'm just asking you would you listen to it and tell me if the thing is worth re-writing, 'cos I think it's a hit." I said, "I'll tell you what I think of the song, but first you have to talk to Barry and Cynthia and ask them if they want us to rewrite it." He called me back ten minutes later. He said, "They would be thrilled." I got the acetate and put it on and I thought, "This is a potential hit. No question about it. But it's gonna need some changes here and there." I called Mann and Weil up and said, "I think this song is a hit but I don't think it was finished right." And they said, "We know there's something wrong with it but we can't figure it out." So all four of us sat around my house one evening and rewrote it together. Mike and I went in and we made the record with The Drifters and it was a stone smash.

Your writing style had changed quite dramatically by the late 1960s. What would you put that down to?

I had been a great deal influenced by Kurt Weill and Bert Brecht and we were kind of looking for a new avenue. We'd done an awful lot of rock'n' roll in all those years and we were also getting a little bit older and we wanted to do something that would appeal to a more mature audience. Although rock'n'roll is great, I think it's mainly a high-energy form for young people. So I started experimenting with different forms. I was looking to write something that was dramatic, theatrical and original. 'Is That All There Is?' was my first attempt at experimenting with a new form. I wrote a series of vignettes that illustrated the state of mind often referred to as ennui. Mike fell in love with them and set them to music. What was missing was a refrain to bind them together and make a whole. I said, "I'm going to go home and try the refrain." He said, "I will too." We both came into the office the following day and he sat down and I started singing the words that I'd concocted overnight and he started playing the notes that he had cooked up overnight and, of all the strangest things, the notes and the words fit. Absolutely perfectly. We've been partners over 50 years: that's the only time that ever happened.

But you do seem to have a certain synchronicity. Does it sometimes feel as though you're not even separate individuals?
I think so. I don't think it's constant and I don't think that it's so intense but I think there are moments when what you describe seems to apply.

Is that a good or bad thing?
I think it could be either. There's something nice about it and something secure about it and sometimes it's a pain in the ass.

How have you found writing with people other than Mike?
I spent about eight or nine months working with [Leonard] Bernstein. We wrote some good stuff but the project never got produced. Bernstein at one point came to me and said, "It's not easy for me to write, I don't have a lot of time, I conduct a lot. If this show doesn't go, do you mind if we separate our interests and you take your words and I take my notes?" I said, "Absolutely fine with me." And when we both found out that the show was not going to be produced, I took my lyrics and he took his music. And I was just as happy because I felt Mike wrote better songs for the lyrics than Leonard had. I don't know whether there were any hits but they were some songs Mike and I both prize very much.

Which of your songs are you most proud of?
'Hound Dog' – and of course I mean Big Mama, so it's not just the song, it's the record – and 'Is That All There Is?', Peggy Lee (*Is That All There Is?* 1969). I think in a funny way that covers the whole spectrum. I could say 'On Broadway' and 'Spanish Harlem,' 'Kansas City' and some others. [Elvis's] 'Love Me' is one of the best records I've ever heard that we've written. I think it's absolutely beautiful. I think 'The Girl I Never Kissed' [recorded by Frank Sinatra in 1995], is one of the best songs we've ever written. Frank was not at the top of his game when he recorded it but we're thrilled that he did. It's the only Frank Sinatra recording of one of our songs.

What are your views on songwriting today?
I think that the keynote and the focus of today's songwriting is virtuosity in the studio. I think it depends upon great playing of instruments, etc. I think it also depends upon great virtuosity vocally. I think the dimension of lyric writing has gotten kind of slim and I think there've been many reasons for it. You see videos where there are all kind of images going on while a guy is singing. When you have images going on you don't really need the images provoked by words, and a tendency to let down your guard and go easy on the lyric writing is there. It's not there musically, 'cos you need the music but you're really not dependent that much on the word, and I think the tendency in today's songwriting is to go with this almost ulterior, subliminal flow of what is needed and what isn't, and that all the kids that are writing songs know that the stuff is eventually headed for the screen, and I think they act accordingly. I think that the lyric writing has gotten thin. There's nobody around today writing like The Beatles. One of the only guys left out there writing anything that is literate, funny, insightful, philosophic is Randy Newman.

Do you still write?
If we write songs, we meet four times a week for three or four hours a day. If we've got anything we really have to do we can go seven or eight but I consider myself semi-retired now because I'm not making records. But I don't know what I'd do with myself if I stopped writing songs.

Extracted with permission from *The Guys Who Wrote 'Em* by Sean Egan (Askill Publishing; ISBN 0954575016)

acknowledgements

Some quotations are taken from *Songs* by Bruce Springsteen (Virgin, 2003), Fred Bronson *The Billboard Book of Number One Hits* (Guinness, 1992), Jim Irvin and Colin McLear's *The Mojo Collection* (3rd ed. Cannongate, 2000), Sean Egan's *The Guys Who Wrote 'Em: Songwriting Geniuses of Rock And Pop* (Askill Publishing, 2004), Berry Gordy *To Be Loved, Smokey: Inside My Life* Smokey Robinson with David Ritz (Headline, 1989), Nelson George *Where Did Our Love Go* (Omnibus, 1985), Hank Bordowitz *Billy Joel: The Life And Times Of An Angry Young Man*, *Innocent When You Dream: The Tom Waits Reader*, edited by Max Montandon (Orion, 2006), 'The Making Of Pet Sounds' booklet included in *The Pet Sounds Sessions* (Capitol 1996), Jimmy Webb's *Tunesmith: Inside The Art Of Songwriting* (1998), and *Songtalk*, the journal of the National Academy of Songwriters in Hollywood, and collected in *Songwriters on Songwriting*, edited by Paul Zollo (Da Capo Press, 1997). Also cited are back issues of *Guitarist, Mojo, Making Music, Melody Maker, Q , Uncut, Guitar World, The Word, YTF Motown Collectors newsletter, Kate Bush Club newsletter*.

For their involvement in the preparation of this book I would like to thank Nigel Osborne, Tony Bacon, John Morrish, Mark Brend, and Simon Smith.

AUTHOR NOTE

Rikky Rooksby is a guitar teacher, songwriter, and composer, and writer on popular music. He is the author of the Backbeat titles *How To Write Songs On Guitar* (2000), *Inside Classic Rock Tracks* (2001), *Riffs* (2002), *The Songwriting Sourcebook* (2003), *Chord Master* (2004), *Melody* (2004), *Songwriting Secrets: Bruce Springsteen* (2005), and *How To Write Songs on Keyboards* (2005). He contributed to *Albums: 50 Years Of Great Recordings, Classic Guitars Of The Fifties, The Guitar: the complete guide for the player*, and *Roadhouse Blues* (2003). He has also written *The Guitarist's Guide to the Capo* (Artemis 2003), *The Complete Guide To The Music Of Fleetwood Mac* (revised ed. 2004), fourteen Fastforward guitar tutor books, four in the *First Guitar* series; transcribed and arranged over forty chord songbooks of music including Bob Dylan, Bob Marley, the Stone Roses, David Bowie, Eric Clapton, Travis, The Darkness, and *The Complete Beatles*; and co-authored *100 Years 100 Songs*. He has written articles on rock musicians for the new *Dictionary Of National Biography* (OUP), and published interviews, reviews, articles and transcriptions in magazines such as *Guitar Techniques, Total Guitar, Guitarist, Bassist, Bass Guitar Magazine, The Band, Record Collector, Sound On Sound*, and *Making Music*, where he wrote the monthly 'Private Pluck' guitar column. He is a member of the Guild of International Songwriters and Composers and the Society Of Authors. Visit his website at www.rikkyrooksby.com

AFTERWORDS

"The world of music is way huger and more life-giving and permanent than the music business will ever be. The real world of music. And that gives me comfort." (Jeff Buckley)[144]

"They are more than tunes. They are little houses in which our hearts once lived. When we hear them we go visiting." (Playwright Ben Hecht on Cole Porter's songs)[145]

footnotes

1
2 *Guitar World*, March 1999
3 *Mojo*, October 2004
4 *Rolling Stone*
5 Bronson
6 *Mojo*, August 1998
7 *Melody Maker*
8 'The Making of Pet Sounds'
9 *Melody Maker*
10 *The Word*
11 *Melody Maker*
12 *Mojo* October 1998
13 Egan
14 *Melody Maker*
15 *The Word*
16 *Melody Maker*
17 *Record Mirror*
18 *Mojo*
19 *Radio Times*
20 *Melody Maker*
21 *Mojo*
22 *Rolling Stone*
23 *Vox*
24 *The Word*
25 *Q*
26 *Melody Maker*
27 *Mojo*
28 *Q*
29 Robinson/Ritz
30 *Q*
31 *Mojo*
32 *Mojo*
33 *NME*
34 Bronson
35 Egan
36 *Mojo*
37 *Mojo*
38 Egan
39 *Melody Maker*
40 *YTF*
41 *Mojo*
42 *Melody Maker*
43 *The Word*
44 *Melody Maker*
45 Gordy
46 Bronson
47 *The Word*
48 *Mojo*
49 *Playboy*
50 *The Word*
51 *Mojo*
52 *KBC Newsletter*
53 *Q*
54 *Mojo*
55 *Mojo*
56 *Q Special Edition: Madonna*
57 *Mojo*
58 Gordy
59 *Rolling Stone*
60 *Melody Maker*
61 *Mojo*
62 Webb
63 *Mojo*
64 Webb
65 *Mojo*
66 George
67 Robinson/Ritz
68 *Q*
69 *Mojo*
70 Egan
71 *Beat Instrumental*
72 *Mojo*
73 *Musician*
74 *Melody Maker*
75 sleeve note, *Tumbleweed*
76 *Melody Maker*
77 Bordowitz
78 *Mojo*
79 The Times
80 *Melody Maker*
81 *Melody Maker*
82 *Mojo*
83 'The Making Of Pet Sounds'
84 *Mojo*
85 *Mojo*
86 Gordy
87 *Melody Maker*
88 Egan
89 *Mojo*
90 *Mojo*
91 *Melody Maker*
92 *Mojo*
93 *Mojo*
94 *Uncut*
95 Rolling Stone
96 *Mojo*
97 *Melody Maker*
98 Life
99 Webb
100 *Melody Maker*
101 *Melody Maker*
102 *Melody Maker*
103 Marsh
104 *Mojo*
105 Webb
106 *The Word*
107 *The Mojo Collection*
108 *Mojo*
109 *Mojo*
110 Egan
111 *Mojo*
112 *NME*
113 *Mojo*
114 *The Beatles Anthology*
115 Gordy
116 *Melody Maker*
117 *Melody Maker*
118 *Mojo*
119 *YTF*
120 *Melody Maker*
121 *Melody Maker*
122 *Mojo*
123 *Guitar World*
124 *Mojo*
125 *NME*
126 *Melody Maker*
127 Webb
128 *Q*
129 *Melody Maker*
130 *NME*
131 *KBC Newsletter*
132 *Life*
133 *Sounds*
134 *Melody Maker*
135 *Mojo*
136 *Uncut*
137 BBC
138 *Mojo*
139 *Mojo Collection*
140 *Mojo*
141 *Melody Maker*
142 *Q*
143 *Mojo*
144 *Mojo*
145 Quoted in *Mojo*